Harold Pinter's Politics

Harold Pinter's Politics

A Silence Beyond Echo

Charles Grimes

Madison • Teaneck
Fairleigh Dickinson University Press

Associated University Presses
2010 Eastpark Boulevard
Cranbury, NJ 08512

The paper used in this publication meets the requirements of the American National Standard for Permanence of Paper for Printed Library Materials Z39.48-1984.

Library of Congress Cataloging-in-Publication Data

Grimes, Charles.
    Harold Pinter's politics : a silence beyond echo / Charles Grimes.
        p.   cm.
    Includes bibliographical references and index.
    ISBN 0-8386-4050-8 (alk. paper)
    1. Pinter, Harold, 1930—Political and social views.   2. Politics and literature—Great Britain—History—20th century.   3. Political plays, English—History and criticism.   I. Title.
    PR6066.I53Z655   2005
    822'.914—dc22   2005001724

Contents

Acknowledgments

I WISH TO ACKNOWLEDGE SUPPORT FROM SAINT LEO UNIVERSITY AND its Professional Development Fund. During my work on this book, Gene Richie, Walter Levy, Leslie Kane, Roger Oliver, Kristen Phaup, Bridget Bean, Kathryn Duncan, and Steven Goldleaf offered advice, criticism, and encouragement, while Bob Vorlicky and Una Chaudhuri graced me with me with wisdom and warmth. Carol Moon deserves thanks for her research assistance; Donald Pharr performed essential editing; Andy Matthews spent countless hours in careful evaluation of this book as it developed. I owe thanks to Malcolm Page, who supplied me with a manuscript of his essay on Pinter and politics, and Frank Gillen, who permitted reprinting of material from the *Pinter Review*. For support and guidance, I am ever grateful to my parents William and Regina Grimes.

I record also my thanks to Harold Pinter, who generously allowed me to quote from papers in the British Library's Pinter Archives, and to Sally Brown, Curator of Modern Manuscripts at the British Library.

Abbreviations

AA	*Ashes to Ashes*
BP	*The Birthday Party*
C	*Celebration*
CS	*The Comfort of Strangers*
DW	*The Dumb Waiter*
H	*The Hothouse*
M	*Moonlight*
ML	*Mountain Language*
NWO	*The New World Order*
One	*One for the Road*
P	*Precisely*
PA	Pinter Archives at the British Library
PC	*Press Conference*
PT	*Party Time*
R	*Reunion*
V	*Victory*
VV	*Various Voices*

References to these sources will be made parenthetically in the text itself using the abbreviations above.

Harold Pinter's Politics

1

Harold Pinter and the Tradition of Political Theater

I'm not a theorist. I'm not an authoritative or reliable com-
mentator on the dramatic scene, the social scene, any scene.
I write plays, when I can manage it, and that's all.
—Harold Pinter, 1962 (*Various Voices*)

I am not concerned with making general statements.
—Harold Pinter, 1970 (*Various Voices*)

We all have to be very careful. The boot is itching to squash
and very efficient.
    Goldberg and McCann? Dying, rotting, scabrous, the de-
cayed spiders, the flower of our society. . . . Our mentors. Our
ancestry. Them. Fuck 'em.
—Harold Pinter, 1958 (*Various Voices*)

Dear President Bush, I'm sure you'll be having a nice little
tea party with your fellow war criminal, Tony Blair. Please
wash the cucumber sandwiches down with a glass of blood . . .
—Harold Pinter (*Guardian*, November 18, 2003)

THE READER WITH A PASSING FAMILIARITY WITH THE PLAYWRIGHT
Harold Pinter will likely be aware of several labels applied to his
work. Early in his career Pinter was credited with inventing so-
called "comedies of menace" such as the widely read *The Birthday Party* and with creating new examples of absurdist theater
in plays such as *The Dumb Waiter*. As Pinter gained fame, the
full extent of his innovative dramatic practices came to be
widely recognized: the withholding of traditional exposition and
the exploration of memory as unreliable, creating a sense of a
mysterious world whose truths cannot be defined, as in *The
Caretaker*; the crafting in all his plays of language faithful to everyday banality but full of mysterious depth; the unrelenting
power and cruelty exercised in friendship, marriage, love, and

family and the concentration upon male violence (and vulnerability) and female inscrutability, especially in plays such as *The Homecoming* and *Old Times*; and the experimentation with form in *Betrayal*, his play about an affair that famously runs backward in time. All these innovations came to be summarized as "Pinteresque," a term that describes his distinctive innovations in both form and content and suggests that this important dramatist constitutes an artistic movement unto himself. However, Pinter has been disdainful of all of these labels and of virtually all the concepts used to categorize and define his writing. The only one he has willingly applied to himself is that of a political writer, a citizen of the world with the duty to speak out about abuses of power wherever they occur. "I understand your interest in me as a playwright," he noted in 1988. "But I'm more interested in myself as a citizen" (Gussow 1994, 71). This book on Harold Pinter takes him at his word by investigating the intersection between his political commitments and his unique dramaturgy.

Even if one had a sense that Harold Pinter's work always contained a political element, albeit an element not always clearly present, Pinter's emergence as a political playwright in the early 1980s might be seen as somewhat surprising. The dominant critical description of Pinter placed him in the "Theatre of the Absurd," a group of playwrights conceptualized by Martin Esslin. Esslin and the numerous critics influenced by him categorized Pinter in the absurdist tradition developed by Eugene Ionesco, Samuel Beckett, and other playwrights. Pinter's earliest plays, *The Birthday Party* and *The Dumb Waiter*, possessed absurdist characteristics: the sense of an ominous yet uncertain fate; the implication of a senseless, random universe; and the use of the stage to present striking images of the human condition. The theater of the absurd is generally thought apolitical, ratifying an agenda of social indifference—by either perception or definition, then, a significant schism divides absurdist from committed drama. This breach was formalized by the 1955 exchange between Kenneth Tynan and Ionesco, in which Tynan urged the political commitment of the author, while Ionesco argued for independence from all external obligations, specifically to fixed political viewpoints (Ionesco 1964, 87–108). According to this supposed opposition between absurdist drama and the theater of commitment, a playwright may address contemporary concerns or humanity's timeless confrontation with a meaningless or hostile universe—yet not both.

Catharine Hughes quoted Pinter's statement that a "thing is not necessarily either true or false; it can be both true and false" as the guiding assumption of explicitly *unengaged* theater (183). Susan Hollis Merritt (1995, 170) has used Hughes's comment to argue that Pinter's political works establish a "freedom from polemics"—they avoid the ideological overcommitment for which political theater is often faulted. Uncommitted theater, in contrast, refuses political statements in favor of examining the difficulty of forming specific conclusions about reality. After his political turn, Pinter acknowledged the potential for contradiction between his principle of ambiguity and his political commitment. Pinter's website (http://www.haroldpinter.org) begins with the 1958 statement about truth and falsity, followed by this comment: "I believe that these assertions still make sense and do still apply to the exploration of reality through art. So as a writer I stand by them but as a citizen I cannot. As a citizen I must ask: What is true? What is false?" This comment distinguishes between Pinter as writer and as citizen, though in other contexts he has portrayed the writing as continuous with his moral duties as public citizen. The contemporary importance of separating fact from untruth illustrates not so much a philosophical distinction or contradiction between Pinter then and Pinter now, but rather a privileging of his moral commitment to politics over intellectual devotion to epistemological nuance.

If the traditional opposition between absurdism and engagement has its share of overstatement, it is nevertheless the case that critics and audiences at the time of Pinter's emergence as a writer identified playwrights in its terms, and authors perceived themselves similarly. Playwrights were either in one camp or the other: either followers of Beckett's and Ionesco's absurdism, such as N. F. Simpson and Tom Stoppard, or political authors linked to the Angry Young Man movement, sparked by John Osborne, and inspired by Brecht, such as Edward Bond and John Arden. Pinter never fit into either camp, as Mark Batty notes, because his drama was stylistically distinct from that of both groups (2001, 91). Two additional factors are involved here: first, Pinter apparently had no early experience with Marxist dialectics as did Brecht, Bond, and Arden. Also, Pinter's individualistic streak prevented him being a joiner at all—in the manner of artists whose rejection of the status quo coexists with irritation at organized resistance to it. Individual freedom from arbitrary power in fact becomes one of the principal themes of his politics.

However, Pinter did not present himself as completely and equally dissociated from absurdism on the one hand and commitment on the other. Given this critical dualism, there is little doubt where Pinter located himself at the time, or at least encouraged others to place him. In 1963 he noted, "There is no question that Beckett is a writer whom I admire very much. . . . If Beckett's influence shows in my work that's all right with me. . . . I admire Beckett's work so much that something of its texture might appear in my own" (Graver 1989, 94). Whether the playwright meant to do so or not, this statement of artistic influence implied Pinter's presumed stances on a variety of issues not limited to theatrical style.

In fact, up to the early 1980s, Pinter's comments on the relationship of politics to writing seemed consistent with Ionesco's apolitical stance against the theater of commitment. Esslin noted that Pinter "himself has occasionally seemed to have wanted to create" the impression of being apolitical (1970, 24). Throughout the 1950s and 1960s, Pinter emphasized abstention from political issues and his distaste for addressing politics through playwriting. In 1961 he declared "I'm not committed as a writer, in the usual sense of the term, either religiously or politically" (1961c, 175). Pinter reiterated this stance in 1966 in a *Paris Review* interview. In 1985, looking back at himself in the sixties, he noted his disconnection from specific social struggles, instead seeing all "politicians and political structures and political acts with . . . detached contempt" (Pinter 1986b, 12). This attitude must be recognizable in terms of the oft-observed venality and shallowness of politicians from both the left and the right. There is honesty too in Pinter's admission that he had strong political views but acknowledged no responsibility to articulate or enact them. He also remarked that the lack of subtlety in Peter Brook's 1968 Vietnam War protest play *US* amounted to an insult to his intelligence, causing him to walk out on the performance (18). "[D]idactic and moralistic theatre" was, Pinter avowed, "sentimental and unconvincing" (Innes 1992, 280). He suppressed his play *The Hothouse*, an expressly political work written in 1958, until 1979. Pinter's most ringing disdain for political theater is expressed in a 1962 speech, in which he denounced

[t]he writer who puts forward his concern for you to embrace, who leaves you in no doubt of his worthiness, his usefulness, his altruism, who declares that his heart is in the right place, and ensures

that it can be seen in full view, a pulsating mass where his characters ought to be. (*VV*, 18)

This familiar attack upon political art deems it intellectually obvious, a simplification of complex situations, and aesthetically flawed, lacking the spontaneity of true art that arises from personal discovery rather than a desire to endorse preconceived messages. Ironically enough, this sort of attack upon political art, which at the time encouraged many to see Pinter as expressly apolitical, was later leveled at his own political works. Esslin, for instance, expressed concern that Pinter's later plays represented a diminution of his gifts, as they abandoned his distinctive ambiguity in favor of proclaiming moral and political truisms: "there is no uncertainty here about what is being shown, nor why it is shown, no multiplicity of levels of possible meanings and interpretations; everything is on the surface, immediately verifiable as what it is and what it intends" (1993, 35). Arthur Ganz's dismissal of Pinter's political works evokes the playwright's criticism of a simplistic, moralizing author: "It is comforting to know that Pinter disapproves of torture and brainwashing as much as the rest of us, but we do not seek out his work because he is an earnest man. His conscience is not the source of his greatness" (1995, 430).

However, a more nuanced interpretation of the evidence concerning Pinter's definition of the author's political role complicates the notion that Pinter disdained all political viewpoints and writing. Rather, it seems more accurate that Pinter objected not to political art per se but rather its occasional obviousness, its tendency to reduce complexity to slogans and clichés. "To be a politician you have to be able to present a simple picture even if you don't see things that way," he said in 1966 (Pinter 1967, 360).[1] Thus the statement that he "distrust[ed] ideological statements of any kind" may be read as indicting the style of leftist discourse, not its content. When he criticizes Brook's *US* in this conversation, his point is that the play failed to portray its subject matter accurately and forcefully, especially compared to representations on media and TV (365). This interview reveals Pinter as a person with political feelings: "I'm in the normal state of being very confused—uncertain, irritated, and indignant in turns" (360). Again, this state of uncertainty must be recognizable and familiar to many. Those people unwilling to entertain political uncertainty are often and understandably labeled ideologues.[2] Also, any well-founded political judgment, it seems, requires considerable research and time to support with facts. Furthermore, these facts appear often in the mode of "spin" and are often the province of experts (frequently partial and partisan ones) whose often contradictory pronouncements the generalist, the concerned citizen, may have little capacity to counter on his or her own terms.

Despite this understandable uncertainty about political expression, then, Pinter always had strong feelings about certain aspects of the world around him. In fact, these feelings are so powerful that rational words are ineffective to express them and the playwright speaks in violent images. When asked about the political connotations of his theater, Pinter responds:

> I don't feel myself threatened by *any* political body or activity at all. I like living in England. I don't care about political structures—they don't alarm me, but they cause a great deal of suffering to millions of people.
>
> I'll tell you what I think about politicians. The other night I watched some politicians on television talking about Viet Nam. I wanted very much to burst through the screen with a flamethrower and burn their eyes out and their balls off and then inquire from them how they would assess this action from a political point of view. (1967, 361)

This statement is intriguingly schizophrenic. Pinter acknowledges deeply felt emotions about current events even as he struggles with the difficulty of taking specific stands and acknowledges that he himself is not directly victimized by oppression. His political views are expressed with great emotion, almost instinctively. They are direct reactions to particular conditions, rather than intellectual conclusions derived by previously held political theory. Austin Quigley believes that Pinter has veered from undervaluing to overvaluing politics (2001, 8). When Pinter proclaims apathy toward politics, and then narrates a fantasy of murdering hypocritical leaders, this rhythm is expressed within the space of a few seconds. His extreme diction shows that Pinter spoke accurately in 1999 when he declared that his social concern emerges from the realization that innocent people die as a result of political decisions (Ross, 22). Thus his unwillingness in the 1950s through 1970s to write explicitly political theater was not solely or mainly due to sociopolitical indifference.

While the author's public comments on politics suggest an awakening dating from the 1960s onwards, it was not until the early to mid-1980s that Pinter explicitly used his art to express his political feelings. Pinter's embrace of the political involves the decision to take public stands on political issues as well as his decision to ally his art with his beliefs and causes. His acute sense of the reductiveness of political discourse, on both the left and the right, was one factor in both decisions.[3] The playwright felt that politicians on both the right and the left engaged in hypocrisy, misstatements, and reductive interpretations of reality.

Another important theme in Pinter's politics has to do with the question of what leads to personal involvement in the concerns of the world. How does one cross the line between disinvolvement and engagement? This transition is imperiled by the ordinary ability simply to ignore the magnitude of social and political problems in the world. As Merritt notes, Pinter is sharply "critical of [his audiences'] unwillingness to face" political reality (1995, 182). Pinter reiterates this criticism in the essay "It Never Happened," which documents widespread public ignorance of or apathy to persistent recurrences of political violence, even genocide, particularly those repressions sponsored or abetted by the United States. Popular opinion and behavior are that such things "never happened. Nothing ever happened. Even *while* it was happening it wasn't happening. It didn't matter. It was of no interest" (*VV*, 198). Disinvolvement is the essence of our lives.

Pinter's political theater could be viewed as emerging from a submerged or subtextual dialogue between his disconnected and his politicized self. The anger of his political theater may relate to the belatedness or lengthy nature of his political awakening.[4] Often his political pronouncements have an apocalyptic tenor, implying that it is too late to change the world for the better (this tone may also be seen as driven by Pinter's early knowledge of the Holocaust). "I believe that there's no chance of the world coming to other than a very grisly end in twenty-five years" he proclaimed in 1985 (1986b, 20). The previous year, the playwright castigated himself for ignoring history: "I in common with a great body of people have been sleepwalking for many years, really, and I remember years ago I regarded myself as an artist in an ivory tower" (Knowles 1989, 25). If it is too much to say that Pinter faults himself for his earlier political inactivity, his political theater dramatizes the interplay and conflict of the opposing poles of involvement and disengagement.

Pinter could be accounted wisely modest in saying in 1966 that he had no cause to feel threatened by political structures.

Even though Pinter was not born into the British Establishment—his origins are lower middle class—for this successful male author to portray himself as the victim of social oppression might well be seen as presumptuous. His judgment that he must see himself as socially privileged, or at least safe, points up the rhetorical excesses of sixties leftism. How do the privileged speak for the unprivileged without a kind of arrogance and moral presumption? On the other hand, personal experience of oppression is not necessary to protest against it. Pinter's political works can be seen as an attempt to grapple with these irresolvable questions. By explaining his personal disconnection from politics in terms of the limits of his own life experience, it seems that Pinter suggests personal exposure to suffering as one likely route to commitment.

While content such as torture, nuclear warfare, and bourgeois triumphalism dominate Pinter's expressly political theater, many of his other works deal with the theme of how the individual comes to acknowledge the political reality around her, what drives this process of connection, and its ultimate results. The plot is that of an individual who existed in a purely private sense, supposedly insulated from the larger social world, suddenly confronted with broad social and political forces, and thus called to political awareness and responsibility. Gus in *The Dumb Waiter*, Mary in *The Comfort of Strangers*, and Heyst in *Victory* all come to glimpse the organized powers arrayed against them and begin to see the necessity of engaging and opposing these forces. (By contrast, the plays that are deemed expressly political often emphasize the overwhelming power of these forces to crush dissent.) Works such as *The Dumb Waiter* are political in the sense that they might be called metapolitical—that is, they concern the conditions under which what is called political perception and (perhaps) action come about. Often, the awakening awareness to the political contours of life is sparked by a personal link to unpleasant historical realities. In *The Dreaming Child* screenplay, for example, Pinter adapts Isak Dinesen's story of a woman whose consciousness is enlarged after "for the first time she felt personally related to the need and misery of the world" (Dinesen 1942, 168). Rebecca in *Ashes to Ashes* struggles with incorporating into her own psyche the historical oppression and political violence of the twentieth century. All these works postulate a combination of imagination and empirical truth as catalysts for a movement from disinvolvement to the beginnings of engagement.

If Pinter, to some extent, always had strong personal reactions to politics, his plays did not explicitly record the traces of these feelings, as Merritt among others observes (1995, 170). However, since the early 1980s, Pinter has often reiterated that his early plays were in fact political, even if they were not first seen as such. In response to public criticisms of his late work, Pinter has drawn attention to the continuity of certain themes and materials throughout his career, maintaining strongly that political dimensions were always in his work. Pinter assumes there is virtue in consistency, apparently believing that his later politicization will seem stronger if this element of his writing can be traced back to his early career.[5] How early is it possible to see the political critique explicit in the later career? To ask this question is to ask also if critics during the 1950s and 1960s were mistaken in not seeing these political implications, or if Pinter's current readings of them are reductive, a problem taken up in the next chapter.

The playwright himself, a valuable if not a reliable source, offers a paradigm of career development centering on the abandonment of humor. The difference between his early and late plays, he notes, is that he believes the present conditions of the world mandate a more urgent, morally focused response. The present moment is politically grave, in Pinter's opinion. "[F]or me the joke is over" he said in 1989 (Gussow 1994, 82). This urgency necessitates a depiction of reality more "rigorous," in his own word, than anything in his previous writing. His late plays are about "one thing" he said in 1993 (102); although, characteristically, he does not say exactly what this one thing is, it is safe to call it abuse of political power. The naked presence of power can be related to the political atmosphere of the 1980s. For many in Britain at this time, the ascent of Margaret Thatcher politicized many who otherwise felt apolitical—as was also the case in the United States in response to the presidency of Ronald Reagan. The stridency of Thatcher's government, her willingness to dismantle fundamental aspects of liberal postwar British society, her abandonment of consensus politics, and her antagonism toward left-wing voices caused many to feel that politics needed to be taken with utmost seriousness and could not merely be treated with, as Pinter observed of himself, "detached contempt" (1986b, 12).

Pinter's activities and consciousness before Thatcher's rise afford more evidence of his conversion to an outwardly political stance. As a private citizen prior to the 1970s, Pinter had a significant experience corresponding to his later political life. When he was eighteen years old, he refused induction into the British armed forces, at the time simply refusing to "join an organisation whose main purpose is mass murder" (Knowles 2000, 187). Pinter, objecting to an institution that he believed cooperated fully in the U.S.-created Cold War, could have gone to jail, but luckily did not. Other than this rather precocious decision, Pinter did not live a political life during the 1950s, '60s, and parts of the '70s—obvious times of great political upheaval. He was not involved in the widespread movement for British nuclear disarmament in 1961, though other prominent playwrights were.[6] In 1962 Pinter responded to an interviewer's question with the statement that he had no interest in the European Common Market. Was Pinter wholly apolitical at this time? The answer is an unqualified yes and no. David Hare offers the paradox that Pinter's disdain of politics was so thoroughgoing it amounted almost to a political stance (Eyre 2000, 20). Upon certain issues Pinter had no pronounced views. Yet on issues such as Vietnam, Pinter certainly had deep feelings—in 1967 he participated in a reading against the Vietnam War (Page 2000, 3). To a significant extent, these political beliefs—such as a moral stand against political violence and a distaste for hypocritical rhetoric and self-justification—were always present; what was lacking was a concept of art and of himself as an artist able to put his writing at the service of his political views.

However, Pinter's disconnection from most forms of organized politics in the '50s through the late '70s suggests a number of important points about his later political theater. His politics of detachment and disdain emphasize the playwright's distance from the traditional postwar political theater in Britain, which looks to socialism for its political vision. Despite Pinter's recent assertions of socialism's necessity and viability (VV, 193), nowhere do his plays critique the status quo through a socialist vocabulary. "[S]ome writers . . . can very easily and properly sit down and write plays from a political kind of ideology. I am unable to do that," Pinter observed in 1981 (qtd. in Merritt 1995, 175). Political playwrights such as John Arden and Edward Bond have criticized Pinter for being insufficiently programmatic, labeling his work unclear, irrational, and uninformative (Billington 1996, 333–34). Merritt critiques radical critic Klaus Kohler, who laments that, beneath the "trenchant debunking" of Pinter's political stance, there exists no "constructive commitment" to a practical agenda of reform (1990, 184). Pinter certainly shows little investment in the politics of class in the manner of many of his British contemporaries such as Hare, Howard Brenton, and Caryl Churchill.

Pinter's leftist politics diverged from those of his contemporaries, and in another sense, as well, his political turn was paradoxically timed, for he turned to political theater as it was entering a period of crisis. His plays began to deal overtly with politics just when the influence of a generation of recognizably left-wing British playwrights—including John Arden, Arnold Wesker, Edward Bond, David Mercer, David Hare, Howard Brenton, Howard Barker, and David Edgar—began to wane. This tradition of radical theater was perceived by critics and its own practitioners as defunct by the time of Pinter's political conversion. The work of such playwrights had been largely marginalized in terms of the established British theater. Critic David Ian Rabey testifies to this crisis. In 1990, Rabey noted the failure of his previous effort to define and extol twentieth-century political theater: "In the early 1980s I wrote a study of modern British and Irish drama which intended to pay tribute to an emergent tradition of radical drama and its subversive potential. In the intervening years, history and experience have taught me that this drama was neither radical nor subversive enough" (1990, 151). Rabey thus defines political theater in terms of its historical failure—its defining goals will be forever unfulfilled. Political theater is marked by an irremediable sense of deficit. Pinter's political theater acknowledges, even underlines, this deficit, by portraying the plot of destroyed rebellion, as well as by not clarifying or endorsing positive ideologies and methodologies of change.

Pinter's transformation is also surprising because it is agreed, at the level of conventional wisdom, that the period after the 1960s was an inhospitable, unhappy time for a political artist to function in. A number of familiar ideas outline the failure of political art. The reality of political conditions is often so grotesque and ridiculous that even a realistic, uninflected version of them would scarcely be believed; when reality is portrayed, it is thought to be literally incredible. Philip Roth, for instance, famously said, as far back as 1960, that political reality in America was so bizarre and extreme that even fiction writers had trouble equaling it.[7] Pinter notes, as one example of the literal incredibility of politics in modern world, that if you told anyone that he and his mates play cricket, at Great Hampden pitch, directly on top the "centre of nuclear operations in Europe," "They would dismiss it . . . 'don't be ridiculous'" (1986b, 21–23). This confusion between the fantastic and the real, argues Jean Baudrillard for one, is endemic to our postmodern society, in which simulations have replaced foundational reality. If reality outstrips the imagination of the political artist, how then can he or she function?

One reason for the inefficacy perceived in "political theater" when Pinter begins to practice it derives from the current status of "politics" itself. In many analyses of the current political moment, political change is thought to be impossible and historical evolution is, literally, a thing of the past. "'Realism' in politics now means considering old progressive ideals as pie in the sky," Christopher Norris remarks of the late 1980s and beyond (1990, 9). Political scientist Geoff Mulgan writes:

> [S]ince the middle of the twentieth century . . . it has been popular to believe that history has come to an end, and that the great transformations are all to be found in the past. The world is stagnant, exhausted, locked into closed loops of bureaucracy and culture that exclude new energies. In such a world no one is in control, and therefore no one is worth opposing or overthrowing. All important decisions are locked into systems—those of finance and money, of bureaucracy, of culture, which are themselves mutually isolated, rendering radical change across spheres all but impossible. In the words of one perceptive German writer, "the rulers have ceased to rule but the slaves remain slaves." . . . If power is no longer exercised by people who can be identified and called to account, most political action will amount to little more than tilting at windmills. (1994, 22–23)[8]

Mulgan's analysis serves as a point of both comparison and contrast to Pinter's political theater. This mood of hopelessness characterizes both the atmosphere of Pinter's political plays, which provide stunning images of repression and victimization, and the pessimistic, even apocalyptic, tenor of some of his public pronouncements on political issues. With history holding out no hope, progressive politics becomes nearly impossible. If so, the primary statement of political theater may be an assertion of its own futility.

Mulgan's image of the "closed loop" evokes Pinter's political plays, where, in varied though always violent fashion, dissidents are marginalized and official power is renewed and strengthened. This image also is reminiscent of the bourgeois society's power to isolate and absorb political opposition, a capacity analyzed by Herbert Marcuse in *One-Dimensional Man*, among other famous descriptions of this phenomenon. The torturer of *One for the Road* even mocks the absence of his prisoner's ideas from the public sphere: "Are you always so dull? I understood you enjoyed the cut and thrust of debate" (*One*, 45), while the two torturers in *The New World Order* joke about newspapers having vanished. In *Celebration*, the Waiter, whose tales of artistic and cultural connections underscore the banality of his nouveau riche customers, is left onstage, isolated and silent, following the echo of a closing door. This pattern of ostracism and expulsion from a central zone of power suggests that political action in Pinter's later plays is not only ineffective; it also exposes political agents to extreme punishment. These plays show us a kind of "loop" closing, often with great force, upon victims of group and state power.

While a postmodern view of politics, such as Mulgan's, sees a world in which rulers are remote and dispersed, Pinter reacts against the supposed facelessness of power. He shows his audience those who are in control—the ultrarich in *Party Time*, a fascist German judge in his screenplay of Fred Uhlman's *Reunion*, the fanatic enforcers of social and political oppression in numerous plays. In fact, Pinter seems to take a sort of pleasure in accenting their ugliness. His villains are clear and obvious, showing his wish to define a politically reachable target. That is, Pinter sees human agency as at the root of political evil.

If the deep structure of Pinter's political plays evokes the postmodern fear that power is inviolate, unapproachable, and unalterable, that "politics" themselves are impossible, the playwright himself has criticized the assumption that politics are moribund. In a 1996 interview, Pinter justified his political theater as a response to the mistaken belief that it is useless to consider political action:

> Political theatre now is even more important than it ever was, if by political theatre you mean plays which deal with the real world, not with a manufactured or fantasy world. We are in a terrible dip at the moment, a kind of abyss, because the assumption is that politics are all over. That's what the propaganda says. But I don't believe the propaganda. I believe that politics, our political consciousness and our political intelligence are not all over, because if they are, we are really doomed. (1998, 60)

Though the ringing tones of this defense of political theater are inspiring, the "critical scrutiny" Pinter urges us to exercise can be applied to his own analysis. His rather vague reference to "propaganda" conflates both triumphalist right-wing theories of the "end of history" with postmodern analyses of the difficulty of comprehending and altering late capitalism. Pinter's definition of "political theater" seems unspecific and unaware of the extensive theorization of this term carried out by political playwrights of his generation. His politics have no reference to specific political groups or ideologies—as he says, he doesn't write out of "ideological desire" (Merritt 1995, 186). If this nonideological focus frees Pinter from representing traditional left/right distinctions in his works, it may also be that to write without ideological desire is to write without ideological focus. Also, the author's just-quoted logic tends to the circular, avoiding the possibility of failure through a logical dodge—a most unusual move for someone influenced so deeply by Beckett's view of failure's centrality to human endeavor. The idea that we are doomed if politics is impossible does not at all prove that politics is possible: it may with equal logical plausibility suggest that, in fact, we are doomed. Early in his political period, the author in fact discussed his political art with reference to Beckett: "I do believe that what old Sam Beckett says at the end of *The Unnamable* is right on the ball. 'You must go on, I can't go on, I'll go on.' Now in this particular reference, if he'll forgive me using his language in this context, there's no point, it's hopeless. . . . Me writing *One for the Road*, documentaries, articles, lucid analyses, Averell Harriman writing in the *New York Times*, voices raised here and there. . . . Finally it's hopeless. There's nothing one can achieve" (1986b, 20). Pinter's ideas about the necessity of oppositional voices beg the question so strongly posed by his plays: how can anything be changed?

In fact, the diminishing possibility of social change came to be the principal concern of avowedly leftist playwrights such as Edward Bond, Howard Brenton, and especially David Hare in the years before and during Pinter's emergence as a political playwright. In 1978 Hare described a political changelessness contrasting with public awareness of political difficulty. This changelessness is Hare's primary explanation for the sense of failure and insufficiency of political theater already noted by Rabey:

> consciousness has been raised in this country for a good many years now and we seem further from radical political change than at any time in my life. The traditional function of the radical artist—"Look

at all those Borgias; look at this bureaucracy"—has been under-mined. We have looked. We have seen. We have known. And we have not changed. A pervasive cynicism paralyzes public life. (1978, 61)

In denying change and in practicing a dystopian political theater, then, Pinter is not being apolitical. Rather, he is aligning himself with playwrights avowedly representing the political left. Politi-cal theater is meant to lead audiences to action or to frame social attitudes so that progress can at least be contemplated; Hare and his leftist contemporaries reach the point at which historical conditions force the heretical realization that systematic change is impossible (or at least not within clear sight). Pinter, though he never invested in the dialectical models of change favored by socialism, begins his political theater exactly with this heresy that Hare and others reached after long experience. The cyni-cism of public life, a well-developed theme both in the popular press and postmodern commentary, paralyzes traditional models of political theater.

Bernard Shaw established twentieth-century political theater as a moralistic attack upon its audience. *The Quintessence of Ibsenism*, Shaw's major account of the operations of a political theater in the modern age, identifies the critical attitude politi-cal theater must create in its audience. Shaw equates political theater with organized religion; the word "conversion" and the phrase "awareness of sin" are used, while the playwright's func-tion is compared to that of a messiah:

> Ibsen substituted a terrible art of sharpshooting at the audience, trapping them, fencing with them, aiming always at the sorest spot in their consciences. . . . The dramatist knows that as long as he is teaching and saving his audience, he is as sure of their strained atten-tion as a dentist is, or the Angel of the Annunciation. . . .
> [Ibsen's] is the technique of playing upon the human conscience . . . in the theatre of Ibsen we are not flattered spectators killing an idle hour with an ingenious and amusing entertainment; we are "guilty creatures sitting at a play"; and the technique of pastime is no more applicable than at a murder trial. (1913, 183–84)

Pinter's plays similarly attempt to make their audiences con-template their guilt. Later in *The Quintessence of Ibsenism* Shaw addresses the nature of such political theatre: "our theatre will be an important place, and . . . will make people of low tastes and tribal or commercial ideas horribly uncomfortable by its efforts to bring conviction of sin to them" (188). Shaw embraces the highest possible moral goals as those of his theater. The association of terms he hints at is theological, referencing the notions of knowledge of sin, shame, moral self-awareness, and a new, cleansed self. He imagines, or pretends to imagine—or pretends to pretend to imagine—that he can make his audience better people intellectually and morally. He wishes to use the stage to convert individual minds to a more correct, enlightened, progressive awareness.

Pinter follows Bernard Shaw in using political theater to address the audience's need for a new moral self-definition. Morality is a keynote in Pinter's speeches about his political plays and his political messages as a public citizen. He emphasized in 1985 the necessity of putting the political actions of one's own country to "critical and moral scrutiny" (1986b, 9). Pinter's plays have at least an implicit moral appeal. The goal of the later plays is to shock audiences into an altered awareness of their true moral condition by exposing the violence done "in their name." While Pinter is not as sanguine as Shaw about achieving this goal, it nevertheless stands as a theoretical ideal towards which Pinter's political plays aim.

The implicit appeal to morality is a legacy of the Shavian model of political theater. In Pinter, morality and power stand in perpetual opposition. Power is the present antithesis to an absent thesis of moral conduct and individual autonomy. There is hope for moral strength as an ideal, but the ideal is never fulfilled. Pinter sees a false, self-absolving understanding of self as a political problem. He often criticizes how individuals in Western society wrongly see themselves as innocent and their political opponents as morally flawed or irredeemably evil, castigating the Western and American attitude that "we" are completely moral and our enemies completely evil (9). Attacking this false moral dichotomy is the aim of Pinter's political theater, yet Pinter the playwright seldom seems to believe that such ingrained moral mistakes can be overcome. Crucially, his late theater tries to place the audience so that it will perceive its own moral complicity with oppressive institutions: "Pinter's political theatre strips its spectators of their conventional invisibility and makes disinvolvement possible only as a conscious choice," writes Jeanne Colleran (1993, 57). Pinter's theater indeed *attempts* such goals, but with no prior assurance and little confidence that entrenched habits of dissociation and apathy can be aesthetically attacked. Pinter wants to break down the spectator's sense of moral isolationism, even as he dramatizes the powerful, who are impervious to opposition, and accepts the aesthetic and protective distance between audience and drama implicit in the proscenium stage.

The distinction between what political theater presents and what its audience receives has troubled political playwrights. The relationship of aesthetic success to political instruction has provoked numerous examinations in the course of twentieth-century theater. Brecht afforded a rather pessimistic view in "The Literarization of the Theatre," in which he argued that theatre, as form and event, encourages a bourgeois audience to see itself reflected in a positive manner. Brecht wanted his *Threepenny Opera* to criticize the bourgeoisie, yet his audiences refused to take the play that way. "The theatre itself resists any alteration of its function," wrote Brecht. "The theatre can stage anything: it theatres it all down" (1964, 43). Brecht's lament, if true, endangers all political art. The idea that theater's inherent properties conflict with political purposes becomes the basis of later self-criticisms of political drama.

Playwright and essayist David Edgar has reflected on reception issues of political theater. His play *The National Theatre* portrays the Shavian theater of moral self-criticism with great skepticism. One character describes how a socially empowered audience misses the point of a theater image meant to criticize itself:

> I went to see a play, at the Old Vic Theatre. It was written 60 years ago, this play, but it was, highly topical, about some national crisis, then. And everyone was talking like they're talking now, no leaders, drift, despair. And at the very end, these bombs came down, and nearly killed the people. And they were sad, the bombs had missed. And that seemed odd. And yet, the audience, who were all people just like these people, middle-class, and rich, and saying just the same, about the crisis, still they clapped and clapped. They surely didn't want a bomb on them. But what they said, about the crisis, now, and what they saw, it didn't seem to fit. Connect. As if, they couldn't see what they were watching. (1989, 131–32)

Through this clever reference to Shaw's *Heartbreak House*, Edgar reflects ironically and skeptically on the actual reception of political art. He doubts that audiences will see themselves reflected upon the stage; when this identification is unflattering, it is successfully resisted. If this is the case, political theater will then fail to foster moral scrutiny or critical self-consciousness in

its audience. Under these social conditions, such political theater as practiced by Shaw, Sartre, Brecht, Miller, and so on has
been neutralized.

Pinter's theater acknowledges audience resistance to seeing itself negatively. Indeed, he assumes that audiences will resist this
identification. These plays underscore the forces that oppose
progressivism and the oppression visited upon social victims
and outcasts. In so doing, Pinter writes a political theater that
denies solace to the audience, that frustrates our desire to find
hope in a brutal world, and that complicates even our wish to
discover reassurance in a clear-eyed depiction of our status quo.

This antagonistic relationship of play to audience is rooted in
the limited receptivity of that audience to any critique of it. According to Christopher Butler, the bourgeoisie supports oppositional art in order to congratulate itself on its social conscience
(1980, 120) so that the enterprise of political art is a charade. The
postmodern critic Peter Sloterdijk also argues that the dominant
mentality of the empowered classes in our contemporary moment is one that combines knowledge of political problems,
analyses, and ideologies, with the nullification both in theory
and in practice of these same ideologies.[9] Sloterdijk summarizes
the postmodern political consciousness: "With schizoids, anything is possible, and enlightenment and reaction do not make
much difference" (1987, 112). We are "clever, instinctive conformist[s]" (109) who live within "the twilight of false consciousness" (3). As well, "this consciousness no longer feels
affected by any critique of ideology; *its falseness is already re-
flexively buffered*" (5).

> The present-day servant of the system can very well do with the
> right hand what the left hand never allowed. By day, colonizer; at
> night, colonized; . . . officially a functionary, privately a sensitive
> soul; objectively a strategist of destruction; subjectively a pacifist;
> basically someone who triggers catastrophes; in one's own view, in-
> nocence personified. (113)

Arundhati Roy predicts the futility of a political or moral address to such a person, in terms of an Indian saying: "You can
wake someone who's sleeping. But you can't wake someone
who's pretending to be asleep" (2001, 68). Both Shaw and Pinter
are concerned about such institutionalized doubleness of the
self in both modern and postmodern society. Shaw saw it as his
political goal in the theater to pierce through such doubleness

by convincing his audience of its truly "sinful" nature. The title character of *Captain Brassbound's Conversion* is an anticoloni- alist exploiter of Ireland who, as one character says, never lets his right mind know what his left is doing (n.d., 440). Such per- sons will, in Sloterdijk's terms, feel themselves already buffered and protected from critique. This carapace of pretended virtue surely deflects the approach of a political theater that attempts to educate its audience morally. Pinter, in his "rigorous," angry and often brutal political theater, attempts to break through this formidable protective buffer in the receptivity of his audience. Indeed, what he stages often amounts to an assault on his audi- ence, as in *One for The Road*, or a dramatization of the very act of being silenced, as in *Party Time, Mountain Language*, and *The New World Order*.

The space that society gives morality to express itself seems to shrink in Pinter's political theater, as power oppresses the in- dividual voices of conscience and opposition. His drama chal- lenges adherents of the Enlightenment tradition—that is to say, those holding mainstream liberal popular attitudes and assump- tions, believing that progress and social justice are possible, identifying themselves as positive moral forces, believing that moral correction of society is possible. This challenge takes shape as the plays depict a power structure seemingly impervi- ous to critique and opposition. In this manner, Pinter's political theater critiques power relations even as the plays themselves dangerously suggest that such critique is, if not impossible, wholly inefficacious. At any rate, the paradox of a political the- atre confessing its own inefficacy is a novel development. Pin- ter's brand of political theater is self-questioning (and, to a viewer, profoundly unsettling) in that the negation of dissent that it enacts possibly applies to the enactment itself.[10]

Pinter's political theater brings us to the verge of the skeptical post-Enlightenment concept of individual autonomy. In this view, individuals are defined by the unequal power relations apart from which they do not exist; individual action, thought, and even experience cannot escape the power interests already in effect. Power, in preserving itself, enables whatever is effec- tively compliant, disables whatever is effectively oppositional. Individual consent (or dissent) is rendered problematic at best. Terms like "freedom," "equality," and "democracy," however appealing, are illusory and worse: they are, in effect, means by which the status quo, the rule of some over others, is main- tained. Language deformation, a classic Pinter theme, attains an explicit political dimension. Beneath these violated terms, Pinter might say, lies the true nature of the status quo: "a body protecting its own power and status . . . in any way at any time" (see 2002a, 24). Indeed, these terms can function to preserve and perpetuate current power structures exactly because of their wide appeal.

Pinter himself testifies to the imprisonment of language within power structures. Though his plays show censorship and oppression as a matter of officialized violence applied to dangerous speakers, he sees a perhaps more insidious process of self-silencing at work in our societies. In his view, oppositional ideas have been rendered impossible to utter or to receive. Speaking of a kind of "self-censorship" affecting those who might oppose their society, Pinter noted, "Nobody actually says, 'You cannot say such and such a thing,' but it is the *case* that you can't. This . . . applies to what we call democratic countries" (see 2002a, 23). Yet there is an irony here concerning the status of speaking out, both in Pinter's political plays and in his life.

Pinter's activities outside the theater emphasize a confidence in the capacity and necessity of the iconoclastic self and the oppositional conscience to resist an immoral or oppressive society. For instance, many of his current political activities center on the resistance of oppression directed at persons and groups. He has protested what he sees as the indiscriminate American use of power, the continued global tolerance of torture, the plight of the Kurds in Turkey, and the fate of writers enduring censorship and persecution. However, the fictive universe of his plays offers no certainty that such resistance to entrenched power is possible. The oppositional individual is characteristically destroyed, either before or after being silenced, as Pinter notes in a conversation with journalist Mel Gussow (1994, 69). Pinter's political theater presents political dissenters as silenced and marginalized, and their opponents as articulate, ruthless, and impregnable.

The status of oppositional speech divides Pinter's playwriting from his public actions, while also distinguishing the plays from contemporary theories of political protest. While in postmodern fashion we might stipulate the futility of countercultural speech, due to its necessary imbrication in social inequalities, the leaders of Pinter's dramatic regimes do not take anything like this view. In fact, these leaders view dissenting speech as dangerous, as something that must be stamped out by any means necessary. The notion of speech as a threat to power is

derided by postmodern theory. If Pinter's late plays exist, by virtue of their date of composition, in a postmodern framework,
there is nevertheless an important irony here: the plays' central
characters emphatically deny postmodern beliefs about the inefficacy of dissent. Pinter's tyrants live in a pre-postmodern world
in which there is a dangerous "outside" to the social world that
must be suppressed. Also, Pinter, as quoted above, often characterizes his political activities in the public sphere in terms of the
necessity of speaking truth to power. The dilemma here is how
to situate Pinter's political plays, symbolized by the silences
with which they culminate, within an appropriate context: as
reified emblems of postmodern social stasis, or as final testimony to a modernist ideal of opposition. One way to resolve this
dilemma is not to resolve it, to insist on the paradox that Pinter's political theater is both things simultaneously, the two
conflicting interpretations serving as correctives to each other.
Clearly, both as public citizen and creative artist, Pinter is pro-
vocatively ambiguous as he explores and exposes the workings
of power.

Sloterdijk articulates one such ambiguity when he considers
the power structure facing enlightenment reformers. Faced with
the steadfast power of the status quo, enlightenment itself must,
paradoxically and ironically, embrace violence as a strategy:

> Of course, enlightenment itself is the first to notice that it will not
> "pull through" with rational and verbal dialogue alone. No one can
> feel the faltering . . . the ruptures, the miscarriage of the dialogue
> more keenly than it. At the beginning of ideology critique there is
> also astonishment because the opponent is so hard of hearing. . . .
> *Hegemonic powers* cannot be addressed so easily; they do not come
> voluntarily to the negotiating table with their opponents, whom
> they would prefer to have behind bars. (1987, 14)

Sloterdijk's thoughts afford one context to view the inherent violence of the address of Pinter's political theater to its audience.
Daniel Mendelsohn, writing in the *New York Review of Books*,
argued that Pinter "has come to resemble his villains" in that
his political plays "bully" his audience and have no other purpose than gratifying their author's aggression (2001, 31). Ramon
Simo remarked in 1996 that Pinter's political works were filled
with "brutality and the obvious" (*VV*, 60), illustrating blunt and
simple messages.[11]

Perhaps, however, to some extent this aggression need not be understood solely as Pinter indulging himself. Rather, Pinter's rage might be prompted by an intuition of the reception his ideas will receive—or, to put this point in extreme fashion, perhaps we deserve to be bullied. The audience of Pinter's political theater is complicit in current deployments of power and unwilling to confront that complicity. Less hyperbolically, although the confrontation of protest versus the status quo may be initiated under the aegis of ideals such as equity, peace, justice, and freedom, this confrontation does not and cannot take shape as a peaceable meeting of equals (Sloterdijk 1987, 15). Entrenched power does not want to listen to contradictory viewpoints; it does not want to listen at all. The condition power prefers is the enforced silence of all opposition. Here can be glimpsed another way into the dilemma of countercultural speech—the status quo seeks to oppress potential opponents in advance of their specific opinions being uttered and without connection to the specific substance of those ideas. The powerful are predisposed against dissenters even before they dissent—*they're going to hate us anyway, so we might as well speak up*. Given this hatred and predisposition to violence by the status quo, the party of critique must then metaphorically arm itself prior to encountering the social forces it attempts to alter. Sloterdijk's metaphor of enlightenment versus power suggests that any communication attempting moral betterment will fail, and that failing, or anticipating its own failure, will bear a measure of violence. Perhaps such violence inheres fundamentally in the initial address of Pinter's political theater to an audience deeply complicit with an unjust status quo.

The status quo's preference for silent opposition is not prompted by the specific content of political critique. Rather, what is fundamentally disdained is anything that questions established social reality, any urge to think new thoughts:

> But even *tradition*, if one is allowed to speak allegorically about it, initially has no interest in granting equal rights of speech to enlighteners. From the dawn of time, human sentiment has regarded the old as the true, the new always as something questionable. This "archaic" feeling for truth had to be subdued by enlightenment, before we could see the new as the true. (Sloterdijk 1987, 14)

Pinter dramatizes this political conflict between the old and the new, as his political villains profess an absolute adherence to "tradition" and the past. Beneath the political battles of left versus right, socialists versus Tories, or progressives versus reactionaries lies an elemental prejudice against anything new. "What is old is good, take my tip," declares Goldberg in *The Birthday Party* (1961a, 70).[12] Attachments to a "tradition" are even less a matter of rational decision and belief than are attachments to a philosophy representing a reasoned, articulated worldview. The emotional basis and intellectual vagueness of an appeal to "tradition" ensures that its defense draws upon irrational energies, including hatred and violence. Perhaps Pinter's political efforts are appropriate to an era marked by ethnic rivalries and religious antagonisms. Murderous allegiances to deep, identity-forming affiliations, whether ethnic, racial, or religious, touch more elemental aspects of human nature than do partisan or ideological commitments. Loyalty to one's "breed," as Goldberg puts it, motivates all varieties of political oppression and protest (52).

Pinter is skeptical that "progress" or an improved civilization can be achieved. Enlightenment is now held in our postmodern era to be an aborted project; somewhat similarly, it seems that Pinter holds little hope that social problems can be ameliorated through reason or moral responsibility. It is not, in the view of these plays, that we are beyond enlightenment, but that it hasn't happened and never will: we are always before it, not past it. Given this, progressives approach their task of enlightenment fully sensing both the internal "faltering" and the violent opposition to be encountered in pursuit of political change.

In one of the most famous of twentieth-century political dramas, *Marat/Sade*, Peter Weiss summarizes the required urgency of the genre. "When will you learn to see / When will you learn to take sides" Roux pleads in the final lines of the play, followed by the wordless assault of the actors upon the audience (1971, 142). Weiss links proper vision with engagement; right seeing leads to right action. In Shaw's vision, accurate seeing leads to corrected thinking. Pinter's political theater truncates the radical program of Weiss, Brecht, and Shaw, hypothesizing no radical revolution, no Shavian-style moral conversion. Pinter wants us to see political reality through the ideological and linguistic obfuscations of a corrupt society, but he does not urge us to subscribe to any program. The plays appear to doubt that we can even perceive the enormity of our political complicity. Nevertheless, Pinter tries, vigorously and variously, to indict us for the political side we have already taken.

2

Early Plays and Retroactive Readings:
The Birthday Party, The Dumb Waiter,
and *The Hothouse*

SEVERAL PARADIGMS ARE POSSIBLE FOR RELATING THE EARLY PLAYS (through 1965) of Harold Pinter to his later ones (1983–present): the expressly political plays are either a fruitful and inevitable development of the earlier work or, contrarily, a diminishment of the work by which Pinter first won critical esteem. Given Pinter's political turn, many critics must now determine if their predominantly apolitical readings of his early plays are still accurate or useful. While important, it is not necessary to defend the political goals of Pinter's later playwriting by finding political messages or strategies in his earlier works (if in fact there are any such messages) or any "messages" at all. An artistic theme or technique is not necessarily made stronger because it can be seen earlier in a writer's career. Themes evolve over a literary career as a writer's particular interests change with time.

In Pinter's case, his political focus in the 1980s and beyond can be considered more instinctual than intellectual, more a matter of feeling than of theory. As several critics note, Pinter has become more political with age, the reverse path to careers such as John Osborne's. Success and celebrity have not softened Pinter's antagonism to the way the world works. Refreshingly, he is an angry old man.

The Birthday Party, The Dumb Waiter, and *The Hothouse,* which approach politics in various ways, do so with increasing directness. The following section on *The Birthday Party* examines how the play has been reinterpreted in light of Pinter's political turn, including by its author, and how history—notably the Holocaust—shapes the play's political vision. The discussion of *The Dumb Waiter* offers the social vision of Michel Foucault as an analogy to the operations of Ben and Gus's "organization," which is not a criminal subculture, but society itself. *The Hothouse* is an overtly angry drama, even more focused than *The Dumb Waiter* on surveillance and control, and Pinter suppressed its publication and performance until 1980. The chapter's last section examines how this early play anticipates his overt representations of power in the 1980s and later.

THE BIRTHDAY PARTY:
THE HOLOCAUST IN THE BACKGROUND

The Birthday Party culminates in silence—according to its author, it is defined by the inability of its protagonist to utter the words necessary to save him. The play has sparked numerous attempts at interpretation, making it Pinter's most written about work. It seems, at least figuratively, as if Stanley's lack of words has initiated a corresponding flow of articulation by readers, spectators, critics, and Pinter himself. The play has also been frequently reinterpreted in the theater since its 1958 debut. More recent reinterpretations attempt to solidify its political nature, examining how *The Birthday Party* dramatizes power structures and the possibility of political action. However, earlier criticisms of the play, including those by Pinter, point toward more apolitical themes associated with epistemological dilemmas, more characteristic of Pinter's absurdist roots. The discussion here is not presented to proffer a "truth" or interpretation of the play presuming to displace all other such interpretations, but to show how different constructions of the play—including those posited by its author—embrace concerns that both are and are not "political." Another goal is to demonstrate some specific historical references to political victimization, including the Holocaust, that ground Pinter's complex allegory of power.

One of the latest productions of *The Birthday Party*, Sam Mendes' 1994 version at the National Theatre, consciously aimed to be political:

Mendes . . . sees Stanley's situation as universal. He is Joseph K, but also anyone arrested under the Prevention of Terrorism Act. He is a victim of the Moonies, but also Salman Rushdie. . . . Usually acted in a tiny, seedy living room, this time the set features several other seedy rooms, the message being that sinister visits can happen to anyone. More plausible now than ever, the danger of arbitrary terror stalks a million homes. . . . (Sierz 1994, 34)

This political conceptualization extended to the play's final moments, when Petey, typically a recessive figure, turns courageous and almost powerful:

> Trevor Peacock's Petey . . . seemed at the end to pose a genuine threat to Goldberg and McCann. This was a point that particularly thrilled Pinter: "When Petey says he's going to look after his peas and not go back to the beach [74], you can feel the hysteria on the part of Goldberg and McCann. For a moment, Petey is the strongest man on stage. Finally he can't resist the invaders, but they are vulnerable, worried, anxious men." (Billington 1996, 356)

Here, Pinter describes a Petey quite different than the one labeled "impotent" in the 1958 poem "A View of the Party" (Pinter 1991, 34).

Interpreting *The Birthday Party*, with its evocations of subjugation, torture, and ethnic identity, provokes confrontation with Pinter's political turn. In 1985 Pinter stated that writing his plays made it "quite obvious" to him that they were about politics, dealing with abuse of authority and the destruction of social and political rebellion (1986b, 7–8). In 1994, Pinter gave an astonishingly honest answer to this question of whether *The Birthday Party* could be considered political:

> I think *The Birthday Party* is certainly shaped by persecution. . . . It's very, very simple, the actual . . . focus of it, I remember feeling when I was asked once or twice what the hell does *The Birthday Party* mean? where do these two men come from? It always surprised me then, the fact that people seemed to have forgotten the Gestapo had been knocking on people's doors not too long ago. And people have been knocking on people's doors for centuries in fact. *The Birthday Party* doesn't express anything unusual, it expresses something that is actually common. . . . I have to be quite clear here and say that I always knew that particularly *The Birthday Party* and *The Dumb Waiter* and *The Hothouse*, which I didn't produce for many years, were all political plays. I knew that at the time. I must say I tended, when asked, on the rare occasions when I was asked, to deny this. I've thought back and wondered why I, in effect, lied on those occasions. I really do believe it was because I didn't want to make great claims, or be pretentious in any way. I thought they [the plays] spoke for themselves already. (O'Toole 1999, 30)

Pinter's seemingly cheerful admission that "I lied" does not clarify in what interpretive context this play can most adequately be placed. Nor does it specify the meaning of a "political play" as named by Pinter.

Pinter's words do, however, point to several important aspects of the political nature of his writing. Pinter believes he is dramatizing not merely the present or the past but recurrent historical patterns—this being the assumption that *The Birthday Party* shows something quite "typical." Second, the Holocaust provokes a good deal of Pinter's political analysis, as evident from the example of *Ashes to Ashes*. Pinter is interested not only in the historical particularities of Nazi oppression but also in the repetition of persecution throughout all history. For the playwright, additionally, being a villain does not require membership in a group that has been categorized as immoral or villainous—a point he makes audaciously by making Goldberg, the head "Gestapo" figure in the play, a Jew. In this sense, *The Birthday Party* becomes "political" in that the play explores an historically specific oppression that we in the present have apparently been fated to experience, mutatis mutandis, again and again.

Pinter's earliest comments on the "meaning" of *The Birthday Party* ask us to reorient our relationship to meaning itself as a possibility of art. In a letter to director Peter Wood from March 30, 1958, Pinter responds to the question "What does it all mean?":

> Meaning begins in the words, in the action, continues in your head and ends nowhere. There is no end to meaning. Meaning which is resolved, parcelled, labelled and ready for export is dead, impertinent—and meaningless. (*VV*, 9)

The meaning of true art must be ambiguous, dynamic, uncertain. Here Pinter aligns his art with that which, as Susan Sontag put it, resists interpretation. Later, however, Pinter addresses the matter of meaning from an opposing perspective, pointing out his conscious control over the play (10) and going on to articulate a political reading about religious oppression:

> We've agreed; the hierarchy, the Establishment, the arbiters, the socio-religious monsters arrive to affect censure and alteration upon a member of the club . . . he collapses under the weight of their accusation—an accusation compounded of the shitstained strictures of

centuries of "tradition." . . . Couldn't we all find ourselves in Stanley's position at any given moment? (11)

Here Pinter, contradicting his belief in the infinite regression of
meaning, embraces a particular meaning without qualifying his
interpretation as merely provisional. The play opposes tradition
(Goldberg, who is frighteningly articulate) against individualist
dissent (Stanley, alarmingly inchoate). Pinter's view that the
play denounces the destructive effects of tradition and established religion anticipates his anti-right-wing politics of the
1980s, when tradition and morality became political tools of the
New Right.

Concentrating generally upon political violence, the play may
be seen as enacting the notion that violence is now the preroga-
tive of untouchable "organizations." Such organizations include
the state, which administers oppression through faceless, anonymous representatives. Violence (recall Stanley's attempts to
control his situation physically, from the attack on Goldberg to
the assault on Lulu) is no longer a viable outlet for rebellion or
social dissatisfaction by the oppressed. There is "nowhere to go"
(*BP*, 26) with any feelings of political discontent. In our one-dimensional society, there is no place from which to contest society's values, modes, and ideologies. What "protest" may exist is
co-opted and absorbed by society itself. The co-optation of dissent, the power of religious conservatives in American politics,
and violent repression by State forces are all important themes
of contemporary history, just as applicable to the present as to
the time Pinter conceived *The Birthday Party*.

Critic Jeanette Malkin offers a social-political reading of *The
Birthday Party*. The play depicts how Goldberg and McCann,
vessels for a language that is pure cliché, convert Stanley to a
supposedly beneficial allegiance to the economic and social
status quo. Incorporation into this social order replaces Stanley's
incipient individualism, his "dropout reclusiveness" (66). In analyzing the play's politics, Malkin focuses on the two long
scenes in which Goldberg and McCann "torture" Stanley, pre-
saging the importance of this subject in Pinter's political theater.

McCann gives one possible answer to the question of the results of such torture after his night with Stanley. "He's quiet
now. He stopped all that . . . talking a while ago," McCann declares (73). This statement echoes the plots of *One for the Road*,
Mountain Language, and *Party Time*: the destruction of dissi-

dent voices by any available means. As the 1950s evolve into the 1980s, Pinter's dissidents are silenced by increasingly direct and violent means. Stanley, after all, is apparently allowed to converse with his torturers. McCann even seems momentarily chagrined over what he has done to Stanley. Goldberg nearly breaks down and must revivify the sense of mission behind his activities. Pinter's later plays seem to present a world even more brutal than one in which torturers may feel guilt or anxiety. In *One for the Road*, Victor has his tongue cut off prior to the play's final scene, while in *The New World Order*, the torturers gloat over an unnamed victim, whose silence extends throughout the play.

Malkin views the effect of torture upon Stanley largely as transformative. He will be "integrated" into a mass, middle-class society of consumers and conformists. He undergoes "mental torture" designed to "gain power over his thoughts" (63), culminating in conversion to Goldberg's and McCann's conformist ways—a transformation signaled by Stanley's final costume as a 1950s "organization man." However, the final visual image Stanley presents strongly suggests a corpse (as Malkin notes). This image parallels Goldberg's earlier remark: "What are you but a corpse waiting to be washed?" In other words, Stanley is not only subjected; he is also destroyed. After his torture, it seems rather more likely that he will become a dead, or broken, man, rather than a model consumer. If the aim of torture is to evacuate desire in its victims, who must learn how little their wishes matter in the world, Stanley's conversion through torture into another "organization man" seems fanciful and unlikely. The transformation of Stanley into a middle-class citizen is a mild, mundane goal compared to what torture in fact accomplishes.

The play may provide a historical hint to Stanley's final condition, one that should not be regarded as conclusive but could hardly be more provocative. Goldberg tells Petey that Stanley needs "special treatment" (85). This phrase is the English translation of the official Nazi euphemism for gassing Jews, *Sonderbehandlung*. Perhaps a theme of the play, which no character is able to express, is hidden in this phrase.

One of the enticements offered to Stanley also has a Nazi ring to it.[1] Goldberg says "You'll be integrated" (84), reusing a word featured in Nazi oppression against those people (not only Jews) deemed antisocial who needed to be "integrated" back into productive society (Noakes 1987, 93). The process by which the

Nazis came to regulate and coordinate all dimensions of human activity (political, social, economic, philosophical, artistic, legal) in accordance with Hitler's vision was called *Gleichschaltung*, literally "parallel switching," often translated as "integration." This system of forced conformity symbolizes in Pinter's political imagination the violent depersonalization of which society is always capable. Stanley certainly qualifies as "workshy," one of a number of groups considered *gemeinschaftsfremd* ("alien to the community") and thus dangerous. This accusation parallels the charges that Stanley has betrayed his land and his breed (52). In act 3, Stanley emerges clean-shaven. The Nazis enjoyed shaving Jews in a sadistic fashion, robbing them of the beards that marked their religion (Daniel Goldhagen's *Hitler's Willing Executioners* has a startling picture of this practice [1996, 93]). Stanley renames himself "Joe Soap" (50), evoking one of the uses Nazis made of incinerated Jewish bodies. Mirroring anti-Jewish propaganda, Goldberg states, "No society would touch you," and a few seconds later McCann accuses Stanley of being vermin (51). Goldberg also describes how his car has just the right amount of room in the front and the back (70–71). This description may allude to the Nazi invention of gas vans to kill Jews prior to the gas chambers. The engineering of these vans proved inefficient. The back was too large in relation to the number of victims; the Jews would move to the rear of the van away from the gas vents, the van would tip over, and the flow of gas would be disrupted. Thus, from the oppressors' point of view, Jews were not being killed quickly enough. This messy and inefficient process was judged unduly upsetting for the murderers, who had to be physically close to the victims. The next step in the technology of genocide, more efficient and less offensive to the killers, was the gas chamber.[2]

The play leads critics to a further historical reference with McCann's famous question to Stanley, "What about the Albigensenist heresy?" (51). Though critics typically see Goldberg and McCann's questions as intimidating by virtue of their linguistic randomness, it is possible to derive referential meaning from McCann's query. The details of this heresy relate to elements of the play, while we can only speculate that Pinter's interest in his own (supposed) status as a Sephardic Jew may provide an intuitive identification with being persecuted as a religious minority. McCann's question about this heresy is one a defrocked priest might ask. Professing the dualist doctrine known as Catharism, the Albigensenists (the name given them by the Church, because the diocese of Albi was a heretic strong-hold) believed that "the sacraments lost their efficacy in the hands of wicked and corrupt priests" (Ruthven 1978, 82). This belief incurred the Church's wrath. Cathars sought spiritual perfection by minimizing the demands of the flesh, following a path of ascetic withdrawal from the world, disdaining pleasure, sex, and procreation, as Stanley does in the play. The more radical of these heretics doubted the efficacy of baptism, distrusting it as transformative magic; this notion evokes the critical attempts to see Stanley's final entrance as rebirth. The Albigensenists were also frequently accused of sodomy and other "unnatural" sexual acts due to their attitude against procreation. This accusation may parallel the sexual tricks contained in Goldberg's briefcase, about which Lulu says "You taught me things a girl shouldn't know before she's been married . . . three times!" (80).

From a historical point of view, the Albigensenist crusade in the twelfth and thirteenth centuries played a significant role in European civilization. The medieval Church, backed by the king of France and northern French nobles, conducted a military assault beginning in the year 1209 against the Languedoc region in the south of France, where the Cathars were established. This attack has been called one of Europe's first examples of "ethnic cleansing" (Naimark 2002, 5). The battles of the church against these heretics also provided major impetus to the use and codification of torture in Europe. Inquisitions, interrogations, and torture were used to persuade heretics to confess and to implicate others. As torture became normalized, its alleged initial purposes were blunted, its use evolved more blatantly into a political tool unrelated to religious orthodoxy. "[I]n the half-century that torture had been institutionalized . . . it had progressed from being an instrument of coercion for use against recalcitrant heretics and their protectors, to a weapon of mass intimidation" (Ruthven 1978, 98). Thus, with one reference, the play gestures to the historical continuity of political violence, specifically of torture, as an enduring fact of Western society.

Pinter's reference to medieval torture has another political resonance as well. While Pinter was writing the play in 1957, rumors as well as news of torture emerged to public view. The French Army and police in Algeria adopted torture in the attempt to repress Algerian rebels. In 1958 Henri Alleg published *The Question,* initially in America due to French censorship, exposing the details of French conduct. These actions shocked European consciences for two reasons: the emphasis on human rights in French law and the victimization of French citizens by the Nazis during World War II. Sartre, who had written the introduction to Alleg's book, articulated the irony that the victimized had become victimizers: "In 1943, in the Rue Lauriston [the Gestapo headquarters in Paris], Frenchmen were screaming in agony and pain. . . . Only one thing seemed impossible in any circumstances: that one day men should be made to scream by those acting in our name" (Sartre 1958, 13). In assigning Goldberg the role of the Gestapo, Pinter animates the irony of the oppressed becoming oppressor. The playwright's interest in torture as a public fact has to do with its sponsorship by governments supposedly on "our" side, on the so-called good side of history, acting in "our" name. Historian Edward Peters notes the Western world has seen two great periods of torture, the thirteenth and the twentieth centuries, a fact that is surely a strong argument against the idea of human history exemplifying moral progress (1985, 18).

The actual psychology of torturers is accurately portrayed in the play through the characters of Goldberg and McCann. Certain men (and some women) are chosen by torturing regimes for their tasks due to a fervent belief in a set of external values that allows the world to be read in terms of an opposition between "us" and "them." These "others" are seen as a threat to the stability of society. The torturer is motivated by a belief that the world is just and that his actions make it more so. These beliefs in the correctness of oneself and one's cause are held with literal fundamentalism and with an absolute absence of doubt. Goldberg exclaims to Stanley in the first torture session, "Of course [we're] right! We're right and you're wrong, Webber, all along the line!" (BP, 51). Pinter recurrently dramatizes this sense of complete rectitude as he creates the political villains and tyrants who populate his theater.

Act 3 shows Goldberg in crisis as he falters three times in his attempt to articulate a personal philosophy of life (BP, 78), seeming to indicate the importance of Goldberg's inner belief as a torturer. Moments after Petey decides to stay and McCann again vents his nervous frustration, Goldberg is apparently rocked to the core. Bizarrely, he asks his friend for succor in the form of breathing into his mouth. Like a salesman discussing his secret of professional success, Goldberg begins to speak of the supposed secret to his strength, his fitness, and his power.

I've never lost a tooth. Not since the day I was born. Nothing's changed. . . . That's why I've reached my position, McCann. Because

I've always been as fit as a fiddle. All my life I've said the same. Play
up, play up, and play the game. Honour thy father and thy mother.
All along the line. (77)[3]

And you'll find—that what I say is true.
Because I believe that the world . . . (*Vacant.*). . . .
Because I believe that the world . . . (*Desperate.*). . . .
BECAUSE I BELIEVE THAT THE WORLD . . . (*Lost.*). . . . (78)

Goldberg rebounds from this low point by invoking the authority of his father. His momentary breakdown, when Goldberg
is unable to recall or articulate what he believes, threatens his
survival and his power. Pinter seems to suggest here that this is
a villain disabled because he has no self, no core beliefs—at least,
none susceptible to articulation. Critics and readers, proud of
their intelligence, may see Goldberg as a man who doesn't know
how to think and who thus loses self-control, a man whose inner
vacuity causes his downfall.

It is my provocative speculation that Pinter invites this attitude toward Goldberg specifically so that he may work against
the condescension inherent in it. This is demonstrated by the
short duration of Goldberg's disablement, by the very fact that
it is containable. Though the means of Goldberg's recuperation
are illogical, they are effective. Goldberg again extols his father
as the bedrock of his own present power and capacity, but he
speaks illogically, as his syntax and sentences fall apart. However, this seems to work as a strategy, as Goldberg soon reemerges as good as ever, abundantly ready for his final
victimization of Stanley. Goldberg's thoughts may be a jumble
of clichés twisting and turning into illogicality, but one should
not presume figures such as Goldberg need cognitive clarity. Au-
thoritarians, reports one sociologist, "make a mockery of the notion that people will feel 'dissonance' or 'imbalance' if their
ideas do not fit together properly" (Altemeyer 1996, 142). Such
people function very well with beliefs that do not satisfy criteria
of order and consistency. Whether we emphasize Goldberg's
breakdown as opposed to his recovery varies according to
whether we prefer an ironic view of power—where power causes
its own downfall—over one that simply sees power as unitary,
ever itself, ever in the process of domination.

The bizarre variety of accusations Goldberg and McCann level
at Stanley, as well as McCann's doubt regarding the purpose of
the visit, illustrates another empirical fact about torture. Once

initiated, torture detaches itself from its original purposes and becomes self-perpetuating and routinized, done for its own sake. Is Stanley the intended victim of the "organization" or "breed" that Goldberg and McCann represent, or is he simply the victim of a confusion of identity—just as some of the unnamed victims in *Mountain Language* are in fact being incarcerated by virtue of an administrative mistake by the oppressors?

Pinter's admiration of the strong Petey in Mendes' 1994 production may betray his own understandable desire as a political being to find someone in this mess from whom to draw positive inspiration. While in Pinter's 1958 poem "A View of the Party" Petey is described as "impotent,"[4] Pinter frequently refers to Petey's line "Don't let them tell you what to do!" in self-descriptions of his political life. To Pinter, this thought summarizes his political theater and his overall stance of political commitment. He declared to Mel Gussow in 1988, "I've lived that line all my damned life. Never more than now" (Gussow 1994, 71).

If so, one hopes Pinter was able to live the substance of the line better than his character, for Pinter seems to ignore that in the world of his own play, it is not at all efficacious. Petey's declaration embraces an ideology of self-determination and courageous independence. Yet its content is belied by the landscape into which it is uttered, as Petey addresses himself to the victorious Goldberg and McCann. These men have nullified Stanley's potential for individuality. Petey is nothing more than a parrot, mouthing meaningless words. His proudest, most moral moment is without moment. When Petey sends out this plea, notes Malkin, "it is too late; [Stanley] has already been told" what to do (67). "[E]ven in his finest hour, Petey can offer only the most token resistance" note Almansi and Henderson (1983, 39). The disjunction between what the words do for Pinter and what they do in his play is stark, almost amounting to a paradox. Pinter is apparently set free by a self-reliant realization of the necessity to speak unafraid against power, but the plot of *The Birthday Party* certainly tells a different tale.

This paradox—wherein political resistance is urged while simultaneously its futility is demonstrated through the play— itself demands explanation. Kenneth Burke argues that one way to celebrate a political cause in art is to depict the suffering of its adherents. The artist works by contradiction; where the essayist favoring a certain cause would argue logically, pointing out its merits while attacking arguments against it, the poet, by contrast would seem . . . to stress the factor of disserviceability. For how better recommend a Cause by the strategies of a fiction than by picturing it as worthy of being fought for? And how better picture it as worthy of being fought for than by showing people who are willing to sacrifice their safety, lives, and happiness in its behalf? Such facts must lead us to search in all deeply felt tragedies the symbol of a birth, and not of the dying we should rationally expect. (1957, 215–16)

Burke concludes that human causes are always recommended in art "by the symbol of the Crucifixion" (217). His analysis provides a way to distinguish between the plot of a piece of art versus its final effect—a discouraging story may nevertheless have an encouraging result. However, not only does the play deny Stanley a clear connection with any named cause or group but it seems also to do its best to trivialize his suffering. Even when he is taken away, we see only that Stanley is shaven and well dressed. He is even offered rewards for leaving—much rougher treatment could be imagined. It could be thought that his restricted life with Meg and Petey is one he has chosen—it's his own fault. When Stanley does emerge as a full-fledged victim or martyr, one never knows (beyond the vague and perhaps unreliable assertion that he has a "unique touch" [22]) why he is marked out for victimization or in the name of what cause he becomes a martyr.

In 1967 Victor Amend described *The Birthday Party* as Brechtian—nearly two decades before the phrase "political Pinter" became common. Because Stanley is so thoroughly dehumanized, one is not able to empathetically connect to him, thus leading to a rational examination of what happened to Stanley and why (166). Put another way, because Stanley is so completely vanquished and Petey's opposition so tentative, we may be led to display in our political lives the resistant qualities the characters demonstrate so minimally. Hall concurs with this notion, though she positions Pinter's political method as postmodernist. With every domestic item in the house conspiring against Stanley, notes Hall, and with Petey's ultimate aversion to confrontation, "Pinter leaves us questioning the means by which we can make a difference in a world of shifting realities and multiple meanings" (1997, 53). Everything Meg and Petey do and fail to do "has consequences," presumably political ones, thus suggesting that "political action can and must begin at home" (52, 53). Yet the paradox remains: everything we have seen in this home allows a unidirectional politics pointing toward (more) repression.

Another way to approach the extreme pessimism in Pinter's political theater is simply to underline the paradox between the necessity of political action and the entrenched power of the status quo. Logically speaking, the impossibility of effective political action does not detract from its desirability or necessity. That is, merely because something is impossible to do doesn't mean it isn't worth trying. Goldberg describes such a condition in his famous pseudophilosophical treatise on the number 846. He states, "It's necessary but not possible. . . . We admit possibility only after we grant necessity. It is possible because necessary but by no means necessary through possibility" (*BP*, 50). This view, applied to the notion of political action, amounts metaphorically to what might be termed a Beckettian view of resistance, one that simultaneously acknowledges the necessity and futility of opposing the status quo. This view is one Pinter himself articulated in reference to the premiere of *One for the Road*:

> You know I do believe that what old Sam Beckett says . . . is right on the ball. "You must go on, I can't go on, I'll go on." Now in this particular reference, if he'll forgive me using his language in this context, there's no point, it's hopeless. That's my view. . . . Because reason is not going to do anything. Me writing *One for the Road*, documentaries, articles, lucid analyses . . . voices raised here and there, people walking down the road and demonstrating. Finally it's hopeless. There's nothing one can achieve. (20)

So there is no ground for believing correct knowledge of the world will ultimately lead to effective action within it. There is a corollary as well: an argument for the necessity of political resistance can never be grounded in its potential success. This is so in that the assumption of viable opposition misrepresents political reality. The notions that everything will turn out all right, that it's all for the best, that knowledge begets truth which begets action, and that things are not as bad as they might have been or as they were in the past or as they probably will be in the future, all represent an evasion of the truth: in a word, bad faith. We are impelled to action, simultaneously as we are forbidden to hope.

This paradoxical condition of hopelessness encasing hope, familiar to readers of Beckett, finds another echo in philosophical considerations of ethics in the era after the Holocaust. After the

Holocaust, concepts of morality, goodness, compassion, resistance, and dignity were no longer available as they were before: if they had existed with as much solidity as we would like to think, the Holocaust should have been impossible. The Nazi genocide, as Theodor Adorno and George Steiner have variously suggested, exploded the myth of "civilization." Moral progress is no longer guaranteed, and there is no certainty that one's well-intentioned intervention in any political or historical situation will be beneficial. As Emmanuel Levinas asks, "Doesn't a phenomenon like Auschwitz invite you . . . to think the moral law independent of the Happy End?" (qtd. in Hatley 2000, 98). His question suggests that ethics must exist without any assumption of its efficacy. Even more simply, *Do whatever you want, but get the idea of a positive ending out of your mind.* Being responsible for those who suffer is an obligation with no inherent justification: "one's responsibility [for or towards others] is revealed to be gratuitous, without precedence, and without the security of a founding principle" (Hatley 2000, 98). Social morality is, to use the word in its root philosophical sense, absurd. To say that ethical duty is without foundation is also to say that it cannot be explained in language—that it resides in silence. As the broken, wordless, and worldless Stanley is escorted to his special treatment, the silence imposed upon him represents the total, brutal destruction of his voice and self. The "gerk in [Stanley's] throat" (*VV*, 10)—his final feeble efforts at articulation— ironically accentuates the completeness of his collapse, his descent into a silence that connotes utter powerlessness. This is a permanent silence, one that conclusively refutes Stanley's belated attempts to speak up for himself, one that contains no echoes of his always tentative, now stilled voice. It is a silence beyond echo, absolute and totalizing. Yet this silence is both absolute and complex; it also represents the necessity of a futile resistance to all analogous brutalities. Virtually all of Pinter's political works end in some variant of this painful, double-edged silence.

Oppression's efficiency increases as Pinter's political focus sharpens. In *The Dumb Waiter* (written in 1957), Pinter again examines issues of power and oppression culminating in and indexed by an ominous final silence; he also uses a comic pairing of two men whose job descriptions include violence, kidnapping, and murder. Pinter dramatizes the particulars of effective repression. Power is always ready to subjugate us—"We all have to be very careful. The boot is itching to squash and very efficient," Pinter remarks in his letter to Wood (*VV*, 10). But oppression would be much easier to administer if we, its subjects, stood ready to subjugate ourselves. Power's activities are more overt and dramatic in *The Birthday Party*, but dominance need not be obvious to be present; the mode of power called banality is just as effective.

THE DUMB WAITER: DISCIPLINE, SILENCE, AND SELF-ENSLAVEMENT

As with *The Birthday Party*, critics argue over numerous, divergent readings of this play. *The Dumb Waiter* has been regarded as a light play, "an hour's worth of sheer, rich fun" (Carpenter 1979, 113), as religious or supernatural allegory, as an existentially flavored vaudeville, as a depiction of postexistential absurdity, or as a play about epistemological uncertainty, charting limits to human knowledge and our attempts as individuals to produce meaning in our lives (van Laan 1987; Quigley 1978). One way to assign political weight to *The Dumb Waiter* is to analyze how the play dramatically embodies Michel Foucault's theories of power by creating a fictive world marked by observation, discipline, punishment, and self-subjection. In *The Dumb Waiter*, Pinter dramatizes, in Michel Foucault's phrase, a "carceral society" built on repressive, continual observation and disciplinary coercion, a surveillance that is subsumed into a system of impersonalized authority perceived as inevitable, unexceptional, even beneficial.

Foucault's view of social power accounts for the complex ways in which political subjects are formed and how social constructs are maintained. In the eighteenth century, according to Foucault's *Discipline and Punish* (1979), a new vision of society was created, one that saw society as susceptible to definition, order, and control through a system of mutually reinforcing observations, classifications, and examinations. Power does more than simply repress; it constitutes the ground on which behavior is judged, individuals are formed, and social truths and norms are established. Subjectivity itself is shaped within social contexts of power and knowledge produced by that power; power is dispersed and decentralized, though not necessarily identified with specific power holders. Foucault calls this system "discipline":

In discipline, the elements are interchangeable, since each is defined by the place it occupies in a series, and by the gap that separates it from the others. The unit is, therefore, neither the territory (unit of domination), nor the place (unit of residence), but the *rank*: the place one occupies in a classification. . . . Discipline is an art of rank, a technique for the transformation of arrangements. It individualizes bodies by a location that does not give them a fixed position, but distributes them and circulates them in a network of relations. (1979, 145–46)

This system of discipline supports a new definition of society that emerged in the transition from the classical to the modern era:

[I]ts fundamental reference was not to the state of nature, but to the meticulously subordinated cogs of a machine, not to the primal social contract, but to permanent coercions, not to fundamental rights, but to indefinitely progressive forms of training, not to the general will but to automatic docility. (169)

This uniquely modern form of power as "discipline" features an array of techniques for managing individuals, for classifying, controlling, testing, and refining human subjects. Power, Foucault argues, comes to operate overtly as well as covertly. Discipline works impersonally, like a machine:

[A]lthough surveillance rests on individuals, its functioning is that of a network of relations from top to bottom, but also to a certain extent from bottom to top and laterally; this network "holds" the whole together and traverses it in its entirety with effects of power that derive from one another: supervisors, perpetually supervised. . . . [Discipline] . . . functions like a piece of machinery. . . . [D]isciplinary power [is] both absolutely indiscreet, . . . since by its very principle it leaves no zone of shade and constantly supervises the very individuals who are entrusted with the task of supervising; and absolutely "discreet," for it functions permanently and largely in silence. Discipline makes possible the operation of a relational power that sustains itself by its own mechanism. . . . Thanks to the techniques of surveillance, the "physics" of power . . . operates . . . without recourse, in principle at least, to excess, force or violence. (1979, 176–77)

Foucault represents ideal discipline using Jeremy Bentham's "Panopticon," a device that enables disembodied seeing and anonymous power. The Panopticon, located at the center of a

circular prison, was to house a warden or watcher, able to perceive the inhabitants of the surrounding cells while remaining
invisible. Embodying observation, surveillance, and hierarchy,
the Panopticon illustrates the "transformation of Western societies from . . . sovereign power to disciplinary power" (Sarup
1993, 68). It aims

> to induce in the inmate a state of conscious and permanent visibility
> that assures the automatic functioning of power. So to arrange
> things that the surveillance is permanent, even if it is discontinuous
> in its action; that the perfection of power should tend to render its
> actual exercise unnecessary; . . . that the inmates should be caught
> up in a power situation of which they themselves are the bearers. . . .
> In view of this, Bentham laid down the principle that power should
> be visible and unverifiable. Visible: the inmate will constantly have
> before his eyes the tall outline of the central tower from which he is
> spied upon. Unverifiable: the inmate must never know whether he
> is being looked at any one moment; but he must be sure that he may
> always be so. (Foucault 1979, 201)

The Panopticon thus perpetuates "dissymmetry, disequilib-
rium, difference" (202). Mark Haugaard characterizes this feature of panoptic surveillance: "Being seen without being able to
see is the ultimate in non-reciprocity" (1997, 82).

"Being seen without being able to see" is the essence of Ben
and Gus's predicament in *The Dumb Waiter*. In one scene, an
envelope is slid under the door of the room where Gus and Ben
are hiding. Gus has been complaining he can't smoke as he has
no matches; he spends about a minute of stage time (nearly two
pages in the script) in deciding to pick up the envelope. When he
opens it, he finds twelve matches. With lengthy directions from
Ben, Gus straps on his revolver to investigate. This reconnais-
sance mission is an absolute failure:

> *He goes to the door, opens it, looks out and shuts it. . . .*
> BEN. What did you see?
> GUS. Nothing.
> BEN. They must have been pretty quick. (*DW*, 96)

From later experience in the play, Gus and Ben learn they are
under observation. Though this oversight is intermittent, it has
the same effect on them as constant surveillance. Gus and Ben
come to realize they are subject to power even when the action
of power is not visible or present. Gus's experience confirms

that there is no escape from this disciplinary system of power; as Foucault writes, there is no "outside" to disciplinary control (1979, 301). What the Panopticon attempts in Bentham's imaginary prison, the dumbwaiter performs in Pinter's play; both create loyal subjects through observation and discipline. The architecture of Pinter's set contains its own panopticon, capable of watching and disciplining those within its purview. *The Dumb Waiter* ends when the centrality of Foucauldian discipline to Gus's life, and Ben's, has been demonstrated.

The Dumb Waiter has provoked sharp disagreement among Pinter scholars, with the play, especially its ending, coming in for criticism. Traditional terms of *The Dumb Waiter* criticism privilege philosophical or religious considerations over sociopolitical analysis. In the midst of British theater's radicalization after John Osborne's *Look Back in Anger*, playwrights were classified either as angry young men with a social message, or as absurdist inheritors of continental writers such as Eugene Ionesco and Samuel Beckett. Pinter's identification with Samuel Beckett led to a view of *The Dumb Waiter* as recapitulating the absurdist vision (a development furthered by the religious signification ascribed to *Waiting for Godot*). James Hollis, for instance, writes that the voice of the dumbwaiter represents a "detached and unconcerned" cosmic power indifferent to human concerns (1970, 50). Several critics deny the play has any intellectually responsible "meaning." Kristin Morrison labels the play "Pinter made easy," an example of craft rather than meaning (1983, 142–43). Thomas van Laan sees the playwright mocking, rather than supplying, meaning in the play (1987, 118), while Charles Carpenter argues simply that virtually all interpretations of the play are overblown, claiming the play's "base metal of silliness" (1979, 113) should not be subjected to a critical alchemy that would yield any serious meaning.

Arguments for the seriousness of *The Dumb Waiter* often cite the murderous nature of the "organization." However, assuming that Ben shoots Gus ignores Austin Quigley's warning that to presume Gus's murder is "interesting but irrelevant speculation"; he further asserts that the play is "climaxed not by a gunshot, nor by the lowering of Ben's gun, but by a long, silent stare" (1978, 1). More specifically, it is Gus who completes this stare by raising his head to look at Ben (*DW*, 121). Therefore, although Ben does not shoot him, Gus recognizes that he may do so at any moment. Gus signals understanding of this fact by returning Ben's gaze; that is, Gus sees how he has always been visible within the context of power. Arguably, he now comprehends that he has always been seen, that the disciplinary system, what he and Ben (echoing Goldberg and McCann) call "the organization," contains him. Since Gus's fate is left inconclusive, it is possible to infer that the system does not require Gus to be dispensed with; it requires only that he become aware how he can be treated.

In the transition to a system of disciplinary power, it was discovered that it is more useful to observe people than to make an example of them through public punishment (Sarup 1993, 67). Power tends to render physical violence unnecessary; violence is too inefficient and too costly a strategy for obtaining Gus's docility. Presumably Gus now faces the responsibility of doing as Ben does; Gus must now oversee himself. This lesson of self-surveillance is the lesson discipline needs to teach. "Disciplinary power," Sarup writes of Foucault, "[is] a system of surveillance which is interiorized to the point that each person is his or her own overseer. Power is thus exercised continuously at minimal cost" (1993, 7). Gus is forced to acknowledge the power that has always been right in front of his eyes, just as Bentham's inmate, according to Foucault, becomes "sure that he may always be" observed by the Panopticon (1979, 201).

Directly preceding the play's end, with its final enclosure of Gus in an all-subsuming system of discipline, he dares to confront Ben about exactly who is observing and tormenting them. This penultimate scene may be read as the emergence of a political consciousness on Gus's part. Gus is perturbed by the meticulous care taken to subordinate him as one cog within a vast machine. The exchange crystallizes a change hinted at throughout *The Dumb Waiter*:

> GUS (*Slowly, in a low, tense voice*) . . . Why did he send us matches if he knew there was no gas?
>   BEN *looks up.*
> Why did he do that?
> BEN. Who?
> GUS. Who sent us those matches?
> BEN. What are you talking about?
>   GUS *stares down at him.*
> GUS (*thickly*). Who is it upstairs?
> BEN (*nervously*). What's one thing to do with another?
> GUS. Who is it, though?
> BEN. What's one thing to do with another?
> BEN *fumbles for his paper on the bed.*

GUS. I asked you a question.
BEN. Enough!
GUS (*with growing agitation*). I asked you before. Who moved in? I asked you. You said the people who had it before moved out. Well, who moved in?
BEN (*hunched*). Shut up.
GUS. I told you, didn't I?
BEN (*standing*). Shut up! (*DW*, 117)

Reaching a climax, the scene shows Gus's worldview dissolving:

GUS (*passionately, advancing*). What's he doing it for? We've been through our tests, haven't we? We got right through our tests, years ago, didn't we? We took them together, don't you remember, didn't we? We've proved ourselves before now, haven't we? We've always done our job. What's he doing all this for? What's the idea? What's he playing these games for? (118)

Gus's assumption that they are being tested and still found wanting provokes mute violence from Ben, who "*slaps him hard, back-handed, across the chest*" (118).

By daring to connect "one thing with another," Gus begins to participate in a way of looking at the world that is embryonically "political." He begins to comprehend that the problem is not with the system itself, or with his immediate superior, Ben. The problem is with him, or rather what he has allowed himself to become in relation to the organization above him. Seeing himself as others see him, docile, Gus may now be on the verge of becoming other than automatic in his obedience. Gus and Ben debate the causality of their situation, seeing themselves as they are seen by others, thereby realizing their fundamentally instrumental importance to an "integrated" system of power (Foucault 1979, 176). Gus and Ben become "political" as they *begin* to elevate their worldview from the personal to the level of groups and hierarchy. *The Dumb Waiter* is metapolitical in the sense that the play investigates the process by which Gus (and in a different way Ben) emerge from mental outlooks that ignore issues of power and violence into an awareness of the world that admits the existence of these realities.

Gus, except in the speech above, does not explicitly criticize the system. While it is Gus who asks the questions, it is Ben who puts forward the idea that they are being watched and judged. Gus's questions, often critically read as evidence of rebellion, are more like requests for information. That Gus is hardly an habitual iconoclast is revealed by Ben's line "You never used to ask me so many questions" (DW, 99). At the play's midpoint, Gus says of Wilson, his and Ben's superior, "There are a number of things I want to ask him. But I can never get round to it, when I see him" (102).[5] Thus Gus's questions, such as "Who clears up after we've gone? I'm curious about that" (103), are never fully asked. Ben generally diverts Gus from talking about what he wants to discuss (as on 86, 87, 91, and 102); either Ben treats the questions as illegitimate and not worthy of response, or Gus fails to verbalize the full ramifications of his queries.

Late in the play, Gus becomes curious about his own habit of obedience. Reflecting on their efforts to satisfy the dumbwaiter's demands to give up all their food, Gus remarks, "Why did you [Ben] send him up all that stuff? (Thoughtfully.) Why did I send it up?" (DW, 113). As with Clov's question to Hamm in Endgame, "There's one thing I'll never understand. Why I always obey you. Can you explain that to me?" (Beckett 1958, 75–76), Gus's question finds no answer, eliciting only a pregnant pause, seemingly full of desperation. Indeed, it is characteristic of the tentativeness of Gus's questioning that he follows his inquiry by irrelevantly marveling at how fully stocked his tormentor's salad bar must be: "Cold meat, radishes, cucumbers. Watercress. Roll mops. (Pause.) Hardboiled eggs" (DW, 113).

In light of Gus's supposed iconoclasm, it is also worth noting that the call to discipline Gus, a call which may, or may not, have upset Ben (DW, 92), had occurred before we see Gus indulge in the "rebellion" that supposedly marks his fate.[6] Gus has glimpsed the arbitrary operation of the system he serves, but he barely articulates his revolt, let alone acts on it. His opposition is contained as a revolt and never nears the threatening status of rebellion. "Gus is *replaceable* if he does not behave *properly*," writes Merritt of a particular production of the play (1986, 58). In the present reading, however, Gus is replaceable without conditions, because replaceability is a property of the power system in which he exists. All elements within discipline are interchangeable. There are no distinctions between different "people," no attitude toward the concept of individual variances other than antagonism. In this regard, we have been fooled as spectators by expectations that dramatic characters are differentiated by personality. We are tricked into seeing personal distinctions as causal, a notion that is simply not part of the system of disciplinary power enmeshing Ben and Gus.

But if the notion of human differences is precisely what discipline tries to manage, this system of power does consider questions of interiority. The system of power represented in the dumbwaiter seems already to know what Gus was thinking before he says it, before he fully thinks it, perhaps. "Intention rather than transgression now becomes the central criterion of culpability" within a system of disciplinary power (Sarup 1993, 67). Merely wanting to ask questions is enough to provoke the display of surveillance. One does not have to rebel actively against this system to call forth its punishment. This is Gus's and Ben's lesson.

Ben may not be completely ignorant of how the "organization" has subsumed him and Gus. Ben's defensive question "What's one thing to do with another?" indicates he can at least conceive that the episode of the matches is connected to the dumb waiter's demands, which resulted in Ben and Gus giving up "all they had" (DW, 111) to the mysterious powers above. The outburst about "our tests" is not answered by Ben, who has *already* asserted that the events of their day have nothing to do with one another. Ben's inability to counter Gus suggests the possible falseness of Ben's position that the events of the day are unconnected.[7]

Ben calls himself the "senior partner" in this duo and acts paternalistically toward Gus (DW, 98). Ben's name has the religious meaning of a paternally favored son (Benjamin being Jacob's youngest son, the favorite of his old age). But within disciplinary power, even the supervisors must themselves be constantly supervised.

Modern power asserts itself through techniques other than panoptic supervision. In addition to surveillance and coercion, the bureaucratic examination further enables the operations of disciplinary power:

> The examination combines the techniques of an observing hierarchy and those of a normalizing judgment. It is a normalizing gaze, a surveillance that makes it possible to qualify, to classify, and to punish. (Foucault 1979, 197)

This analysis echoes Gus's cry of despair over their seemingly infinite testing. He asks, "What's he doing it for? We've been through our tests, haven't we?" (DW, 118). By focusing on the progressive, unceasing nature of the duo's "tests," it can be seen that discipline's treatment of Gus is nothing personal, nor is it specific to either Gus or Ben. What the play shows is not Gus's execution on the grounds of inefficiency, rebellious nonconformity, or emergent intellectualism, but simply one more test in a series of tests designed to keep Gus and Ben, as functionaries, in practice, to increase the store of surveilled information about them, and to remind them of the power system in which they are enmeshed. The terrifying, although banal, truth is that Gus has made only one "mistake." He assumed the tests he already passed were the only ones he would ever have to take.

The play thus ends on Gus's recognition that he is, has been, and will forever be vulnerable to discipline. The contrast between Ben and Gus may be related to other terms belonging to Foucault's later analyses of discipline and power. About a decade after *Discipline and Punish*, Foucault broadened his analysis of power through the concept of "governmentality," a level of power involving, among other things, regulation and self-regulation. During this time, he extended his notion of how power forms subjects. Modern power shifts responsibility for "conducting conduct" from the state or sovereign to the individual. Barry Hindess explains this concept:

> Government . . . aims to regulate the *conduct* of others or of oneself. In addition to acting directly on individual behavior, it thus aims to affect behavior indirectly by acting on the manner in which individuals regulate their own behavior. (1996, 106)

"We live," Foucault emphasizes "in the era of a 'governmentality' first discovered in the eighteenth century" (1991, 103).

The difference between Ben and Gus can be clarified through the concept of how conduct is conducted within the mode of governmentality. Unlike Gus, Ben accepts that his personality and "self" are created within a structure of power. Ben serves as his own judge, internalizing an externally enforced perspective on his own conduct. Pinter dramatizes Ben's submission to hierarchical standards through his deferential dialogue with the voice at the other end of the speaking tube (*DW*, 111). Ben's craven tone here contrasts to his rough and scornful attitude toward Gus. When it appears that the pair will not be able to obey the dumbwaiter's orders, Ben "*despairs*" (113). At one point in their dealings with the dumbwaiter, Gus hides an Eccles cake for a snack, reasoning "Well, they don't know we've got it, do they?" Ben ripostes, "That's not the point" (106). Ben knows that safety lies in assuming that one is being observed, that one must always act *as if* one is being watched: "Self-enslavement is the moment of horror" (Sarup 1993, 76).

If the soldier is the model personality of the modern era (Foucault 1979, 135), then Ben is a man of the times, while the dyspeptic, restless Gus is all too clearly out of joint. Ben exemplifies this new style of personhood because he self-governs; he conducts his own conduct. Ben's identity is an effect of power, determined by the "interests" of others even though he believes his behavior is self-regulated:

> BEN (*lowering the paper*). You kill me. Anyone would think you're working every day. How often do we do a job? Once a week? What are you complaining about?
> GUS. Yes, but we've got to be on tap though, haven't we? You can't move out of the house in case a call comes.
> BEN. You know what your trouble is?
> GUS. What?
> BEN. You haven't got any interests.
> GUS. I've got interests.
> BEN. What? Tell me one of your interests.
> *Pause.*
> GUS. I've got interests.
> BEN. Look at me. What have I got?
> GUS. I don't know. What?
> BEN. I've got my woodwork. I've got my model boats. Have you ever seen me idle? I'm never idle. I know how to occupy my time, to its best advantage. Then when a call comes, I'm ready.
> GUS. Don't you ever get a bit fed up?
> BEN. Fed up? What with?
> *Silence.* (DW, 90)

Ben boasts how he accommodates himself, his personal life, to the order that governs him; his personality is a creation of the power that arranges his life. He has effectively taken on the task of governing his behavior. Discipline allows its subjects to believe that their lives are self-designed, as Ben does. He is governed from within, while Gus cannot get used to being (self-) controlled in this manner.

In the previously noted scene in which Ben discusses his interests, and indeed throughout the play, Ben allows Gus no language in which to manifest his discomfort. Gus's silence in this early scene, and his overall inability to articulate discontent meaningfully, are different versions of the inaudibility into which Gus sinks at the end of *The Dumb Waiter*. This silence announces the victory of Ben's accommodationist vocabulary over Gus's.[8]

Pinter anticipates something about contemporary power with Ben's victory. The task of conducting one's own conduct is pleasant, virtuous, and necessary to Ben, who never loses his cool, who advises his partner Gus he is getting "slack" (*DW*, 108), who appreciates that under the current regime of power, wherein each person must adopt the role of "his own overseer," that "things have tightened up" (93). This quality of self-regulation earns Ben his survival, at least temporarily, demonstrating how Pinter dramatizes the enveloping, formative power against which everyone, not merely the pathetic Ben and Gus, must contend.

The abyss that opens in the play's final silence between Ben and Gus has always been present. The lives of Ben and Gus are defined by coercion and violence, directed from the pair onto others, and onto Ben and Gus from their organizational supervisors. If the audience is inclined to reflect on surveillance and violence after watching the play, the characters also discuss their relationship with violence—a metatheatrical discussion of one of the play's themes.

When in the beginning of the play Ben denounces the horror of a "child of eight killing a cat" (*DW*, 88), the interchange with Gus is comic due to the limited perspective brought to bear on their participation in the world's violence. A guilty creature projects his guilt on to others. Ben fails to connect his own violence with those acts that provoke in him such disgust and moral outrage. "Whatever moral sense made them 'want to puke' when reading of deaths distanced as 'story,'" according to Morrison, "seems not to operate in those murders they intend to perform" (1983, 148). Ben verges on the schizophrenic: what he denounces in others, he does himself. His mind has split itself up into separate compartments, or we might say along with Ben, departments, thus disallowing true recognition of what he does versus what he believes himself to be: "Have a bit of common. They got departments for everything," Ben replies to Gus's question about who cleans up their victims (*DW*, 103). Ben's self-conception works the same way. Sloterdijk's postmodern self perceives itself as a force for good while objectively causing disaster; similarly, Ben regards himself as positive and moral, in a way impartial judgment would disallow. This self-perception—Robert Jay Lifton, scholar of the Nazi medical doctors, would call it "doubling" (1986)—stabilizes rather than disintegrates over time.

Ben and Gus's sense of propriety amid their murderous occupation evokes notions of those "good Germans" who committed genocidal violence even while seeing themselves as moral. Ben's petit-bourgeois shock marks the conceptually thin though existentially useful moral boundaries he creates between himself and others. Breaking down such boundaries, and bringing his audience to a full sense of responsibility, though it is denied, would seem to be a goal of Pinter's political theater. Ironically, Ben's behavior announces the near impossibility of such a goal. The irony extends to Pinter's political project as a whole. Ben stands in for the occluded, self-deluded audience member who refuses to see his own political nature even when it is mirrored to him with perfect clarity. This moral equivalence raises the troubling notion that we may never be capable of seeing ourselves and our public actions accurately.

THE HOTHOUSE: VIOLENCE AND RECUPERATION

In *The Birthday Party*, Stanley fears being watched even when in hiding, while *The Dumb Waiter*'s logistics of total visibility index power's insidious reach. This correlation between observation and control appears even more strongly in the earlier play *The Hothouse* (written in 1958). The Foucauldian dynamics argued for in *The Dumb Waiter* characterize with even greater force the social world of the hothouse. *The Hothouse* depicts an institution, specifically governmental, whose purpose is to control, observe, regulate, and imprison human beings. The theme of observation combined with coercion becomes not only unmistakable but is explicitly connected to the operations of a State, and not to an unidentified subculture or criminal underworld.

For motivations not entirely clear, Pinter suppressed this angry, obviously political play. In 1980, he directed its first production. In a 1966 interview with Lawrence M. Bensky, Pinter recalls

> I have occasionally out of irritation thought about writing a play with a satirical point. I once did, actually, a play that no one knows about. . . . It was called *The Hothouse* and was . . . heavily satirical and . . . quite useless. I never began to like any of the characters, they

really didn't live at all. So I discarded the play at once. The characters were so purely cardboard. I was intentionally—for the only time, I think—trying to make a point, an explicit point, that these were nasty people and I disapproved of them. And therefore they didn't begin to live. Whereas in other plays of mine every single character, even a bastard like Goldberg in *The Birthday Party*, I care for. (1967, 361)

In 1999 Pinter offered a more practical reading of his decision. Following the box-office failure of *The Birthday Party* in 1958, he decided that *The Hothouse* would likely have no more chance of success: "I didn't think anyone that year would produce 'The Hothouse'" (Ross 1999, 23). It is hard enough to find a paying audience for a new, experimental play, without further presenting the play as "political," a fair enough point. Fintan O'Toole, however, goes so far as to state that Pinter suppressed the play to forestall being seen as a political writer (1999, 30). Pinter's analysis of his play as uselessly satirical and overly explicit raises interesting questions. Did Pinter find a way to humanize characters such as Nicolas in *One for the Road* or Terry in *Party Time*, or did he determine that the goal of making his characters likable or human was no longer crucial? Are satire, exaggeration, and a certain degree of didacticism justified by the extremity of political catastrophe? Perhaps so, as Pinter evidently felt that 1979, the dawn of the Thatcher era in Britain, was the right moment for the play to emerge from its suppression.[9]

Following his political turn, Pinter revealed a view of *The Hothouse* different from his negative 1966 evaluation. In 1985 he declared "*The Hothouse* . . . could be defined as a totalitarian society . . . each of the plays [*The Hothouse*, *The Birthday Party*, and *The Dumb Waiter*], I would say, dealt with the individual at the mercy of a certain authoritarian system" (25). In 1988 he further described this opposition between dissent and authoritarianism. These plays, he said, are

> much closer to an extremely critical look at authoritarian postures—state power, family power, religious power, power used to undermine, if not destroy the individual, or the questioning voice, or the voice which simply went away from the mainstream and refused to become part of an easily recognisable set of standards and social values. (Knowles 1989, 25)

Society's assault upon individuals is explicitly, painfully obvious in *The Hothouse*. The play is the strongest possible evidence that Pinter's political conscience has always been part of his artistic imagination.

The actual hothouse in the play is a restrictive and corrective institution currently under the management of Colonel Roote. The patients are "not criminals," Roote notes, but "only people in need of help" who need to regain self-confidence (*H*, 9). Nearing Christmas, several crises arise: one "patient" or inmate, number 6457, has been murdered, and another, 6459, is pregnant. Roote must investigate both the murder and the pregnancy. Aiding Roote in his investigation is his paramour, Miss Cutts; opposing him are a hostile lieutenant, Lush, and Gibbs, a sneaky second in command who frequently attempts to one-up Roote. In the middle of this power struggle is the new lock tester, Mr. Lamb. The "patients" or inmates are kept out of sight. The play implies that Roote has fathered 6459's child and murdered 6457, while the blame is placed on the hapless sacrificial Lamb. Because of his actions, Roote is seamlessly replaced by Lobb, who takes over the hothouse at the end of the play.

The politics of *The Hothouse* belong both to the moment of its writing and its premiere. The anodyne promises the institution makes to its patients—they will be confident, secure, and happy—allow a specific analogy between the hothouse and the postwar British welfare state which aimed to equalize opportunity and grant everyone heightened enjoyment of life. If so, Pinter's play is an early leftist critique of the oppressiveness of the welfare state and its bureaucracies. In addition to the play's satire on conformity and institutionalism, and its possible allusions to the institutions of the welfare state, *The Hothouse* anticipates plays such as *Mountain Language* and *One for the Road*. The bureaucracies in *Mountain Language* and *The Hothouse* are both prone to murderous "clerical errors" (updated in *Mountain Language* to a computer malfunction [*ML*, 41]). The character of Roote, the head of the institution, may be linked to Nicolas, the interrogator in *One for the Road*. Nicolas speaks contemptuously of what others may perceive as his insane deployment of power. He assumes his power is beyond reproach and explanation; it is simply a fact, as he states to Victor:

this is my little finger. I wave my big finger in front of your eyes. Like this. And now I do the same with my little finger. I can also use both . . . at the same time. Like this. I can do absolutely anything I like. Do you think I'm mad? My mother did. (*One*, 33)

The "anything" Nicolas can do is performed by Roote in *The Hothouse*, as he is confronted by a subordinate asking Roote to account for himself:

> LUSH. You can't explain yourself.
> ROOTE. I can't?
> LUSH. Explain yourself.
> GIBBS. He's drunk.
> ROOTE. (*moving to him*) Explain yourself, Lush.
> LUSH. No, you! You explain yourself.
> ROOTE. Be careful, sonny.
> LUSH. (*rising*) You're a delegate, are you?
> ROOTE. (*facing him squarely*) I am.
> LUSH. On whose authority? With what power are you entrusted? By whom were you appointed? Of *what* are you a delegate?
> ROOTE *hits him in the stomach.*
> ROOTE. I'm a delegate! (*He hits him in the stomach.*)
> I was entrusted! (*He hits him in the stomach.*)
> I'm a delegate! (*He hits him in the stomach.*)
> I was appointed.
> LUSH *backs, crouched, slowly across the stage,* ROOTE *following him.*
> Delegated! (*He hits him in the stomach.*)
> Appointed! (*He hits him in the stomach.*)
> Entrusted!
> *He hits him in the stomach.* LUSH *sinks to the floor.*
> ROOTE *stands over him and shouts:*
> I AM AUTHORISED!
> LUSH *remains heaped on the floor.* ROOTE *goes back to the desk, pours a drink for himself and* GIBBS. (*H*, 102–3)

Here, Pinter's suggestion is simply that authority is always violence. Founding itself on oppression, authority will always resort to force. Roote's childishness as he states "No, you!" merely underlines the suggestion that all power is illegitimate. The extravagant display of personal violence—seven stomach blows—points to the lengths to which the status quo will go to maintain itself. Power exists in a register of physicality rather than of reason or articulation. Power can never explain itself in words. It doesn't need to and doesn't want to. Just as with Goldberg's near breakdown in act 3 of *The Birthday Party*, Roote is a Pinter character who experiences the limitations of his worldview. Crucially, however, these characters recover from their moments of existential despair; they successfully evade debilitating self-knowledge and resume their roles as victimizers.

From a different perspective, the supplanting of Roote at the end of the play, unaccompanied by satire, suggests that Pinter believes that most serious abuses of power are not tied to direct violence. The play flirts with the notion that power reveals its weakness when resorting to force. In *The Hothouse*, Pinter delineates the power of individuals in institutions while shifting to the even more frightening, if less palpable, power of the institutions themselves. These institutions are capable of preserving themselves and their repressive ways even when the individuals inside them lose legitimacy, credibility, status, or position.

In his Christmas speech to the institution, Roote praises corporate identity, in his final words of the play:

> Remember that you are not alone, that we here, for example, in this our home, are inextricably related, one to another, the staff to the understaff, the understaff to the patients, the patients to the staff. Remember this, as you sit by your fires, with your families, who have come from near and from far, to share this day with you, and may you be content. (*H*, 113)

These bathetic sentiments resemble Nicolas's in *One for the Road*:

> We are all patriots, we are as one, we all share a common heritage . . . I feel a link, you see, a bond. I share a commonwealth of interest. I am not alone. I am not alone! (*One*, 50–51)

Roote and both Nicolas see "being alone" as ultimate horror. Solitude may be mentioned but it is too frightening to be articulated. If aloneness connotes the existential awareness of one's own situation and smallness in life, the antidote to its terror is group identity, an awareness of the organic relation between oneself and others. Pinter presents allegiance to group identity as a mark of all his political villains.

Another similarity between Roote and Nicolas is that both exalt the past in extreme, emotional terms:

> ROOTE. The men who gave their lives so that we might live. Who sacrificed themselves so that we might continue. Who helped keep the world clean for the generations to come. The men who died in our name. Let us drink to them. (*H*, 75)

Recalling the past as he tortures a female dissident, Nicolas declares:

Your father fought for his country. I knew him. I revered him. Everyone did. He believed in God. He didn't *think*, like you shitbags. He *lived*. He lived. He was iron and gold. He would die, he would die, he would die, for his country, for his God. And he did die, he died, he died, for his God. (*One*, 66)

Both characters are particularly obsessed with the purity of dead ancestors. To these fundamentalist selves, to use Robert Jay Lifton's words, the past is a sacred, though imperiled, guarantee of present meaning (1993, 163). The type of personality represented by Roote and Nicolas attempts, against all odds, to see history as a continuum, thus endowing life with stability and meaning. Such a person cannot face the possibility of the past having no sense of order, revealing no sense of continuum, and adding up to no coherent whole. This postmodern perspective that history is chaos is something leaders such as Nicolas and Roote must combat.

The fact that the conservative exaltation of the past may fail to provide individual security becomes material for Pinter's satire. Roote, in his valorization of social and political icons, implements a metaphor that dominates Pinter's political thinking in the 1980s plays. He speaks of a world that needs to be "kept clean," anticipating *The New World Order* of Lionel and Des, who are entrusted with the task of "keeping the world clean for democracy" (*NWO*, 60). Roote expresses his attachment to the past and to a dream of social order in the following speech, addressed to the hothouse's staff:

As my predecessor said, on one unforgettable occasion: "Order, gentlemen, for God's sake, order!" I remember the silence, row upon row of electrified faces, he with his golden forelock, his briar burning, upright and commanding, a soldier's stance, looking down from the platform. The gymnasium was packed to suffocation, standing room only. . . . "Order, gentlemen," he said, "for the love of Mike!" As one man we looked out of the window at Mike, and gazed at the statue—covered in snow, it so happened, then as now. Mike! The predecessor of my predecessor, the predecessor of us all, the man who laid the foundation stone, the man who introduced the first patient, the man who . . . opened institution after institution up and down the country, rest homes, nursing homes, convalescent homes, sanatoria. He was sanctioned by the Ministry, revered by the populace, subsidised by the State. He had set in motion an activity for humanity, of humanity and by humanity. And the keyword was order. (*H*, 23–24)

This authoritarian mind-set is comically literal, as Pinter overtly ridicules a conservative attitude toward the past. By making Roote not credible, the play perhaps takes itself less seriously than it might otherwise have. Behind Roote's literalism, however we take it, we can see that authority stages and solves its own legitimacy crisis by constructing idols from the revered past. The speech illustrates the fundamentalist mentality, a "mode of being which draws primarily upon a sacred past" (Lifton 1993, 60). This reverence became a potent political force in Britain and America at the time of the play's first production. The sacralization of the past recurs in *Party Time*, in which the past is one of "values" that are never quite defined, as well as in Pinter's *Reunion* screenplay, in which the past is of Aryan supremacy. Since that past is so revered, by comparison the present always suffers, and so, by definition, any measures are necessary and morally permissible to reestablish the glorious past in the present.

Pinter dramatizes horror differently in his presentation of the character Lamb, perhaps the play's ultimate victim. Pinter, in signal fashion, uses silence to dramatize the horrific triumph of power. Lamb's naiveté, marking him out for maltreatment, leads him to take the therapeutic rationale of *The Hothouse* at face value: "I've thought out a number of schemes, you know, ideas, for a really constructive, progressive approach to the patients" (*H*, 21). He is oblivious to the apparent fact that the institution he serves intends to harm these so-called patients. He is tortured, presumably just for sport, by Gibbs and Cutts, who attack his sexuality and virginity, and assault him with unanswerable, contradictory questions. At the close of act 1, Lamb is defeated and glad to be so; he is apparently eager for more torture: "You haven't finished your questions, have you? I'm ready whenever you are." This offer is met with a resounding silence (57), the silence of a power that has attained maximum status. It is a silence that dramatically indexes the destruction of Lamb and by extension the murder of any innocents. This frightening silence swallows up attempts at its ironical description or summary.

In Pinter's political plays, those in power assume that the family is a dangerous threat. The mere fact of biological relatedness—having a mother, a father, a name given by one's parents—serves as evidence to the powerful that the powerless may retain the capacity to speak and have a voice. Accordingly, the fact of family is viewed with alarm by agents of established state power. Nicolas in *One for the Road* attacks Gila for initially making her husband's acquaintance; he also insinuates that little Nicky is wrong to love his parents. In *Mountain Language*, when a prisoner mentions that he has a family like that of his guard, he has committed obscene treason mandating renewed torture (*ML*, 31). Roote unconvincingly worries about the deindividualizing effects of calling the occupants by number. In doing so, he accurately articulates this tactic's goal of destroying the family as determinant of personal identity:

> I often think it must depress them . . . somewhat . . . to have a number rapped at them all the time. After some of them have been here a few years they're liable to forget what names their fathers gave them. Or their mothers. (*H*, 10)

The process of dehumanization aimed at by totalitarian systems could not be more openly stated.

Roote, facing his own exposure as the father of 6459's child, later becomes incensed about the mother of one inmate. He hysterically attempts to assert the meaninglessness of maternity:

> ROOTE. How do you know she was his mother?
> LUSH. She said so.
> ROOTE. She was a liar!
> LUSH. No, she wasn't.
> ROOTE. How do you know?
> LUSH. She looked like a mother.
> ROOTE. How do you know what mothers looks like?
> LUSH. I had one myself.
> ROOTE. Do you think I didn't? . . .
>
> ROOTE. I was fed, Mister Cleverboots, at my mother's breast.
> GIBBS. So was I.
> LUSH. Me too.
> *Sudden silence*
> ROOTE. WELL? AND WHAT ABOUT IT? (*H*, 81–82)

The state's secret dream is to generate its subjects on its own, independent of biological reality. The family seems to stand as a source and reminder of love, loyalty, and conscience outside of and opposed to society. All of these qualities must apparently be supplied by and through the authoritarian state.

The connection between a stern, authoritarian father and the state recurs in *Moonlight*. Andy, a strong father who has alienated his sons, describes his life as a civil servant:

I inspired the young men and women down from here and down from there. I inspired them to put their shoulders to the wheel and their noses to the grindstone and to keep faith at all costs with the structure which after all ensured the ordered government of all our lives, which took perfect care of us, which held us to our bosom, as it were. I was a first class civil servant. (*M*, 17)

Moments earlier, his two sons have provided another view of the stern authority of their father as encompassing both law and physicality:

JAKE. My father adhered strictly to the rule of law.
FRED. Which is not a very long way from the rule of thumb.
JAKE. Not as the crow flies, no. (11)

Here, the sons' personal lives are colored by the vision of the "father of the country" who perpetuates the principles of law and force. Andy describes an inversion by which the State becomes explicitly parental, in his case maternal. The citizen must submit to the overwhelming and suffocating comfort of the maternal bosom into which the State has made itself, or which it attempts to emulate.[10]

Parallel to the state's antagonism to family is a tendency to sexual violence and the manipulation of women. The bureaucracies both of *The Hothouse* and *One for the Road* routinize misogynistic force. Also, sexual violence is an inextricable part of the world of *One for the Road*:

NICOLAS. How many times have you been raped?
GILA. I don't know.
NICOLAS. And you consider yourself a reliable witness? (71)

Misogynist oppression is ubiquitous also in *The Hothouse*. When Roote asks who impregnated 6459, Gibbs responds,

She was ... noncommittal, sir. She said she couldn't be entirely sure since most of the staff have had relations with her in this last year.
ROOTE. Most of the staff?
GIBBS. According to her statement, sir.
ROOTE *rubs his mouth*. (*H*, 25)

While Roote's gesture hints at personal guilt, clearly sexuality becomes an aspect of power in the hothouse. Nicolas, in more vulgar terms, also sees female sexuality as instrumental to his national cause:

> We have a first class brothel upstairs, on the sixth floor, chandeliers, the lot. They'll suck you in and blow you out in little bubbles. All volunteers. Their daddies are in our business. Which is, I remind you, to keep the world clean for God. (*One*, 77)

The violent oppression of an outgroup merging with misogyny recurs in Pinter's political plays.

Pinter's extremely skeptical treatment of the themes of power and the state versus freedom and the individual can be clarified by comparing *The Hothouse* to Tom Stoppard's *Every Good Boy Deserves Favor* (1978, 1977). *The Hothouse* and *Every Good Boy Deserves Favor* diversely reflect the practice of incarcerating political dissidents as if they were mental patients. Stoppard's play was prompted by the case of Vladimir Bukovsky, who accused the Soviets of misusing psychiatric facilities as prisons for political opponents (Innes 1992, 324); Bukovsky was promptly imprisoned in just such a facility. In March 1974, Pinter wrote a letter to the *Times* of London protesting Bukovsky's imprisonment (Knowles 1989, 24). This letter was one of Pinter's few overt political acts since his 1948 conscientious objector declaration. In 1988, three decades after writing his play, Pinter notes the hothouse is "a home for political dissidents . . . who are kept, as it were, in a psychiatric hospital . . . which actually preempted the now well-known facts about how psychiatric hospitals were used particularly in Russia" (25).

In Stoppard's play, Alexander Ivanov is imprisoned in a psychiatric facility for telling others that a perfectly sane friend was imprisoned in a psychiatric facility. Alexander's cellmate, also named Alexander Ivanov (the script labels him by surname), is a "genuine mental patient" (1978, 9) who hears an orchestra in his mind. The audience hears the same orchestra as does Ivanov, Stoppard's device to depict the permeable boundary between sanity and insanity. Alexander resists attempts to get him to admit he has been cured, while Ivanov is ironically cured of his delusions. With great pomp, a KGB colonel confuses the two patients and asks Ivanov if he believes Soviets imprison the sane, and receives a negative answer; then he asks Alexander if he still has an orchestra, and again hears a no. He orders both released— bureaucracy loses, and the individual triumphs. As Alexander's son says, it is possible that "Everything can be all right!" (39).

A stylistic difference between the two plays is that Pinter is not specific about setting while Stoppard locates his play specifically in the Cold War-era Eastern bloc. Moreover, Pinter suggests that such oppression is a feature of any society, or perhaps a fact of hierarchy itself. Pinter *dares* us to connect the events of the play to a possible England, while Stoppard assumes his object of representation is geographically and politically distant and distinct from his audience. This stylistic contrast can be seen as a foundation for a later strategy of Pinter's playwriting, in which a historically vague or polyvalent setting suggests that political monstrosity can exist anywhere.

The strength of the carceral bureaucracy as revealed in the plots of the two plays suggests another political difference between the playwrights and their plays. Quite simply, there is a happy ending in Stoppard's play and a depressing one in Pinter's. Stoppard's system is inefficient and fallible, thus allowing the release of the play's two central characters, a political prisoner and a true mental patient. Comedy inheres in Stoppard's worldview, as human weakness and misprision are stronger than institutions or ideologies. Stoppard allows for the preservation of individual moral rights as he demonstrates that, either by design or absurd accident, such moral efficacy can survive. In *The Hothouse*, the State responds to internal challenge and chaos by further and fatal victimization. Pinter's play is more pessimistic about the survival of freedom and nonconformity. Pinter denies audience sympathy for his characters; he also denies onstage presence to the victims of the system, the evidence of their rebellion limited to "Whispers, chuckles, [and] half-screams" (*H*, 113), which ominously cease just as Roote is replaced (or uprooted, perhaps) by his successor Lobb.

In this drama about an institution that is both synecdochical with and a symbol of society, Pinter portrays power as stabilizing itself at the expense of some of its agents and all of its subjects. A certain amount of change—limited to the switching of figureheads—is *in* the order of things, yet fundamental change is not, to paraphrase Roote's distinction (*H*, 9). Individual representatives of power may or may not be vulnerable; power itself is not. When Pinter returned to politics in the 1980s, he returned also to the theme of how power renders itself ever more invulnerable.

3
Pinter against the (New) Right: *Precisely,*
One for the Road, and *Mountain Language*

Pinter's theater begins, in the early 1980s, to feature plays that demand interpretation in terms of the realities of public politics. The early plays in this period have a stylistic brevity that is key to their political vision. They offer precise yet resonant images of ruthless power in the act of silencing and destroying dissenting individuals. In restricting his plays to image rather than extended narrative, Pinter focuses on the triumph of power in the irrevocable moments of its assertion, depriving his audiences of consolation or political encouragement. Even if analogous facts in contemporary public affairs are well known to educated audiences, these plays may nevertheless break through intellectual knowledge to a present at least an intimation of what it would be to directly experience political oppression. The responsibility for preserving the project of opposition in the face of a vicious, unrestrained status quo belongs not to the plays or their author but ultimately to the audience itself.

The sketch *Precisely* begins Pinter's dramatization of specific political issues. In March 1983, Pinter accepted an invitation from the Peace Movement to contribute a sketch to a theatrical evening about disarmament; this event premiered December 18, six months before massive public protest against the American nuclear missiles stored in Britain. (And about two years after Pinter noted, "I am myself a convinced nuclear unilateralist but I don't see there is any . . . way I can write a play about it" [qtd. in Merritt 1995, 175].) In the final work, two men, designated A (Stephen) and B (Roger), drink and argue about a "figure." B tentatively refers to unnamed others who define this "figure" as thirty million or more, but A pressures him to stick with the original figure of twenty million. The nature of this figure is not directly given—"They could be discussing anything, from the cost of a proposed new motorway to a company's unit sales," observes Peacock (1997, 137)—and it is not made certain until A insists at the end of the sketch that they are talking about civilian casualties: "No, no, Roger. It's twenty million. Dead" (P, 37).

At (or perhaps before) this point, we infer that these two bureaucrats are talking about "acceptable losses" in a nuclear war, specifically in a retaliatory second strike (Howard 1996, 130). That is, if country X decides to drop nuclear bombs on country Y, Y will respond automatically with a counterattack, thus killing a certain amount of people in country X.[1] According to this "logic" of mutual assured destruction, the price of using nuclear weapons is the death of some millions of one's own countrymen. Pacifists and opponents of nuclear war seek to define "acceptable losses" as high as possible, in order to portray nuclear war as maximally horrifying, while proponents of nuclear feasibility would want the figure as low as possible. Given this conflict, the "figure" here is established not in a disinterested, sober manner, but in a political context. The "figure" being discussed may refer to the number of people who would likely die in a counterstrike against the initiators of a nuclear war or, rather, to the number of people that country X's government is willing to state would probably die in such circumstances. The single figure A insists upon elides this crucial distinction between reality and propaganda. *Precisely* underlines the dual nature of language: language as (ideally) conveying facts, truth, and knowledge, pitted against language refracted through the interests of power.

The language use of the characters is itself informed by their power struggles, as speech becomes a contest of wills. The outward rationality of the men—their politesse, their commitment to "objective" figures, their language of official procedure—belies the irrationality of their advocacy of mass death. Superficial rationality masking actual savagery sets a pattern for the villains in Pinter's political theater. This sketch both alludes to and represents violence, specifically the violence of nuclear confrontations, through the verbal antagonism of the two characters.

Through depicting speech as power struggle, Pinter captures the nature of the nuclear balance of terror. What looks like a merely statistical argument becomes something much broader. For nuclear weapons are (or were) successfully threatening only insofar as their owners could be perceived as possessing the will to use them. As the U.S. and U.S.S.R. developed their arsenal of atomic weapons, these weapons were intimidating only to the extent to which their owners could credibly threaten to use them. Nuclear weapons altered the nature of war, as Jonathan Schell writes: "War was displaced from the battlefield to a realm of appearances—of 'credibility,' in the jargon of the nuclear trade—in which terrifying shows of nuclear power were meant to have the influence that actual fighting had had under the old war system" (2003, 40). If B does not perceive A's estimate as serious and sincere, then A has lost not just an argument but the actual threat his country's nuclear arsenal is intended to pose. Mutual deterrence displaces violence from the physical realm to the verbal: "violence [becomes] not so much an instrument for producing physical results as a kind of bloody system of communication, through which the antagonists delivered messages to one another about their wills" (42). The battle of wills in *Precisely* illustrates this condition, in which any lack of (murderous) intent in the guardians of nuclear weaponry is fatal to those weapons' supposed power. Personal power enables the force of nuclear weaponry, and vice versa.

If uncovering the truth about power involves displaying power as the potential for large-scale as well as interpersonal violence, it also means displaying power as the suppression of dissent, the invalidation of what the disempowered think as well as what they feel and experience. *Precisely* dramatizes how the empowered caste labels dissent and how this fact of labeling illustrates society's involvement in its own disempowerment. Discussing those who wish to raise "the figure," Pinter uses the language of medieval revenge to portray contrary opinion as treason:[2]

> A. I'm going to recommend that they be hung, drawn, and quartered. I want to see the color of their entrails.
> B. Same color as the Red Flag, old boy. (*P*, 37)

Labeling opposition, of course, enables it to be seen as unpatriotic or treasonous. The references echo the past in several ways: first, their calumny of Communism evokes an hysterical, McCarthyite Cold War rhetoric; second, Pinter as a youth was sometimes called a Communist (the personal as the political, indeed);[3] thirdly, being hung, drawn, and quartered was historically the punishment for those who committed regicide. Roger and Stephen imagine themselves as ruling by divine right, unapproachable by the common masses they govern.

The conflict between A and B, both elites, seems to raise the possibility of internal division among the empowered. As does

Pinter's other political theatre, *Precisely* hints—but only hints—at a power struggle within the privileged class. The debate, abortive as it is, becomes a red herring, as it were, that covers the persistence of power. The conflict is one of the incipient cleavages within the ruling class that always comes to naught, Marx writes in *The German Ideology* (1975, 173). The image of power as self-divided and unstable appeals to the liberal conscience that imagines the status quo can be improved. Hopes that regnant power might fail, however, remain unfulfilled in Pinter's political theater, as it continually challenges its audiences' liberal hopes for social improvement through the immanent failure of power.[4] As the plot of *Precisely* disappoints the desire to see B resist or puncture A's authoritarian position, it enacts a sort of defeat that echoes in the frightening aporias and concluding silences in Pinter's later political works.

In the case of *Precisely*, this possibility of resistance begins as B edges toward declaring that A is misrepresenting the number of deaths a nuclear war would cause. B floats numbers to see how A will respond, hoping for any sign of agreement. For the most part, though, B echoes A with responses such as "Quite," "Indeed," and "I know." B seems to view opponents as A does: "I'd put the bastards against the wall and shoot them" (37). B's behavior is cautious and fearful, never forthright or bold in contradicting A, as if he is shamefully aware of his relative lack of power, lacks confidence in his own beliefs, or fears retribution from A.

B's tentative behavior and his ultimate condition of silence evoke a unique theme in Pinter's political theater. His plays illustrate the silenced, marginalized nature of liberal opposition in the sphere of public politics. Do liberals and progressives seem more doubtful and self-questioning, less secure, less aggressive, and less confident in articulating their opinions and enacting their beliefs than conservatives? (Liberal pundit James Carville gave this advice to the left on the December 4, 2003, CBS *Morning Show*: "Quit conceding the other side has a point.") The idea that the left lacks self-belief and self-assertion certainly exists at the level of popular perception and commentary. Conservatives, especially the forces of the New Right, do not hesitate to use verbal attack for political effect: "conservatives . . . have been notably more aggressive in tearing down their opponents. Partly that is because liberals are less cohesive and angry, more timid and easily cowed. Even when liberals have strong beliefs, they act as if they were not quite sure they actually agree with them," writes Walter Isaacson in the *New Yorker* (2003, 98). Perhaps, observes James Traub in the *New York Times*, "today's liberals, unlike today's conservatives, don't believe in any particular set of ends ardently enough to blind themselves to the means they are using to achieve them" (2003b, 10). As politics are inevitably a matter of perception, the truth of these contentions matters perhaps less than their very existence. In parallel with such ideas is the commonly voiced complaint on the left that those who should be speaking up for left and progressive ideas have been cowed into silence or consensus with mainstream ideologies. To be explicitly oppositional was to risk being expelled from any possibility of attaining power. Such dissatisfactions were especially rife in the 1980s and beyond in Britain and America, as Margaret Thatcher and Ronald Reagan, each in his or her own distinctive fashion, dominated the terms of public discourse.

If there is a reticence to leftist opposition to the (new) right, are its causes temperamental or contingent—or both? If opposition is *inherently*, in its very nature, committed to fairness and self-doubt in its struggle against an unfair, repressive, unreflective status quo, then there is no use contemplating change in how opposition works. However, in the ruthless power struggles of politics, parties evincing evenhandedness and self-skepticism, not to mention lack of self-belief, will inevitably suffer negative consequences. Also, the phenomenon of liberal reticence involves another constitutional factor in power relationships: the elemental bias for the old and established against the new and the questioning. But the issue is temporal as well as temperamental. A distinguishing feature of political life in the time of Thatcher and Reagan was the success each had in branding oppositional ideas as morally unworthy, beyond the pale of respectable consideration, and the manner in which they mobilized a force akin to "common sense" against dissenting voices. This mainstream "common sense" was defined either in terms of the numbers of those who already consented to it, or as self-evident correctness. The tendency, irrespective of cause, for oppositional voices to end in an enforced or a quasi-accepted accommodationalist silence is a dilemma Pinter's political theater continually evokes.

The sketch leaves undetermined the extent of B's capitulation. The audience may wonder if he abandons all opposition, or if the possibility of opposition somehow remains open despite B's final silence. Is Pinter, by suggesting that the possibility may remain open, partially fulfilling audience hopes for changing an unjust order? Or perhaps B does agree to A's "figure," and thus to his agenda and worldview, submitting to A's will. This agreement can be seen as power invariably consolidating itself at the expense of dissent. The view that social change has limited possibility involves, for Pinter, the weakness of society's oppositional forces as well as the strength of its privileged caste—the weakness derives from the strength, and vice versa.

Pinter scholars have access to an extraordinary resource, the Pinter Archives housed at London's British Library. The author has generously donated his working papers, drafts, notes, correspondence, and other materials related to virtually every piece of his writing. This study of Pinter's expressly political plays is supplemented by recourse to these notes and drafts (my examination of his *Reunion* screenplay also features the author's process). Pinter has often spoken of his writing process in instinctive terms: as a writer he listens to what his characters say and attempts to let them say it (*VV*, 8)—as if, like Pirandello's six, his characters exist independently of their creator. Examining the drafts underscores how incomplete is this instinctive account of Pinter's artistic process. Like those of any other creative writer, the works reach their finished state after a process in which the author consciously shapes, refines, builds, and edits a number of drafts. While the ultimate object of analysis must be the finished work, Frank Gillen notes (2001, 63), examining that work through the process of its development and refinement permits important insights that would not have been available otherwise.

Analysis of how Pinter developed *Precisely* yields insights into the nature of his political theater. As the playwright revised his script, he underscored the process by which B is silenced by A's deployment of power while emphasizing B's action of withdrawing from conflict. The initial holograph draft is as follows (see Merritt [1994, 30] for a different but similar version):

A—You're asking me to give you another two?
B—Yes.
A—No, no, Charley. It's 20 mill. Dead. ~~Precisely~~.
B—You mean precisely?
A—I mean dead.
Precisely. And I want you to accept that figure.
B—Mmm. It's just that someone told me—
A—Nobody told you anything! There are no more questions to be asked! There is nothing more to be said!

The next draft is a single-spaced typescript with some holograph changes. The last exchange, which matches the published script, is as follows:

> A—(Handwritten in: "*Slowly.*") No, no. ~~Jack~~. Chris. It's twenty mil-
> lion. Dead.
> B—You mean precisely?
> A—I mean dead. Precisely.
> *Pause.*
> I want you to accept that figure. (Handwritten in: "*Pause.*") Accept
> the figure.
> Pause. *They stare at each other.*
> B—Twenty million dead, precisely?
> A—Precisely. (PA, Box 60)

In the first version, B's protest is more elaborate; his capitulation is emphasized in the finished script. In the holograph, B is still introducing new ideas into the conversation, granting presence and credence to the "others" who have opinions contradictory to the status quo, showing no signs of surrender. In the final version, B significantly echoes A's words in his penultimate speech, and thus apparently accepting them as A defines them, abandoning reference to the ideas of others. Seconds later, B ends in silence.

The dynamics of interpersonal and social power have long fascinated readers of Pinter. Elias Canetti gives one central model of the activity of power. The basic instrument of power is the command: one who is powerful can command another to perform a specific activity. This activity of commanding another, according to Canetti, produces two reactions. Those who wield power experience the "anxiety of command," a fear of revenge from those commanded, while those who must submit to orders feel the "sting of command," an atavistic memory of pain that never leaves consciousness (1962, 303–9). The anxiety and sting of command provide a starting point for describing the emotional dynamics of Pinteresque dominance and subjugation. Goldberg's quasi-hysterical breakdown in *The Birthday Party* is a product of this anxiety of command, the feeling that the foundations of his dominance may crumble, exposing the former leader to revenge. However, as Pinter's dramas evolve from *The Birthday Party* on to the more explicitly political works of the eighties and beyond, and as the institutions of power represented in them come to be more severe and destructive than in *The Birthday Party* and *The Dumb Waiter*, the empowered feel less and less of the anxiety of command. They assume with blithe arrogance that no vengeance upon them will ever be possible, while the disempowered are ever more immobilized by the sting of command. ("The power of those who give commands appears to grow all the time," Canetti observes [1962, 305].) A's final outburst above might seem to betray signs of the anxiety of command; the string of exclamations hints at anxiety or loss of composure. In the next draft, however, Pinter makes A a much cooler and more suavely triumphant character. A no longer declares in the final version, as in the draft, that there is nothing more to be said. In the revision, A simply wins and does so without the frustration or nervousness readable as subtext between the early draft's lines; the anxiety of command has, to all effective or observable purposes, departed. This change indicates how Pinter's empowered characters bury or transcend the "anxiety of command" by glorying in the condition of triumph, of belonging to the winning side.[5]

In fact, A *compels* B to say no more about their conflict, thus making the play an enactment of the silence in which A declares incipient protest must end. The draft's statement that there is "[n]othing more to be said" accurately describes the ultimate situation A creates and enforces in the final version of the sketch. Wordlessness becomes, as well, a greater feature of the finished sketch's dramatic style—as he amends the typescript by hand, Pinter adds a pause to A's final attack and extends the final pause into a mute confrontation, the final stare between the two men. In ending this sketch with a wordless gaze that announces deployed power, Pinter initiates a motif that continues in many of his explicitly political plays. Power produces silence.

If silence is the endpoint of this confrontation, it is also the goal of all torture. The fact of voicelessness links the antinuclear agenda of *Precisely* with Pinter's later plays about torture. Pinter told publisher Nick Hern in 1985 that before his turn to political theater, he was conscious of two political issues: "One is the fact of torture, of official torture, subscribed to by so many governments. And the other is the whole nuclear situation. I've been a member of CND [Campaign for Nuclear Disarmament] for some years" (1986b, 12). The phenomena of torture and nuclear weapons can be seen as mutually reinforcing: both create a situation that deprives a populace of political will, agency, and voice. Elaine Scarry presents torture as a rhetorical device designed to make its subject speak the language of the state and to experience the silence of his or her own voice (1985, 36). Torture teaches the solitude before death, the futility of all action contrary to power, the necessary fate of opposition in final silence. This goal consistently defines the attitude of Pinter's torturers, as in Goldberg's and McCann's treatment of Stanley, as well as *The New World Order*'s dismissal of its victim: "Before he came in here . . . he never stopped questioning received ideas. Now. . . . he's stopped all that, he's got nothing more to say, he's more or less called it a day" (*NWO*, 58). The effect of torture is to turn political subjects, capable of speaking and avowing particular beliefs, into political objects (49). It is exactly this overall political condition, Scarry argues, which the ideology of nuclear weapons both assumes and reinforces.

If the goal of torture is to render opposition silent and futile, nuclear war depends upon a population that has been rendered incapable of effective speech and thus effective consent. Scarry argues for the unprecedented moral obscenity of nuclear war by demonstrating that nuclear conflict more closely resembles torture than it does conventional war. As opposed to nuclear conflict, traditional war requires a degree of consent from its participants. Before going to war, a draftee leaves his job, says goodbye to friends and family, dons a uniform, and performs other acts that establish his consent; later, he may again put that uniform on, renewing consent, or else go AWOL or abandon fighting (Scarry 1985, 153).[6] Additionally, the consent of the populace is at least theoretically necessary: full-scale conflict "cannot be carried out without the 'authorization' of . . . the population" (153), to which the government must argue the war's rightness. Even if this case is clichéd, fraudulent, perverse, or otherwise logically empty, it must still be made, and that necessity implies popular agency.

By contrast, "Consent is in a nuclear war a structural impossibility" (Scarry 1985, 154). Nuclear war, depending on missiles that need be fired only once, invalidates the need for a government to rely on popular consent or even to make its case for war. Not even manufactured consent is necessary, while dissent becomes futile. In a war that may last only hours, no renewal of popular or individual consent is possible or necessary. By their very nature, nuclear weapons do not need informed consent to function, and this fact is integral, not incidental, to their power (152). Nuclear war, therefore, assumes and creates a population that has been converted from political subjects into political objects. The people of a country going to nuclear war are not agents with a role to play in what happens to them. In this way, the existence of nuclear weapons resembles the use (or threat) of torture, because both serve to establish popular silence and disempowerment.

The agon of *Precisely* is not how many people might be killed in a nuclear war or who may legitimately establish the most authoritative estimate of such a figure. Rather, the question is whether the government will continue to possess the unquestioned capacity to allow its people to be killed without consideration of their status as living human beings and without their consultation. Roger wishes a dialogue on the issue of nuclear casualties. Stephen aims not so much to prove his outlook superior to Roger's—that would imply a contradictory outlook is even notionally possible—but to deny that Roger can have an agenda at all. A is not arguing for "twenty million" because of any importance to this figure. Rather, his point, as encapsulated in the word "precisely," is the impossibility of the government permitting any numerical estimate authored by any other group, the impossibility of granting credence to any voice other than that of power. This democratic government enforces, through the existence of nuclear weapons, the right to determine its citizens' fates without consultation with or consent of those citizens. This enforced segregation of the vox populi from the power of the state unites Pinter's political plays.

In *One for the Road*, Pinter depicts a confrontation between power and powerlessness, between voice and voicelessness. It culminates in a silence that announces the brute fact of power as domination. The play examines the relationship between individual psychology and power, exploring the notion of whether there is a type of personality attracted to positions of power and dominance. *One for the Road* also investigates the psychology of a torturer or leader who kills or sacrifices others for his ideals, country, group, or faith, posing the recurrent, but perhaps unanswerable, question of how such a person may reconcile murderous deeds with a positive self-image.

The short, four-scene play is set in an unspecified country. The play's central character, the placid torturer Nicolas, speaks urbane English while commanding an institution that incarcerates and tortures political dissidents. In the play Nicolas verbally assaults three members of a family imprisoned in this torture center.[7] In the first scene, Nicolas interrogates Victor, the ironically named father of the family, who is battered and largely silent. However, Nicolas does not seek a confession or any specific information. We assume all pertinent information has been gathered and that no confession is necessary, probably because "proof" is irrelevant to the regime Nicolas serves. His bizarre conversation digresses to include the leader of his country, the quality of the cheese at a posh cocktail party, ominous hints about the fate of Victor's wife and son, the uselessness of despair, and the metaphysical appeal of death.

In addition to being metaphysically inclined, Nicolas believes himself divinely connected: "God speaks through me. I'm referring to the Old Testament God, by the way, although I'm a long way from being Jewish" (*One*, 36).[8] Imposing arbitrary demands upon Victor, Nicolas demonstrates his power over him, verbally flaunting his capacity to inflict pain. Issuing commands does not just satisfy Nicolas's apparent sadism but creates an intense, secular experience of connection: "I feel a link, you see, a bond. I share a commonwealth of interest. I am not alone. I am not alone!" (51). At this, Victor asks Nicolas to kill him, a plea Nicolas belittles.

In the next, much briefer, scene, Nicolas meets Victor's son and is surprised to discover the boy's name is Nicky. As Nicky plays with a plane, Nicolas intimidates him, noting that their country's soldiers detest Nicky. Next in line for Nicolas is Gila, Victor's wife, whom he browbeats with unanswerable questions and sexual innuendo:

NICOLAS. How many times have you been raped?
GILA. I don't know.
NICOLAS. And you consider yourself a reliable witness? (71)

Nicolas's wrath peaks when Gila mentions her father, apparently a national hero: "Your father fought for his country. I knew him. I revered him. Everyone did. He believed in God. He didn't *think*, like you shitbags. He *lived*" (66). The scene ends as Nicolas airily dismisses his victim: "But I should think you might entertain us all a little more before you go" (74).

The final scene returns to Nicolas and Victor, now "tidily dressed" (*One*, 75). "How have you been? Surviving?" Nicolas asks, perhaps with overt sarcasm. After Nicolas releases Victor, Victor tries to speak but cannot:

NICOLAS. I can't hear you.
VICTOR. It's my mouth.
NICOLAS. Mouth?

VICTOR. Tongue.
NICOLAS. What's the matter with it?
Pause. (76–77)

When Victor inquires about his son, Nicolas answers:

Your son? Oh, don't worry about him. He was a little prick.
VICTOR *straightens and stares at* NICOLAS.
Silence.
Blackout. (79–80)

In a masterstroke, the play uses language to index murder: its horrifying violence is presented indirectly through Nicolas's subtle reference to Nicky in the past tense. The play ends in a complex silence. This silence indicates that no words could adequately describe the horror of what has happened—as Primo Levi (whose works Pinter is familiar with) noted of the Nazi death camps, "Then for the first time we realised that our language has no words to express this offence, the demolition of a man" (1985, 26). This culminating silence is in another sense a product of pain: the experience of pain, according to Elaine Scarry, deprives its sufferers, even its witnesses, of the ability to conceptualize and articulate, to use language: "pain . . . tends to appropriate and destroy the conceptualization abilities and language of persons who only observe" it (1985, 279). The final silence of *One for the Road* indexes too the brutal, and brutally simple, fact that power is experienced by the powerless as a disabling mixture of shame, fear, resentment, and vulnerability.

This short, resonant, unforgiving play has provoked difficult questions of interpretation and classification. Nicolas's freedom from restraint, according to Austin Quigley, is such that both he and *One for the Road* itself defy interpretation by any explanatory scheme (2001, 11). One initial debate is whether this play is too much invested in psychology to be properly political. Pinter's colleague Simon Gray locates Nicolas in the tradition of Gothic villains (1985, 54), and he also notes Nicolas's extraordinary aura of freedom: "What I like best about it is the ghastly richness of Harold's monster . . . [who has] gone beyond absolute corruption on to complete freedom of spirit" (Eyre 2000, 39–40). Benedict Nightingale sees the play as illustrating Nicolas's "psychopathology" (147). The character, indeed, seems to agree, remarking, "Do you think I'm mad? My mother did" (*One,* 33). The reading Pinter himself offers, though we need not grant it ultimate authority, discusses the play in universal psychological terms, noting that it provokes the realization that we all would be tempted by the "absolute power" Nicolas possesses (1986b, 45).

This psychological focus has implications for designating *One for the Road* as a political drama. Political drama, by one definition, must explore social issues in ways that refer to political structures rather than invoking universal (and thus ahistorical) qualities (Rabey 1986, 2; see also Merritt 1995, 180–183). Paradoxically enough, then, this play might exceed—or fall short of—the category of "the political." Read or misread in a certain way, that is, the play might support the oft-cited illusion of political liberals that rooting out the evil in individual hearts and minds can correct political evil. As Pinter evolved through the 1980s as a political playwright, he emphasized character and psychology considerably less, in order to avoid identifying abuse of power with single, aberrant personalities.

However, as if to stress the force and power of a particular personality, the production of *One for the Road* at the 2001 Lincoln Center Pinter Festival starred Pinter himself. Onstage and off, Pinter is known as a charismatic figure, both graceful and commanding, who can convey threat and anger (reviews of his early acting career noted he was best at playing villains, and it has been suggested that Pinter is the best Pinter actor there is). His performance as Nicolas alternated the pleasing musicality of his voice with moments of tangible horror, as when he manhandles Gila, pinioning her arms and forcing her into an embrace. Another significant choice in this production was its focus on the internal psychology of the torturer. Pinter entered in half-light to the sound of church bells and sat in the chair he reserved for his victims, as he rubbed his chin in a seeming bout of self-pity. This man is not unaware of what pity is; however, he reserves it only for himself.[9]

Another intriguing performance moment, dealing with silence and powerlessness, was the close of the play, when Victor lifts his eyes to look at Nicolas. In its use of a conclusive, wordless confrontation through the act of looking, *One for the Road* is sometimes compared to Beckett's *Catastrophe* (1984), the most clearly political of Beckett's plays (it is dedicated to Václav Havel, then still imprisoned by the Communist government of Czechoslovakia). In this play, an unnamed actor is harassed by a controlling director. At the end of the play, the actor breaks the director's rules through one small gesture: he raises his eyes and looks at the audience in front of him. This gesture Beckett read as strong defiance: you're not done with me yet. According to Judith Roof, for instance, the stare concluding *One for the Road* hints at Victor's defiance and suggests that hierarchies and ideologies of power might yet be subverted: "Nicholas' need to display his potency gives the victim/audience some power. . . . [Victor's] final voluntary gaze at Nicholas is characterized as a 'stare' instead of a look, a difference which may indicate either shock or the beginnings of a subversion of Nicholas' system" (Roof 1988, 15). In the 2001 New York production, as if in denial of this hope for subversion, Victor's face at this moment clearly expressed fear, subjugation, and suffering rather than defiance. The look was unwilled, an instinctual reflex prompted by shock. This moment above all in the play presented Victor as reduced to a nameless essence existing only in the biological sense. After Victor raised his eyes, Pinter's Nicolas returned the gaze, slowly raising his gaze to smirkingly savor his triumph. Victor's "stare," then, seemed provoked by Nicolas exactly so it could be framed and subsumed by him. Pinter's stare showed absolutely no sign of the "insecurities" Mark Batty sees Nicolas as betraying at this moment (2001, 106). The audience was denied the satisfaction of seeing even a momentary reversal of power's triumph and forced to focus on the overwhelming force and cruelty of the status quo. Defiance of immoral power is subsumed by ongoing oppression.

Nicolas's fierce admiration for Gila's father is founded on the latter's faith, certitude, and preference for vitality over intellect: "He believed in God. He didn't *think*, like you shitbags. He *lived*" (*One*, 66). Pinter's political villains disdain thinking, regarding it as a threat to a natural, harmonious, ordered way of life and to the State that preserves that way of life. Stephen Watt observes that contrary to the postmodernism exemplified by Baudrillard, who argues that resistance to the status quo is impossible, figures such as Nicolas do not characterize intellectual dissent as always already impotent (1998, 108). Rather, Pinter's regimes, especially in *One for the Road* and *Party Time*, viciously attack those who allegedly use "thought" to oppose the status quo.

In these plays, dissent calls forth a massive retaliatory apparatus that successfully silences resistance. The fate of dissident voices is to be destroyed. The plots of these plays tend to the ultimate triumph of power, while the pattern of Pinter's plays is a complete defeat of one person by another (Sakellaridou 1989,

45; Knowles 1995a, 11). What these defeated characters undergo is something rather more than subjectification or interpellation. Watt maintains that according to the state, "the individual must become a subject in that sense of the term that underscores the positionality of one in subjection" (1998, 108). Victor suffers a bleaker, less metaphorical fate. To put it bluntly, if you want to interpellate someone into reigning ideology, it is unnecessary—and probably counterproductive—to mutilate his or her tongue. These portrayals of resistance's brutal, iterated defeats, occurring throughout his oeuvre, suggest that though Pinter the citizen does not regard resistance as already or a priori futile or complicit with regnant power, the precise images his plays offer depict how power crushes its would-be opponents.

The origin of this power in Nicolas's sense of self is an important critical issue. Marc Silverstein has analyzed *One for the Road* in Foucauldian and Althusserian terms, arguing "the 'link' he [Nicolas] 'feels' does not arise from unmediated experience but is discursively produced" (1993, 147). From Silverstein's perspective, this sense of belonging is ultimately fraudulent; it is the signal of a disruption or contradiction in Nicolas's ideological myth of legitimation. A reading that locates potential weakness in the monstrous Nicolas and his legitimating discourse has obvious appeal. The pleasure of ironically deconstructing his self-presentation is tempting. The concrete facts we are confronted with in *One for the Road* bear no suggestion that such a deconstruction will occur. The play provides us with a graphic experience whose very force can be invoked to counter the abstract logic of an Althusserian or Lacanian analysis. The very fact that we, as critics operating from a knowledge of postmodern theory, can spot a contradiction in Nicolas is morally gratifying in light of Nicolas's villainy and intellectually gratifying in terms of being able to treat Nicolas's self-definition with irony. To dwell on this irony while looking at what happens to Victor and the victims he represents is a troubling sort of bad faith, and to suppose that a sort of logical contradiction within Nicolas's discourse renders his power less secure in effect is (to borrow a phrase from Austin Quigley) an interesting speculation irrelevant to the observable facts of the play.

Moreover, Nicolas's sense of connection can be read without irony. It does for him what he says it does for him, what the play shows it does for him. Other models of the relationship between self and society are equally, perhaps more, relevant to Nicolas than is Silverstein's. According to Canetti, for example, the relationship between subjectivity-as-agency and power is opposite what it is for Althusser. As a response to the "anxiety of command," it is beneficial to have a bond with others and to merge oneself with that group, because the desire for revenge on the part of the commanded is likely to be inefficacious against a strong group (Canetti 1962, 328). For another instance, Nicolas can be seen as an instance of the fundamentalist self identified by Robert Jay Lifton, as an individual whose existence is organized by devotion to extrapersonal, fixed sources of value located in a sacred past that is meant to endure through the contingencies of history and change. The fundamentalist self excludes the uncertainties, the dimensionality of an introspective mode of being: he or she "distrusts intellectual or spiritual suppleness" (1993, 163–64). He *lives*, as Nicolas says; he doesn't have to *think*. This swerve away from doubt characterizes Pinter's tyrants. Another model for Nicolas's status is the monolithic individual, analyzed by Jacques Ellul, who looks to the past for verification of traditional social values. Through this buttressing of self-beliefs by tradition, the monolithic individual is relieved of any existential doubt, thus being able to move "forward with full assurance of his righteousness," "formidable in his equilibrium" (1965, 165). Nicolas, frightening and formidable in his cold sangfroid, boasts both of his righteousness and his poise. His insistence that worthy people "live" rather than "think" again suggests that such poise and self-acceptance are gained precisely by the abandonment of reflective thought. Ellul depressingly predicts that such individuals will sway history in ever greater, more dangerous ways.

While Silverstein is led to ponder the self-contradicting foundations of power in ideology, Pinter's depictions of suffering caused by political violence focus powerfully on the graphic realities of repression. Silverstein's analysis, emphasizing questions such as ideology and identity, perhaps fails to account for *One for the Road*'s full emotional impact. The horror the play elicits has to do with its tragedy of absolute victimization and the relentless way this victimization is specified in terms of bodily consequences: Victor's tongue being cut out, Gila's being raped, Nicky's murder. Pinter's political morality stems from the literal, actual consequences of oppression, the corporeal truths of torture, pain, death (Knowles 1991, 72). Silverstein's argument that Nicolas's position is subject to a kind of internal schism, that power can never be so absolutely lodged in one person, uses Althusserian terms that predetermine his answer; we arrive inevitably at the postmodern cliché that no specific subject position has a monolithic, unshakeable hold on power. As readers of the play, we may lose something of the full response to it if the play is taken as an embodiment of Althusser's vision of state power as opposed to Pinter's.[10] The critical issue is temporal scale: a balance must be created between the local effects and the long-term theoretical potentialities of power. To contemplate the idea that no subject has definitive power may be a comforting theory as we contemplate what may happen in the future to Nicolas and his regime, but it is hard to imagine it as relevant to Victor or his family. If a postmodern account of power valuably hints at its hidden internal paradoxes, such a reading may discount the specific violence depicted in the play and its tremendous human cost.

Silverstein ultimately wonders if Pinter's plays are collusive with the ideologies and power structures they seek to oppose. In Pinter's plays, "the cultural order" and its "forms of power" are "unshakably homogeneous and monolithic" to the extent that "the totalizing nature of [the plays'] analysis of cultural power tends to reify that power" (1993, 142, 152). Here the assumption, a common one among politically oriented critics, is that political theater must provide tools for change or at least establish hope for change. If Pinter reifies power, he also creates images of it in action that are extraordinarily painful and forceful. This focus on forms of cultural power and their rhetoric displaces attention from the specific violence of the plays, the presence of power in its physical dimension. Fredric Jameson writes that "history is what hurts," (1981, 102) and Pinter's dramas attempt to make us experience history in just this sense: as the corporeal consequences of suffering. (Even here there is ambiguity, of course, as Pinter's dramas of torture, pain, repression, and oppression are largely verbal and deal allusively with the fact of violence.) Pinter writes a political theater that is heterodox, even heretical, on the basic assumption that such theater be oriented to change. If political theater tells us to rebel against what exists, Pinter's version obliges by rebelling against the prevailing definition and procedures of that political theater.

It may well be true that something about how *One for the Road* affects its audience exceeds any intellectual attempt to explicate the play. Specifically, a literal focus on human pain may be lost in a postmodern reading emphasizing the self-contradictions of ideology. If the contemplation of pain leads to aporia— when we witness pain, we lose our ability to think and to speak—this condition of enforced muteness must nevertheless be included in critical analysis of Pinter's political dramas.

While *One for the Road* aims to produce a stark, shocking effect, Pinter's next play, *Mountain Language*, is arguably even bleaker, more pessimistic. The oppression *Mountain Language* dramatizes is a matter of governmental policy, not the cruel whims of one individual. The theme, atmosphere, and experience of *Mountain Language* intensify those of *One for the Road*. Pinter indicts abusive power more generally, depicting the bureaucratic machinery of torture. By featuring a wider vision of a repressive regime, Pinter illustrates a wider level of its function; in contrast to *One for the Road*, which centers on the villainy of one extraordinary person, *Mountain Language* illuminates an extensive apparatus of ethnic and political repression.

Mountain Language is set in an unspecified country in which "mountain people" reside, as opposed to those in "the capital" (*ML*, 21). The play examines the relationship between power and prejudice, limning a fascist society that represses an ethnic minority. The first scene, outside a prison wall, shows a number of women waiting to visit their imprisoned men. An Officer harasses a young woman when she observes that an older woman has been bitten by a dog:

> What was his *name*? . . . Every dog has a *name*! They answer to their name. They are given a name by their parents and that is their name, that is their *name*! Before they bite, they *state* their name. It's a formal procedure. They state their name and then they bite. What was his name? (17)

An Officer announces the regime's agenda: "You are mountain people. . . . Your language is dead" (21). The Officer discovers that the young woman's husband is not a "mountain person," but both Sergeant and Officer continue to demean her: "She looks like a fucking intellectual to me," says the Sergeant, adding, "Intellectual arses wobble the best" (25).

The next three scenes are briefer, even more concentrated. Inside the prison, the elderly woman sits with her son. They are commanded to speak the language of the capital, but the old woman cannot do so. The prisoner appeals for sympathy—he, like the guard, has "a wife and three kids" (*ML*, 31). The lights dim, motion onstage ceases, and the Prisoner and his mother speak in voice-over—we hear their unspoken thoughts. The old woman tries to comfort her son: "The baby is waiting for you. . . . They're all waiting for you. . . . They're all waiting to see you." The guard calls for the Sergeant to punish this "joker" (33).

Scene 3 depicts the violence so ominously promised. The young woman, by accident, comes upon her husband, hooded and thus presumably about to be tortured. In another voice-over scene, the young woman and the man speak a romantic memory: "I watch you sleep. . . . You look up at me above you and smile" (ML, 39). The lights come up, interrupting this moment of communion; the man collapses and is dragged offstage. The Sergeant mocks the woman's plight while hewing to bureaucratic language, blaming the snafu on a computer with "a double hernia" (41). The young woman grimly attempts to bargain her body for better treatment: "Can I fuck him? If I fuck him, will everything be all right?" (41).

The final scene returns to the son and mother of scene 2. The Guard tells the prisoner and his mother that the rules have changed; they can use their mountain language. However, the mother cannot or will not respond to her son, who repetitively beseeches her to talk, to no avail.[11] He trembles and collapses, beginning "to gasp and shake violently," but the Sergeant dismisses this suffering: "Look at this. You go out of your way to give them a helping hand and they fuck it up" (ML, 47).[12]

The author has discussed the import of the play in numerous statements, attempting to direct its interpretation.[13] His stance toward his own play is illustrated in a letter to the *Times Literary Supplement*:

> In your advertisement . . . you state that the play was "inspired" by my trip to Turkey with Arthur Miller and is a "parable about torture and the fate of the Kurdish people." These assertions were made without consultation with the author. The first part of the sentence is in fact true. The play is not, however, "about the fate of the Kurdish people" and, above all, it is not intended as a "parable." (Pinter 1988b, 1109)

Pinter evidently believes his political plays are too direct to be seen as metaphors or parables. He states that though he began the play in 1985 following his return from Turkey, "this play is not about the Turks and the Kurds. I mean, throughout history, many languages have been banned—the Irish have suffered, the Welsh have suffered and the Urdu and the Estonians' language banned" (http://www.haroldpinter.org). In other statements, he disclaims the notion that the play deals in any proper way with the overall fate of the Kurds in Turkey or anywhere else: such a play would have to be far longer than *Mountain Language* and necessitate more historical research than Pinter did in preparing the play (Gussow 1994, 68).

The author's interpretive suggestions are not unproblematically helpful. Pinter seems to mean that the play is not *only* about the Kurds in Turkey but illustrates other, similar situations as well. Pinter creates "political parables that are universally applicable" as Batty writes (2001, 113). This approach is interesting in terms of the history of political theater, which generally defines the situations it portrays, and the purposes it serves, in topical ways. By contrast, Pinter delineates his political issues as recurrent, even continuous throughout history. The plays deal with an essential historical truth that shows itself in different countries and various eras.[14] This reasoning has intriguing consequences. Shaw accepted that political theater could be measured by immediate effects. Plays which addressed political issues will always be topical, writes Shaw, but they need not shy from this condition. "A Doll's House will be as flat as ditchwater when A Midsummer Night's Dream will still be as fresh as paint," he proclaims, "but it will have done more work in the world" (1958, 63; Shaw writes the titles without italics). Pinter, in contrast to Shaw, seems to want to avoid topical references and purposes in his political theater. His model of political theater may assume that if the audience defines the play in terms of one specific situation, it will more easily be able to think that that one situation is caused by foreign "others" who can be regarded as morally inferior (as in, "Oh those Turks, they should be civilized and reasonable like we are"). Alternately, if a play denotes a particular situation, we may be tempted to focus on that one situation and ignore other, similar ones happening elsewhere.[15]

Mountain Language conducts its political analysis by featuring signature elements of Pinter's dramas: language as attack and as silence. Language is the domain of the powerful in this play: specifically, the verbal violence of the Sergeant and Guard strikes a familiar tone to readers of Pinter. The techniques of illogical aggression through language, backed up with real threats of physical violence, link Pinter's earlier absurdist plays to those meant to serve a clear public purpose. The verbal assaults in *Mountain Language* are reminiscent of those in plays such as *The Homecoming*, for instance, Lenny's, whose specious authority on varied subjects, philosophical speculation, and blithe violence are echoed in the former play's Officer.

Despite this similarity, *Mountain Language* is stylistically and formally distinct not only from Pinter's full-length plays but even from its immediate predecessor *One for the Road*. Pinter pushes his drama structurally towards postmodernism, with surface characters and abbreviated, disrupted narratives.[16] As personalities, none of the characters in *Mountain Language* are as psychologically developed as characters such as Lenny, Goldberg, or Mick in *The Caretaker*. Pinter does not want the figures in *Mountain Language* to exert psychological fascination upon the audience. He attempts to minimize the predominance of character in his political plays. In this sense, Pinter's political theater moves in the direction of Brechtian techniques.[17] Depth of character is replaced by something like Brecht's concept of gestus, in which "character" is nothing more than the expression of historical location and power status through action. People behave the way they do because of their position in society, the purpose of this behavior being to preserve asymmetries of power and privilege.

In *Mountain Language* the tortured prisoners are prohibited from speaking their language. In the last scene this stricture is arbitrarily reversed. The old woman is told she can speak her language, yet she remains silent while her son collapses under the strain of imprisonment. The arbitrariness of the Guard's command must be understood as deeply wounding, not as an expression of mercy or reform. The Guard even emphasizes the change will be transient: "Until further notice" he says three times (*ML*, 43, 47). This inconsistency points out a discrepancy between the fact of domination and the ostensible justifications of power.

Consistency in rule making is necessary to the "inner morality" of law, according to legal philosopher Lon L. Fuller.[18] Prior to any distinction between "good" or "bad" laws, the system of law itself may break down if, for example, the rules contradict each other, or if they require behavior beyond the capacity of the subject, if they are administered inconsistently, or if they are changed so frequently that no one can orient his or her actions by them—all of which occur in *Mountain Language*. It is this state of disorientation—one that outlasts the specific tortures shown in the play—that Pinter dramatizes through the old woman's final muteness and her son's collapse. This regime ex-

ploits the rule of law to complete the victimization of its enemies.

This cynical exploitation of power parallels the regime's lack
of interest in justifying its procedures. According to what is
called the "just-world theory," torture may be tolerated because
people believe that their representatives are on the side of right
and that any victims, are, therefore, wrong and deserving of punishment. If someone is ill treated, this is seen simply as an unfor-
tunate accident, the work of the proverbial bad apple, not the
intentional result of governmental actions or policy. The behavior of authority is assumed to be ordered and systematic (Crelinsten and Schmid 1994, 4).[19] Such a belief is contradicted by the
actual practice of torture, which features arbitrary rules and chaotic brutality: "Arbitrary and gratuitous punishment are frequently accompanied by explanations of motive that they seem
intended as demonstrations of contempt" (Scarry 1985, 278).
The *Mountain Language* regime is ostensibly imprisoning the
mountain people for some reason; however, the revelation that
misidentified people have been imprisoned—"He's in the wrong
batch"—is dismissed as trivial and barely regrettable. This regime doesn't bother to follow its own rules, and isn't even
obliged to pretend to do so.

The language of *Mountain Language* raises key issues about
the behavior of ruling classes, especially the ways in which they
attempt to legitimate or rationalize their conduct. As critics
have noted, the pronouncements of the regime are logically contradictory and do not bear rational examination: if the mountain
language is dead, efforts to outlaw it are then redundant and look
silly (Watt 1998, 109). If the regime rationalizes its conduct
through language that is transparently and obviously fraudulent,
how can it win consent or support from its general populace?
The illogicality of the regime's outward justifications for oppressing the mountain-people minority extends beyond this irrational absurdity of banning an extinct language. The grounds for
prejudice and governmental action against this minority are arbitrary, loose, fungible, shifting, and syncretically accepting of
self-contradiction. The initial prohibition against the mountain
language is schizophrenically both a military decree and a law, a
condition the Officer highlights rather than minimizes (*ML*, 21).
The distinction between dictate and legislation belongs to a
world that cares about logical and intellectual niceties—not to
this one.

If the domain of governmental pronouncements does not

serve to justify hatred, other concepts can be borrowed for the occasion. Thus, the young woman who protests the system hasn't committed a crime, as the Officer points out. Nevertheless, as the Sergeant declares and the Officer seconds, she is a creature of sin and thereby rightfully subject to punishment (*ML*, 23). Here religion, in the form of Christian associations between the flesh and sin, permits the abuse that the powerful wish to perform, even when such oppression is not justified by the quasi-legalistic dictates against the mountain people. Perhaps, though, this distinction between religious-moral motivation and a legal one disappears if one follows the development of law from morality far enough back in human history (to the roots of ancient Greek thought, for example, or before, say, the Enlightenment's translation of moral compassion from religion to philosophy). In any case, as we have been reminded before and after the 2003 war in Iraq, consistent justification is needless to support actions one wanted to take anyway.

The logical contradiction is given one more twist here. If the young woman is an intellectual, she must not be sensual, according to the prejudice against intellectuals and the philosophical life, but the Sergeant mixes his terms: "Intellectual arses wobble the best" (*ML*, 25). Again, the behavior of the rulers combines contradictory notions in a syncretic manner. Logical opposites are seamlessly combined. No weakness follows this embrace of self-contradiction. This logical absurdity in the language use of oppressors is explained by Jean-Paul Sartre in a way that matches Pinter's characters. In Sartre's famous *Anti-Semite and Jew*, he outlines the verbal behavior of the adherents of anti-Semitism, an organized and active prejudice similar to the destructive hatred of the capital people for the mountain people and to the overall attitude of Pinter's oppressors for their victims. The anti-Semite, writes Sartre, treats language as a game not as a way to convey referential truth—a type of *parole* that should be familiar to any students of Pinter's drama. This rhetorical mode exempts the anti-Semite from arguments grounded in logic and grants him the joys of freedom and style:

> The anti-Semite has chosen . . . to devaluate words and reasons. How entirely at ease he feels as a result. . . . Never believe that anti-Semites are completely unaware of the absurdity of their [language]. They know that their remarks are frivolous, open to challenge. But they are amusing themselves, for it is their adversary who is obliged to use words responsibly, since he believes in words. The anti-Sem-

ites have the *right* to play. They even like to play with discourse for, by giving ridiculous reasons, they discredit the seriousness of their interlocutors. They delight in acting in bad faith, since they seek not to persuade by sound argument but to intimidate and disconcert. (1995, 19–20)

This analysis suggests the practical attitude to language and communication generally taken by Pinter's oppressors and clearly seen in *Mountain Language*. (*The New World Order* makes this emphasis explicit, as its torturers embrace logical contradiction at every opportunity.) Sartre implies that logical dissections of oppressors and their thoughts are irrelevant; such people have preemptively disassociated themselves from claims of or arguments based on truth. And he offers an appealingly direct explanation for such behavior: it's fun; it's play. *Mountain Language*'s regime, which does not care if it imprisons the wrong people, anticipates the later plays such as *Press Conference* (2002), in which the ruling regimes simply do whatever they want without convincing logical justification. It may be that there are logical contradictions in forbidding that which has already been defined as impossible. But doing so is fun. (For proof, read aloud the officer's speech about the dog in *Mountain Language*, or imagine the *jouissance* of a grinning Pinter playing the Minister in *Press Conference*.) In forbidding the impossible, or breaking the supposed rules of legitimation for one's actions, one experiences the perverse joy and total freedom of Nicolas in *One for the Road*. One gets to break the rules of rationalist either/or logic and still be, in a deep and fundamental sense, absolutely right.

The irrelevancy of logic and thought links to another important theory of political power. Hannah Arendt's familiar, though controversial and often misapplied, idea of "the banality of evil" connects to the vision of political malfeasance suggested in Pinter's plays. The link is not just the empirical fact that evil is best accomplished by functionaries working in bureaucracies that exempt personal conduct from moral examination (the delineation of such a system differentiates *Mountain Language* from *One for the Road*). It is also the depthlessness of evil as a principle: its imperviousness to thought, reflection, and analysis. Oppression is most efficiently accomplished by people without psychological depth. The dynamics of lying, often applied to Pinter's characters, apply here: people who harm others often attempt to believe their actions are positive. Such self-deception is easier to accomplish the shallower one's "self" is. Even more fundamentally, in an historical sense, evil persists precisely because it frustrates tactics of accountability that rely on intellectual tools—it is "thought-defying," in Arendt's words. Any attack on evil must avoid going into depth about it, just because evil makes such an approach irrelevant:

> It is indeed my opinion now that evil is never "radical," that it is only extreme, and that it possesses neither depth nor any demonic dimension. It can overgrow and lay waste the whole world precisely because it spreads like a fungus on the surface. It is "thought-defying," as I said, because thought tries to reach some depth, to go to the roots, and the moment it concerns itself with evil, it is frustrated because there is nothing. That is its "banality." (2000, 396)

Arendt's notion that political evil is, paradoxically, both systemic and superficial expresses the ineradicable threat of oppression as dramatized by Pinter.

Mountain Language has other important implications about the nature of state power. This regime has untethered itself from the rule of law; it exists principally to oppress. It is not the case that the oppression occurs as the exception to this country's activities adhering to rules, laws, and established governmental processes. Rather, all those political niceties have been proclaimed irrelevant. The state exists solely to repress its enemies. What laws it does promulgate serve only to oppress. This condition evokes several political theorists who sought to describe (or prescribe) how state power changed in the twentieth century. According to Arendt in *The Origins of Totalitarianism*, the state after World War I came to be perceived as the instrument of domination by a "community" or in-group, rather than as an embodiment of law—it is ever more "difficult . . . for states to resist the temptation to deprive all citizens of legal status and rule them with an omnipotent police" (1966, 290). The Nazi political theorist Carl Schmitt described a similar view in his philosophies, which were used as rationale for the Third Reich. Schmitt defined politics and the purpose of the state in terms of the distinction between friend and enemy (as he argued in 1928's *The Concept of the Political*).[20] From here, once this enemy was found, it must be fought with any means. This idea conjoins with another of Schmitt's, that the state must ultimately rely on sovereign, nondemocratic, extralegal authority. A true state exists in a perpetual state of emergency, dispensing with laws in favor of the higher, more elemental, and urgent task of defeating its enemies—just as Hitler's Germany was founded in the suspension of the Weimar constitution, granting unlimited powers to the head of state. No need exists for such a state to explain or apologize for violations of law, procedure, and customary morality, because the nation may break any laws in its quest for safety and protection from enemies. All of the regimes in Pinter's openly political theater define the task of government in similar terms. The logic is clear and, in its own way, admirably efficient: the existence of invented enemies justifies all acts of power. In *Mountain Language*, as in *One for the Road* (and even more so, perhaps, in *Party Time*), Pinter demonstrates how attractive such a concept of governmental power is to entrenched leaders, and he suggests that we compare this vision of the state against the ones we live in.[21]

Obviously, Pinter's play is not an abstract lesson in political philosophy: the play dramatizes subjugation in practice, not in theory. The ultimate import of *Mountain Language* derives from the action it depicts, an action culminating in the final, frozen silence of the old woman as she watches her trembling son. Faced with this rigged system, with a regime that regards rules as inconsequential, the old woman's ultimate nonresponse does not necessarily indicate surrender. Her final silence is ambiguous. The woman may be choosing not to speak since to speak in her own language would be to obey and succumb to the government imprisoning her (Gillen 1988, 4). Is her silence a positive act of "final defiance" (4), a demonstration of renewed power (Adler 1991, 7) in the same way that Victor's silent stare in *One for the Road* may be a token of future subversion (or, to be more precise, a symbol offering a faint promise of the future possibility of subversion)? Perhaps her silence suggests a reserve of power, the power of reserve: "The power of remaining silent," writes Canetti in *Crowds and Power*, "is always highly valued" (1962, 294).

However, the political meaning of this choice is uncertain, since it gives the old woman only the negative capacity of withdrawal. Another view of her silence is just as compelling if not as comforting; that is to envision the old woman as defeated, beaten, therefore silent. She has been deprived of means to alter, to endure, even to describe her condition. This state of powerlessness is ascribed by philosopher Emmanuel Levinas in a discussion of tyranny and freedom. It is true, he notes, that one might refuse a command even at the risk of death, thus achieving a kind of freedom. But, in such a case, this freedom is merely nominal; substantively, it is fraudulent or illusory. "A freedom of thought reduced to itself, a freedom of thought which is nothing but a freedom of thought is, by that very fact, [only] a consciousness of tyranny. . . . In these conditions would not the tyrant [be] the only free being?" Levinas asks rhetorically (1993, 15–16). Freedom and tyranny can coexist given such a definition of freedom. The old woman's silence, if it can be termed a free act, represents such an illusory "freedom of thought," a reduction to the pure awareness of being commanded. Canetti, as well, sees silence not just as refuge but also as imprisonment—if keeping silent is a kind of power, it is always a highly qualified, ambivalent one. "Silence is an extreme form of defence, whose advantages and disadvantages are almost equally balanced," Canetti writes (1962, 286). "[N]o one can remain silent forever. . . . Silence isolates. . . . Silence inhibits self-transformation" (294). The dispossessed exist not in a silence of wisdom but a silence of poverty, as Joseph Roth observes. Silence is passive, even if actively chosen. Ultimately, it supports reigning power: "Through silence, the status quo is more likely to remain secure" (Sloterdijk 1987, 14). *Mountain Language* thus illustrates how reigning power prevents the marginalized from expressing themselves in words or action.

The experience of silence is difficult to transmit through the written page. The perception of time and suffering involved in *Mountain Language* demands the medium of performance. Katie Mitchell's 2001 production of *Mountain Language* at the Pinter Festival used inventive staging to amplify the play's content. The sound design simulated the violent, reverberating clang of prison bars, an assaultive noise that both contrasted with and underlined the profound silences of the play. For each scene, lighting and curtains literally framed the visible action in different ways, cutting off the fullness of the proscenium stage. "Lighting" may be the wrong word: each scene was unusually dark, forcing the audience to strain to see the action. These performance effects had a touch of the Brechtian about them. The experience and difficulties of perception were forced upon the audience's attention so that the spectators became self-consciously aware of their spectatorship. However, this self-conscious distancing, in a Brechtian paradox, did not lessen but arguably increased audience involvement with the play. The fake snow dropping on scene 1's lengthy line of eleven women appeared sharply real despite its clear theatricality; the bag of apples spilled in scene 4 was both visually striking and a brazen, though apt, symbol of assaulted innocence. This moment was intensified when the Guard picked one up and started munching.

Mitchell's production emphasized the social otherness between the victims in the play and the sophisticated, middle-class, urban audience watching it. The military characters spoke their lines with inhuman lack of inflection and correspondent excess of volume, enjoying their power without showing emotion or vulnerability. Their routinized depthlessness was just as frightening, if not more so, than a willful malevolence. The old woman whom the guards victimized was visually defined as a peasant, socially and psychologically other to the play's urban audience. The old woman's wrinkled face betrayed no absolutely signs of inwardness, no reaction at all to the happenings around her. This blankness frustrated audience impulses toward empathy, adding another alienating effect to this performance. To an extent, this passivity can be read realistically, as manifesting fear or confusion. In a metatheatrical sense, the image of age and social otherness forced the audience to recognize and consider its own disconnection from what it was witnessing, as we continually desired but were denied some emotional reaction consonant with onstage events, some portrayal of the old woman that registers and communicates the suffering we see in the play. The audience's customary desire to identify empathetically was at least partially frustrated and thereby made problematic.

Morally speaking as well, the suffering of the old woman resists being possessed by the audience. The role of empathy was put into question through this production's portrayal of the elderly woman. According to philosopher James Hatley, the spectacle of age frustrates the impulse to empathy: the other's aging is not mine and cannot be suffered as one's own is. Suffering and age index a life history of vulnerability that is absolutely specific and "untranslatable" to the observer:

> The past held in this face *as face* resists any interpretation of it that would have it translated into a presence of what is the now the case or even might be the case for me. . . . The other's ageing submits me to a time that could never be mine, not even in sympathy. (2000, 84)

To act otherwise, as if the life of another could be suffered as if it were one's own, is an act not of "compassion" but of profound self-approval and moral arrogance (84). To translate another's suffering into the terms of one's own life is dangerously, even offensively, presumptuous.

The old woman's corporeal reality, emphasized through her final silence, thus serves to demonstrate the disjunction between her suffering and our experience of it. This silence can be seen as a moral indictment of the audience achieved metatheatrically. Such a fraught silence can be seen in an 1989 CSC Repertory production which paired the American premiere of *Mountain Language* with *The Birthday Party*. Petey's impotence and silence at the end of *The Birthday Party* evoke the play's audience; both are "decent, well-intentioned, knowledgeable, but" ineffective (Gillen 1989, 97). Values such as sympathy, decency, concern, and awareness are all futile in the face of what actually happens in the world. "Understanding is not enough" (97). While political theatre in general tries to make one see, to understand, with the assumption that accurate seeing can be the precursor to right action, Pinter's political theater exposes the fragility of this hopeful assumption.

4

Pinter and the Permanence of Power:
Party Time, Celebration, Press Conference, and *The New World Order*

Pinter's political theater means to be disturbing. The plays themselves seem to depict a power structure that is impervious to critique, while they dramatize the triumph of power in destroying opposition. Power, in preserving itself, enables whatever is effectively compliant, disables whatever is effectively oppositional. Individual consent, or dissent, is rendered problematic at best. Pinter's political plays suggest the effective irrelevance of individual experience against a determined and violent status quo: they dare us to contemplate the destruction of progressive action. Furthermore, structures of power systematically pervert terms of political discourse, in a double process. First, the status quo disables dissent by rhetorically marginalizing its ideas and vocabulary; opposition then nears the condition of silence, a final silence that appears as the tendency of unchecked power to legitimize itself. Any debate over whether or not this silence is historically inevitable should not distract from its frightening and debilitating presence, whether as possibility, likelihood, or certainty.

Power silences opposition in another way as well: the status quo claims positive ideals and terms as alibis for violence and repression. Words such as freedom, equality, and democracy are used in ways divorced from their original meanings and become rhetorical tokens by which the status quo is maintained. Elites exploit the malleability of language: worthy words—democracy, human rights, morality—have been corrupted and stolen to legitimize conduct that contradicts the received meanings of these concepts. Indeed, these terms defend and maintain present power structures due to their popular appeal. *Party Time, Celebration, Press Conference,* and *The New World Order* explore

101

how rhetorical justification exists on a social level and proceeds through language deformation to sanction, and often sanctify, violent repression.

In 1991's *Party Time*, Pinter explicitly shifts his focus from abroad to England. Rather than representing a foreign situation and implying that the play refers to its audience's society, Pinter depicts a recognizably English setting. *Party Time* is ambitious and inclusive, with a more extended plot and a larger cast than in the earlier political plays, amounting to a dramatization of the mores and modes of bourgeois triumphalism. The play satirically denounces its own audience, portraying a lifestyle concerned with prestige, luxury, and fitness, not all that far removed from that of our own upper classes. While it more explicitly defines its locale, this political play continues the self-questioning of political theater's goals and assumptions, just as *Mountain Language* moves in the direction of questioning ideals of empathy and the possibility of resistance. Daringly, perhaps even perversely, *Party Time* subverts the hopeful assumption that there may exist an alternative to our status quo of Western capitalist power. The play records the marginalization of the social protest it urges, hinting at the end of political theater. With an ending that features a silenced character named "Jimmy," the play seems to self-consciously close the period of British political theater inaugurated in 1956 by the iconoclastic Jimmy Porter of John Osborne's *Look Back in Anger*.

Party Time suggests that in contemporary England, dissent has been criminalized and made abject. It indicts a Thatcherite, neoconservative embrace of "values" and social refinement as fascist. In *Party Time*, Pinter portrays the so-called "Culture Wars" of the late '80s and '90s consistently with a 1996 public statement: "The conservatives are beyond redemption."[1] Military repression follows the verbal characterization, demonization, and domination of an already vanquished "other." Pinter employs satire to imply that England is (becoming) a fascist prison in which human rights and personal freedoms have vanished; fascism coexists with "democracy" and with a presumption that the elites and what they stand for is moral. In this brutal world, social privilege is both justification and vehicle of repression—privilege is moral. Hierarchy is justified simply because the underprivileged "have less world (property, knowledge, ambition, style, professionalism, and so forth)" (Scarry 1985, 331). The notion that society and government serve morality is unmasked as a perverse fraud perpetrated in two ways: by force and by deformation of language use.

A *langue* promoting democratic ideals conceals a *parole* mocking notions of human morality and worth. Politesse, culture, distinction, refinement, social hierarchy, and other practices of "everyday life" disguise an ugly, otherwise naked will to power that determines how all political, social, and personal life is to be conducted. The language of the play shows the powerful force of social euphemism backed up by physical strength and military might. Power determines how this elite group uses language. Euphemisms and unacknowledged double-meaning expressions replace reference to unpleasant reality, while a dependence on cliché and banality demonstrate the extent to which individual thinking has been replaced by a conceptually thin social propaganda, amounting to brute hatred of those who differ from or doubt the status quo. The elite become ever more desperately insistent upon their morality as their ostensible beliefs of social goodness conflict with reality, just as Marx notes in *The German Ideology*: "But the more the conscious illusions of the ruling classes are shown to be false and the less they satisfy common sense, the more dogmatically they are asserted and the more deceitful, moralizing, and spiritual becomes the language of established society."[2]

Party Time illustrates how metaphors are socially constructed to define community members in moral opposition to outsiders, considered less than human, whose existence serves to justify any means of preserving the in-group's lifestyle. As power structures focus on who controls public discourse, language games become deadly. The "reality" instituted by such games legitimates physical repression—murder, to put it plainly—of the losers. The play also satirizes a specific form of public language use contemporary with the play's writing. *Party Time* portrays the discourse of neoconservatism, which argued that traditional morality be enforced with renewed vigor across all society. This discourse is used to demonize (and then destroy) those who would regard morality, truth, and politics as relativistic matters open to inquiry or examination.

Party Time uses Pinteresque techniques to dramatize the lived experience of the oppressors as they go about their daily business of oppressing. The subjugation of females is one large aspect of this oppression. In the fascist regime of *Party Time*, women are valued only for childbearing and are feared for their uncontrollable, disruptive sexuality. The play identifies power with men (defined as would-be protectors) and powerlessness with women (in need of protection). There is psychological tension in this opposition as women contest how they are being defined. Here, as in *The Comfort of Strangers* and *Ashes to Ashes*, Pinter explores social and political conflict through the example of gender relationships. Power hates what it controls; the most visible evidence of this tendency in the world of *Party Time* is its rampant, casual, and violent misogyny. Misogyny is an example, a readily visible one, of how power in general works and how it appears to its victims.

These themes rest on a fairly simple plot. A group of upper-crust socialites gathers at the apartment of one of them, Gavin, for a refined cocktail party, though an unspecified disturbance on the local streets has delayed some partygoers. Envy, social climbing, and quarrels over status dominate the conversations of the guests, who boast of their social connections, their yachts, their wives, and their affairs. Gavin is entreated to join one especially exclusive club, an establishment that offers "pure comfort" and has "real class" (*PT*, 3). Terry brutally berates his wife Dusty, who keeps asking about her brother Jimmy, apparently persona non grata at this level of society. In other interactions, a woman named Charlotte tangentially confronts Fred, a military officer whom she suspects is responsible for the death of her husband. The elderly Dame Melissa gives a speech lamenting the breakdown of social cohesion and morality, and Gavin then apologizes for the disturbances his guests endured. Jimmy enters; stage movement ceases; the lights dim. Issuing weakly out of the darkness, his disembodied voice provides haunting, paradoxical testimony to his own absence.

One readily apparent dimension of this world is its misogyny. The society of *Party Time* assumes that women are baby factories and that anything they do other than bear children and tend to their husbands destabilizes society. "It's the root of so many ills, you know. Uncontrollable wives" (*PT*, 23), Gavin says. Power and influence, in this martial society—at least three male characters are military—are marked as male virtues. (There is a pun here, correlating the play's many references to virtue to the root Roman meaning of *virtu* as military ability.) Women's valued roles are limited to reproduction and a traditional, self-denying motherhood. All the men in this society hold such a belief; the few male-to-male conversations in the play, full of banality and empty phrases, are notable for their superficiality. The sole legitimate purpose of women, the men assume, is to create new humans to carry on old traditions. These men have their eye on history and the future; they want not just to achieve sociopolitical power but also to extend that power indefinitely into the future. Thus they must use the present to perpetuate a pure and unchanging future. (One is reminded of the goal of the Nazi genocide: not merely to destroy all Jews but to wipe the existence of Jewry from the record of human history.) Douglas fulsomely praises his wife and his devotion to her. "[M]y little girl here had given birth to twins" (39) whom "she looked after . . . all by herself. No maid, no help, nothing. . . . And that's why we're still together" (41). The reference to twins reveals the society's dream of reproduction as a variety-denying duplication of the status quo.

In *Party Time*, the ideological definition of woman as mother leaves the female characters of the play with very little to do except idle activities and competing for men. There is, however, ideological blurring, as female behavior emulates the animal viciousness and force characterizing male behavior in this society. Stereotypically male language and conduct infect female experience. In one conversation, Liz and Charlotte discuss a man with whom Liz has previously fallen in love, a man seduced by another woman. "I could have cut her throat, that nymphomaniac slut," Liz claims, judging that this "bigtitted tart" "raped" her "beloved" (*PT*, 12–13). This paradoxical use of language illustrates that, in this male-dominated society, action must be expressed in conventionally male terms, while viciousness and hierarchy corrupt any personal relationships.

Pinter further connects motherhood and family with politics through Terry and his wife Dusty. Her sibling relationship to the dissenter Jimmy leads Terry to imagine sadistic, misogynist punishment for those who question society:

TERRY: Easy. We've got dozens of options. We could suffocate every single one of you at a given signal or we could shove a broomstick up each individual arse at another given signal or we could poison all the mother's milk in the world so that every baby would drop dead before it opened its perverted bloody mouth.
DUSTY: But will it be fun for me? Will it be fun?
TERRY: You'll love it. But I'm not going to tell you which method we'll use. I just want you to have a lot of sexual anticipation. I want you to look forward to whatever the means employed. . . .
DUSTY: But you still love me?
TERRY: Of course I love you. You're the mother of my children. (*PT*, 30–31)

The ideological split between motherhood and personhood, and the definition of sex as violence, are unmistakable. Power is registered through corporeal, sexual terms.[3]

If Terry's violent and crude language is one index of his rage, *Party Time* demonstrates in numerous other ways a connection between spoken language and power. The empowered use language in the modes of euphemism, tautology, and cliché. To use language with denotative accuracy seems forbidden; doing so would reveal unacceptable truths about this social world. As a character of British playwright Howard Barker says, "The more mature you are, the less you use the word you want" (1982, 45). Moral laxity and dependence on cliché over authentic communication are clearly satirized:

> DOUGLAS. Oh, it matters. It matters. I should say it matters. All this fucking-about has to stop.
> FRED. You mean it?
> DOUGLAS. I mean it all right.
> FRED. I admire people like you.
> DOUGLAS. So do I.
> *FRED clenches his fist.*
> FRED. A bit of that.
> *DOUGLAS clenches his fist.*
> DOUGLAS. A bit of that. (*PT*, 14–15)

After this stunningly banal exchange, Douglas amplifies his vision of society's purpose:

> DOUGLAS. We want peace and we're going to get it. But we want that peace to be cast iron. No leaks. No draughts. Cast iron. Tight as a drum. That's the kind of peace we want and that's the kind of peace we're going to get. A cast-iron peace.
> *He clenches his fist.*
> Like this.
> FRED. You know, I really admire people like you.
> DOUGLAS. So do I. (17)

Pinter's dramatization of banal repetition, his exposure of tautology, has two effects. Pinter drains this representation of humor, intentionally denying comedic distance. The first time one hears Doug and Fred's repeated banality, it is a laugh line, as one assumes one's own intellectual superiority over these cliché spouters.[4] The second time the repetition happens, the joke is exhausted, no longer funny; retroactively, one may question the first laugh. Also, this regime's habit of tautological repetitions parallels theoretical accounts of the nature of bourgeois society. Roland Barthes in *Mythologies* and Guy deBord in *The Society of the Spectacle* identify tautology as characteristic of bourgeois society. The "spectacle," as deBord sees it, is a representation of society that subsumes all that can be seen, perceived, and thought, a representation that excludes everything outside itself: "The spectacle is the existing order's uninterrupted discourse about itself," saying "nothing more than 'that which appears is good, that which is good appears'" (1983, paragraphs 24 and 12). Bourgeois society, endlessly and approvingly, displays itself to itself in a perpetual, all-encompassing, and repetitive representation.

Power's self-absolving euphemisms appear most strongly in Gavin's speech welcoming his guests. He pacifies the partygoers with a neutral, reassuring explanation of the circumstances of their evening and their political situation:

> GAVIN: Thank you very much indeed. Now I believe one or two of our guests encountered traffic problems on their way here tonight. I apologize for that, but I would like to assure you that all such problems and all related problems will be resolved very soon. Between ourselves, we've had a bit of a round-up this evening. This round-up is coming to an end. In fact normal services will be resumed shortly. . . . That's all we ask, that the service this country provides will run on normal, secure, and legitimate paths and that the ordinary citizen be allowed to pursue his labours and his leisure in peace. Thank you all so much for coming here tonight. It's been really lovely to see you, quite smashing. (*PT*, 45–46)

Gavin's presentation of this military action as innocuous is meant to be odious, as is the acceptance of that action's normality by the partyers. What is passed off as "normal," Pinter reminds us here, may well be inhuman, even deadly.[5]

The language in Gavin's speech is studded with paradoxical meaning. Doubleness reigns, as Gavin's casual words, considered in their actual meanings, indict the political world he administers. "The service this country provides" images the state as a waiter, a subservient presence guaranteeing the pleasure of the citizens in this sanctum, citizens thus redefined as consumers. (Here the play anticipates the leftist critique that globalization reduces individuals to passive consumers.) This punning image is visually corroborated when a number of waitresses enter immediately after this speech. That this country is pic-

tured as a provider of pleasure belies the partygoers' notion that
their society embodies moral ideals. Gavin's locution that government programs "will run on normal, secure, and legitimate
paths" tangentially echoes the phrase "At least they got the
trains to run on time," a popular joke about Mussolini and other
fascists, justifying oppression through supposed efficiency. The
line also estranges the concepts of normality and legitimacy,
showing these matters as socially defined. In the phrase "ordinary citizen," "ordinary" means privileged and the concept of
citizenship has been negated. "Pursue" refers to the actions off-
stage, namely the successful pursuit of dissidents such as
Jimmy. "Peace" ironically invokes the civil war of repression the
State is fighting, while "labours" glances at labor camps, perhaps Jimmy's fate. "Thank you all so much for coming here to-
night" can be read as an ironic address to the play's spectators.
The statement seems to question the audience's capacity as witness. This metatheatrical sarcasm might be directed at the smug
sense of denial that Pinter has observed in his audiences—their
ability to maintain that what they see is not real and has nothing
to do with them. The conditions these plays present, he noted
in 1988, are something "most people prefer understandably to
ignore, to pretend don't exist" (Nightingale 1990, 136). Gavin's
"smashing" is another pun, as one meaning of the word ex-
plodes, as it were, from beneath another. The word carries the
obvious meanings of exciting and entertaining but more literally
describes what is happening place outside the party: the State's
physical destruction of its enemies.

If Gavin's address represents the height of evasive language,
euphemism also characterizes elite speech in general. Whatever
is happening "outside" the hermetic world of power must be
minimized in language.

> MELISSA: The town's dead. There's nobody on the streets, there's
> not a soul in sight, apart from some . . . soldiers. My driver had to
> stop at a . . . you know . . . what do you call it? . . . a roadblock. We
> had to say who we were . . . it really was a trifle . . . (PT, 7)

Language verges on sheer euphemism and denotation is
avoided as much as possible. These elites seem to believe that
not knowing the word for an unpleasant part of reality will make
that reality disappear. If language precedes reality and thought,
thereby constituting society, then controlling language use determines subjective psychology and objective reality. Melissa's

ellipses are minipauses charged with the threat of unutterable political content. These hesitations are not psychological transitions, but a way of negotiating precision in language in accordance with a self-protective, self-serving view of the world.

Given that the language of the state carries such shadowed meanings, one key language strategy of the play's disempowered characters is the revelation of puns. Powerful characters employ euphemism, while the marginalized attempt to question language as it is used around them, seeking to air the actual meaning underneath the social alibi. Instead of collapsing two meanings, or substituting a literal for a metaphorical meaning, Charlotte, for instance, attempts to highlight the social meaning of the word "regime":

> God, your looks! No, seriously. You're still so handsome. How do you do it? What's your diet? What's your regime? What *is* your regime, by the way? What do you do to keep yourself so . . . I don't know . . . so . . . oh, I don't know . . . so trim, so fit? (*PT*, 38)

Fred's individual exercise program merges with the dictatorship he serves. The point here is that no one onstage perceives this as a pun, but we in the audience do easily. It is as if the capacity to experience language as complex, the basis of humor, is not available to the powerful. Terry explicitly denies having a sense of humor: "I never joke. Have you ever heard me crack a joke?" (19).[6] (Tyrants must be dull, Brodsky notes [1986, 116].) The euphemisms of the powerful characters should not, from a logical standpoint, be very hard to see through. To see the massive self-deception in the language of the powerful is, intellectually, rather easy. This obviousness underlines that the social conditions alluded to in *Party Time* are, once again, "past a joke": while we may laugh at how Charlotte outwits Fred, we should not forget that the massive physical repression the joke protests against will certainly outlast it.

Another aspect of the play's denunciation of politicized language engages a political movement contemporary with the play. *Party Time* particularly satirizes the neoconservative language of morality and "values" that was so popular and important a tool of the New Right in the 1980s and 1990s in both Britain and America. The peak of this discourse was in the early 1990s, the time of the play's writing and first productions. In America this movement was led by a number of conservative political figures such as Bill Bennett.[7] These conservatives believed that governments must become more moral and more concerned with inculcating morality in their citizens. Themes of caring and morality were annexed by the political right, which assumed itself to be the only proper guardians of moral values. "[A] growing public discourse . . . actively articulates care and community to the New Right. . . . [A]s selective as their 'caring' is, the right's reclaiming of 'fundamental' values constitutes an appealing platform," wrote one commentator in 1992 (Probyn, 508). Also, crucially, these figures believe that there is only a single and universal, hence nonrelativistic, morality, one labeled Judeo-Christian (with the accent on the Christian, in practice). This movement attracted bipartisan support. David Edgar, in *The Second Time as Farce* (1988), argues that in the United Kingdom, as in the United States, this idea was used to demonize a variety of the right's favorite political targets: the tradition of the welfare state, the 1960s as a whole and its progressive politics in special, and any approach to morality or politics that uses intellect or introspection to examine the values of the past.

This appeal to "values" and a simple, traditional, antirelativistic "morality" was a potent aspect of the New Right, establishing a populist appeal and so allowing it to proceed with an antipopulist agenda. Words relating to morality, values, and principles occur nineteen times in the play, illustrating the play's satire of neoconservative language. Alluding to fundamental values, one character notes, "What is right is right, that's what I say . . . We're talking about principles" (*PT*, 27–28). This tautology, in which a thing is defined as itself and further debate about it therefore cut off, captures the anti-relativistic conception of morality. The vision of morality and the world held by the powerful is the only one possible. There is only one way to explain anything, everything: questioning established values is a sin. *Party Time* captures a condition that may well be perceived as achingly familiar: the elites in the world of the play believe both that the great majority of society's members are right-thinking people who agree with them, and that, paradoxically, society is growing ever more dissolute. This downward devolution can be corrected only when moral standards have been enforced anew across society.

Under these antirelativistic conditions, there is the opposite of the fair, neutral conversational dynamics central to government by participatory consensus. In a world of neoconservatism, to question established morality is to be immoral, and, of course,

it is never necessary to listen to immoral people. Dame Melissa
expresses the need for stable morality to make society work:

> MELISSA: The clubs died, the swimming and the tennis clubs died
> because they were based on ideas which had no moral foundation,
> no moral foundation whatsoever. But *our* club, *our* club—is a club
> which is activated, which is inspired by a moral sense, a moral
> awareness, a set of moral values which is—I have to say—
> unshakeable, rigorous, fundamental, constant. (*PT*, 42–43)

Melissa's repetitions of the word "moral" and her bizarre conjunction of morality with luxury and ease clarify Pinter's satire
of those who use the badge of morality to justify privilege and
oppression. The elites' professed devotion to moral values contradicts the extreme greed of their lifestyles and the punitive
measures which support it, a disjunction captured in Norman
Mailer's aphorism about American conservatives: "They [have
the] moral equivalent of teflon on their soul" (2003, 50). Despite
such contradictions, strict adherence to orthodox values (or proclaimed adherence to these values) divides those accepted by society from those it excludes.

The society in *Party Time* uses a variety of means to enforce
its division between an inner "us" and an outer "them." One is
a metaphorical opposition between health and disease: Fred
leads a "clean" life while the musician is an "infection." Nazi
rhetoric pictured Jews as a virus infecting European civilization.
Power's tendency to disparage its enemies as unclean and impure characterizes fascist societies (Watt 1998, 113). The metaphor of disease is only one example of a classificatory use of
metaphor to support social segregation—such moral metaphors
implement the ruling ideas of a society, overtly fascist or not.
Antinomianism—the construction of opposed pairs, such as
dirty versus clean, up versus down, and so forth—is the term
given to this use of metaphor. Antinomianism yields to Manicheanism as metaphorical oppositions of us versus them are subsumed in an overarching distinction between good and evil.
Ellul argues that the propagandee lives in a Manichean universe
(1965, 69), constructing dualistic categories to separate truth
from error, as does Canetti: "Man has a profound need to arrange
and re-arrange in [two opposing] groups all the human beings he
knows or can imagine. . . . Judgments of good and bad are an age-
old instrument of dualistic classification, but one which is never
wholly conceptual, nor wholly peaceful" (1962, 297). In a draft

of *Party Time*, one character proclaims his Manicheanism: "But also—I say this—there are your people and my people," receiving this reply: "Absolutely" (PA, Box 44).

The characters in the play are all members or prospective members of a social club that quite literally excludes this society's in-group from its out-group. Behind this meaning of the word, however, is that of "club" as a weapon. This pun brings these two meanings together: exclusion goes with violence. This word features in Pinter's analysis of *The Birthday Party*; Goldberg and McCann are part of a "club" which uses the "shit-stained strictures of centuries of 'tradition'" as justification for oppression. There is substantial continuity between the two plays. Scene 11 of *Party Time* puns on elements of *The Birthday Party*:

> SAM: . . . We're talking about principles. I mean, I met a man at a party the other day—I couldn't believe it—He was talking the most absolute bloody crap—his ideas about the world, that kind of thing—he was a complete and total and utter arsehole—a musician or something—
> SMITH: Stoddart?
> SAM: That's it. Now you see, these kind of people, they're an infection.
> SMITH. Don't worry about Stoddart. We've seen him off.
> HARLOW: We've had him for breakfast. (*PT*, 28)

The references to a "party," to an iconoclastic, free-thinking musician, and to the famous opening and closing of *The Birthday Party* (breakfast and Stanley's removal) connect *Party Time* and *The Birthday Party*. But with this exception: in the world of *Party Time*, the earlier duo McCann and Goldberg have metastasized across all society. The socio-religious monsters are back, and everyone is one. Goldberg and McCann's menace originates in their private selves as well as their quasi-official status as members of a particular group. In *Party Time*, by contrast, menace is stripped of its psychological particularity and becomes a social generality.

Even the outer architecture of power in *Party Time* is invulnerable to disturbance. The mechanisms of state power are more durable than in any other play. There is in the society of *Party Time* a potential split between the managers and the actual perpetrators of state violence (hinted at in the first scene's contention between Gavin and Terry). But, since Gavin makes it into the club, this split is healed. Females contradict male authority only in indirect, tangential ways. And there is a potential rupture between those with social refinement, such as Dame Melissa, and those who are rougher and more vulgar. But again this split is resolved without apparent conflict. The final seamlessness of power, syncretically combining those who seemed to be opposed, renders *Party Time*'s analysis of political and cultural power ultimately dispiriting. The so-called set of moral values so often broadcast by this society does not exist; only power does.

The invulnerability of power links the plays from *One for the Road* through *Party Time*. Pinter consistently emphasizes the frightening assurance and strength of his empowered characters. Their grandiose assurance and self-exaltation ("God speaks through me," Nicolas says [*One*, 40]) provoke horror and disgust, as if they were villains in a Gothic tale. Such characters inhabit a number of Pinter's plays: Goldberg's appeals to patriarchal and bureaucratic authority provide him with a protectedness that adds to his aura of menace, while Mick in *The Caretaker* sparks fear through the image he presents as an expert in finance and fashion. In Pinter's explicitly political plays, the position of empowered characters within an entrenched system, whether government or class, serves only as added support for the corrosive power that seems to be theirs through innate personality or presence. The presence of such figures throughout Pinter's career may be illuminated through accounts of the type of character that is formed through a relationship with social power.

Jacques Ellul, Robert Jay Lifton, and Theodor Adorno are three writers concerned with the relation between sociopolitical conditions and personality. In his account of the propagandized individual, dating from the middle of the twentieth century, Ellul speaks of how "propaganda" causes values and standards to be "crystallized" until they dominate the whole of the propagandee's self, thus constructing a "monolithic" individual whose behavior expresses not himself but his group or society (1965, 160–71). He maintains that this sort of individual attains an internal consistency and self-confidence which translate into power, security, and surety, and which completely counteract any negative effects ensuing from the alienation of the individual from society. Propaganda, when it is successful, "eliminates inner conflicts, tensions, self-criticism, self-doubt. . . . Such an individual marches forward with full assurance of his righteousness. He is formidable in his equilibrium" (165).

The opening moments of *One for the Road* illustrate precisely this equilibrium, while the dominance of these crystallized standards, the reduction of self to a pure and empty articulator of socially provided themes, is everywhere implied in *Party Time*. "A bit of that," as Douglas says to Fred and Fred to Douglas, is a characteristically inarticulate expression of the social self ruling the world of *Party Time*. A propagandized society, Ellul believes, creates a humorless, dimensionless, internally consistent subject. "I never joke," says Terry to his wife, Dusty, capturing the solidity that is his distinguishing feature as a character (*PT*, 19). Terry is the most propagandized and the most crystallized character in the play. His importance is stressed in that he dominates the play's opening scene and is the source of its most shocking, yet utterly uninflected, verbal violence (30).

Ellul's concept of crystallization is an image of solidification. Doug wants not mere peace but an impermeable one: "a cast-iron peace" with "No leaks. No draughts" (*PT*, 17). The depthless men of *Party Time* have become crystallized, solid, unchanging. The play provides images of liquefaction, such as the bar where "[p]eople swim at you, you see, while you're having a drink" (5). In this context, a line such as Liz's "I love everything that flows" (26) may suggest a counterprinciple to this propagandized, crystallized society, promising change instead of rigidity. Julia Kristeva links fluidity as a metaphor with possible destabilization of the self and its society through her concept of the "abject." The abject is everything that the self and society attempt to expunge from themselves. Abjection reveals society's tenuous control over the fluid, untidy, irrational aspects of psyche and body, as Kristeva explains throughout *Powers of Horror: Essays in Abjection* (1982). The principles of flux and fluidity thus offer themselves as subversive opposition to the tight logical transparency and ideological and personal solidity of the ruling class. However, flux, movement, and freedom are precisely what the society of *Party Time* eliminates, or rather incorporates into itself—as if they've read Kristeva and are one step ahead of her. As indicated by the corporate control of liquidity in the bar, the world of *Party Time* has seemingly contained the subversive potential of fluidity.

Another theory links the body, psyche, and ideology in a way that sheds light on *Party Time*. Robert Jay Lifton, a sociologist who has studied the Holocaust and modern personality structures, speaks of the "fundamentalist self" as engaged in a continuous battle with a more protean self, locked in the same self, the same body (1993, 160). The corporeal self becomes a ground upon which constitutive political and ideological struggles are fought. The fundamentalist persona fights an internal battle on the space of its own body. From this perspective, the elite's focus on the body and its orifices becomes understandable. Terry's perverse plan for destroying his enemies bespeaks, then, a submerged battle with illegitimate aspects of himself. Of course, this psychomachia—unrelated to the people upon whom it is exercised—means that no amount of killing will necessarily reduce the motivation for further killing.

It is a common characteristic of Pinter's villains, such as Terry and Nicolas, to be obsessed with the death of their enemies. Images of these deaths become psychically indispensable to the lives of these tyrants. The plays make this obvious. "I love death," Nicolas declares (*One*, 45), adding helpfully that this is not an existential anxiety about his own mortality—he adores the "death of others." Terry creates erotic fantasies of killing his society's internal enemies. The act of murder provides existential meaning to figures such as Terry and Nicolas. Christopher Hudgins reminds us that in Pinter's early plays, death has two effects on personal behavior: it is "the motivation for our repressing much of our experience and for aggressive behavior" (1984, 289). If the thought of our own death prompts us to violence, this suggests a virtually limitless provocation to violence. While Bert in *The Room* strikes out against the blind Negro, a symbolic reminder of death, leaving him as if for dead, characters such as Terry remove the "as if" from this equation, effecting literal rather than metaphorical assassination. The death of others, presumably a psychological counter to insecurity, is what they aim at and what they achieve.

Fundamentalism posits itself, in Lifton's analysis, as a social struggle for meaning against dying that (ironically) uses murder in rhetorical and literal forms. Fundamentalist societies are motivated, as is the one in *Party Time*, by the sense that valued, sacrosanct aspects of self and society are being destroyed and that social life is suffering from moral dissolution (1993, 160). This cast of mind is obvious in *Party Time* (as in Melissa's speech about the club standing for moral values [42–43]). The supposed goals of fundamentalism refer both to the sacred past and to a hoped-for future of harmony and order. Fundamentalist movements defend "sacred, literalized text in a purification process aimed at alleged contamination—all in the name of a

past of perfect harmony that never was, and of an equally vision-
ary future created by a violent 'end' to impure, profane history"
(161). These references to a sacred past and of a utopian future
run through the discourse of all Pinter's autocracies (Watt 1998,
113).[8]

Curiously, however, the regime in *Party Time*, while it exhib-
its the idealizing look backward at a pristine era of moral order,
is a rather secular version of this fundamentalist impulse. No sacred text or belief system is referred to; no apparent theological
mandate underwrites female submission. If there is a blank
space in the regime's rhetoric of legitimation, does this make the
regime more or less frightening to us? Perhaps this regime is no
less solid for having no identifiable justification in the customary mode of fundamentalist societies. This regime justifies itself
through the very fact of its existence—"What's right is right"
being proximate to "Whatever is, is right." It may be that the
regime does not require rhetorical legitimation at all; it may
have simply sprung free of this need. A society that does not
need to justify itself cannot be delegitimized. (This point does
not mean that such a society cannot be opposed, but that ideology critique is not an effective form of opposition.)

The world of *Party Time* is traditionally fundamentalist in
designating its enemies as a contamination of healthy social
order. Murder's meaning as the attack on contamination has social, political, even moral dimensions. The process of identifying social others as victims deserving to be oppressed or
destroyed is what Lifton calls "false witness" (1995, 139). Cate-
gorizing humanity into *us* and *them* is often prelude to violence
against *them*. This is so not only due to the fact of difference,
but because violence provides meaning. The process of killing
solves the anxiety of death:

> False witness tends to be a political and ideological process. And
> really false witness is at the heart of most victimization. Groups vic-
> timize others, they create what I now call "designated victims," the
> Jews in Europe, the Blacks in this country. They are people off whom
> we live not only economically . . . but psychologically. That is, we
> reassert our own vitality and symbolic immortality by denying them
> their right to live. . . . *That's* what false witness is. It's deriving one's
> solution to one's death anxiety . . . by exploiting a group of people
> and rendering them victims. (139)

The meaning that is created from such practices is not fraudulent, Lifton explains. "What is perverse is that one must impose

death on others in order to reassert one's own life. . . . And the problem is that the meaning is real. It's *perceived* as meaning" (140). Officially empowered murderers garner meaning and security from their actions. As a thinking, moral being, one wants to maintain that there is something false, self-contradictory in the process by which this immoral victimization leads to meaning. But there is not, from the viewpoint of its perpetrators. Killers acquire all the meaning they need from the process of classification, division, and destruction that Lifton terms false witness. Lifton goes farther in this direction, alluding to the work of sociologist Jack Katz. Even in murder, writes Katz, the criminal will often speak as if his (or her) action was taken to correct an egregious moral wrong. The murder is seen as "morally necessary," allowing Lifton to conclude "you cannot kill large numbers of people except with a claim to virtue" (140). Murder thus produces moral self-approval in addition to existential security and life meaning. This aspect of murder explains and links the moralism of all Pinter's tyrants and torturers, their conviction that they are acting for God or in the name of transcendental principles.

There is a familiar idea that in the act of murder, power forsakes what it seeks from the powerless: "Power abrogates itself in the act of killing. The death of the other puts an end to the social relationship" (Sofsky 1997, 294). The logic is this: the powerful seek service, respect, awe, obedience, labor, and so forth from those they subjugate. If in the course of commanding the powerless to render these objects, power destroys those it commands, then it will never attain these objects, making murder thus self-defeating. According to this view, then, the powerful are cast as victims (albeit of their own actions), and a certain kind of victory is granted to the powerless in the moment of their death. In other words, an ironic reversal has occurred in the drama between powerful and powerless; a twist, a thickening complication, disrupts the straightforward plot, the static situation, of asymmetrical power and unilateral dominance.

This view is essentially a summary of Hegel's paradigm of the master-slave relationship. This paradigm conditions our thinking about the relationships of dominance and subservience that insistently characterize Pinter's theater. As described by Camus in *The Rebel*, the master-slave paradigm arises out of man's desire to be acknowledged by others, a desire that does not characterize the life of animals but that defines human life. Two kinds of consciousness are postulated here: that of the master, who desires recognition from others, and that of slaves, who do not desire such recognition and are content to exist on the animalistic level. The twist comes about in this way:

> Undoubtedly the master enjoys total freedom first as regards the slave, since the latter recognizes him totally. . . . However, this autonomy is not absolute. The master, to his misfortune, is recognized in his autonomy by a consciousness that he himself does not recognize as autonomous. Therefore he cannot be satisfied and his autonomy is only negative. Mastery is a blind alley. (Camus 1991, 140)

If the desire for full recognition, allied with conditions of asymmetrical power and material domination, leads the master to kill the slave, this has two effects. For the master, a loss, as there is no one there to recognize him anymore. "[T]he victorious consciousness . . . cannot be victorious in the eyes of something that no longer exists" (139). For the slave, his murder has a benefit, although one that is incorporal, immaterial, transcendent: "The very agony of death experienced in the humiliation of the entire being lifts the slave to the level of human totality" (141). In the death of the subservient, the killer loses and the murdered wins.

This analysis of subjugation serves to distinguish between different conceptions of power that can be used to describe Pinter's plays. First, there is another way of seeing power and murder, and it is that murder is simply the ultimate, purest expression of the will to power over another. Canetti holds exactly this view: the penalty of death is implied in any instance or use of power (1962, 227). Power in fact is simply the ability to inflict pain and death (231). The ruler maintains power by enforcing death sentences: "[T]he autocrat's only true subject is the man who will let himself be killed by him. . . . He will order an execution for its own sake, the victim's guilt being almost irrelevant. . . . His most dependable, one might say his truest, subjects are those he has sent to their deaths" (232). The view of power implied in Hegel's master-slave paradigm contrasts to Canetti's blunt, forceful concepts. To Canetti, power is iterative and unidirectional; the other view is more hopeful by contrast, positing change, the partial defeat of the master, and growth, albeit spiritual or on the level of consciousness, for the slave. Canetti's point is blunt; the Hegelians' is complex.

It is possible to regard the Hegelian-inspired view of power as a myth: a fictive, consoling assumption that certain people hold unquestioningly. What kind of people value immaterial gains and prefer a story to a situation and irony to simplicity? In a word: intellectuals. The consoling allure of the Hegelian story, which served as philosophical underpinning for twentieth-century discourses of liberation, is powerful. The need to see the powerless as potentially or implicitly powerful, the wish to see power as self-defeating, as prey to its own internal self-contradictions, is consistently tempting.[9]

Judith Roof adopts a homologous stance when she argues that Nicolas, in *One for the Road*, needs Victor as an "other" to reflect back upon him (1988, 9). This reading is something like Hegel's theory of recognition. However, the results don't work out the way they would if the drama of frustrated recognition guided the action of the play. Nicolas does not act the way he would if he were Hegel's sort of master, and neither do Terry or the officers in *Mountain Language*. As Nicolas casually dispenses with Victor, the partyers seem to ignore the spectacle of the humiliated outcast Jimmy, as if their triumph over him is a minor, casual thing, a sort of nonevent. The brutal dramas of Pinter's political theater dare us to contemplate politics and the possibility of political change without the reassurance that power will necessarily destabilize itself. Pinter rejects the Hegelian myth and exposes the powerful in Canetti's terms.

This distinction between portraying power in terms of anticipated dialectical reversal rather than immediate moments of domination relates the formal distinctions between Pinter's implicitly versus explicitly political dramas and also the stylistic shifts within those political works. Pinter has discussed his move toward a kind of minimalism as he pursues dramatic expression of his political feelings. "I find that I'm writing shorter and shorter pieces which are more brutal and more and more overtly naked," he remarks (qtd. in Merritt 1995, 188). As he shortens and tightens his dramas, he shifts focus away from narrative development to the presentation of images, moments without temporal extension. Mark Batty perceptively observes that the political plays are understood by audiences in terms of such images which "remain in the memory long after we have witnessed a performance of the piece" (2001, 102). These images are always of the ruthlessness and triumph of power (as most clearly in *Mountain Language*). By focusing audience perception on these ultimate moments in which power has asserted itself definitively, as opposed to a narrative of power which supposes the dramatic and dialectical possibilities of reversal, these plays demand emotional engagement with the prospect that political change is simply not forthcoming. That such a possibility is heretical to leftist definitions of political drama and politics as a whole is another example of Pinter's characteristic penchant for paradox, self-questioning, and ambiguity.

The masters or elites evade the supposed self-debilitations of empowerment in several ways. First is the simple fact of demographics: there are always more victims to create, more people to be made into slaves and thus to serve as reflectors of the elite's self-conceptions. Secondly, the intended benefit of mastery is not, as Hegel suggests, autonomy or recognition, but as Canetti notes, simply the pleasure of destroying others. The sight that has most pleased tyrants throughout history, the latter writes, is a pile of corpses (1962, 233). Novelist Tim Parks analyzes power's unrestrained sadism and its preference for ultimate, irrevocable solutions: "Death pushes back the horizon of predictability to the infinite. . . . There is no longer any danger of getting things wrong" (2000, 157).

Party Time's frequent animal imagery suggests another way the citizens of this regime have evaded detrimental effects of power. They have embraced life at the animal level, that of creature comforts and physical security, where consciousness exists only to aid basic tasks of survival and reproduction. These people then require no recognition from others, this being the Hegelian distinction between advanced human consciousness and a prehuman or animalistic way of life. In *Party Time* human life is described in animal terms; the human nearly merges with the animalistic. Pamela notes of another woman, "At Oxford she was fully expected to marry a dog" (*PT,* 18); Suki conflates Emily's husband with his horse (15); Douglas boasts "I could take a wild animal on" (27); Gavin waxes lyrically about charming squirrels: "I had no idea how many squirrels were still left in this country. I find them such vivacious creatures, quite enchanting" (23–24). These peculiar images suggest that human desires have settled at the unreflective, unself-conscious level of the bestial.

If human life has become bestial, and power always sees murder as a positive strategy, the social realm of articulation is nevertheless an obsession with the privileged members of *Party Time*'s regime. The processes of demonization, of false witness or moral "othering," and of social exclusion are interlinked with the goal of controlling discourse. In a world of neoconservatism, to question established morality is to be immoral, and, of course, it is never necessary to listen to immoral people. Terry makes this fact clear, specifying that he controls what can and cannot be uttered and heard. His intimidating language uses images of articulation:

> I don't know what it is. Perhaps she's deaf or perhaps my voice isn't strong enough or distinct enough. . . . Perhaps there's something faulty with my diction. I'm forced to float all these possibilities because I thought I had said that we don't discuss this question of what has happened to Jimmy, that it's not up for discussion, that it's not on anyone's agenda. (*PT*, 22)

With power setting the "agenda," discourse becomes one-dimensional. (The title is a pun on this monolithic aspect of politics: there used to be multiple political parties, with varied viewpoints and agendas, but now there is only a single party.) There are, then, no opposing viewpoints to negotiate with or even consider, because these have been, as it were, outlawed. This community is defined, conveniently, as the people who already agree with dominant opinions. Austin Quigley sees Pinter's political plays as proffering an image of contractual discourse, in which individuals communicate to establish provisional, changeable contracts guiding social life (2001, 15). In *Party Time*, what happens is exactly the opposite of this conversational paradigm. The tendency to moral Manicheanism, labeling others as deserving victims, unworthy outcasts, or irrational deviants, fundamentally negates the possibility that diverse viewpoints be equally weighted.

In drawing this picture of silenced speech, is Pinter relying upon satirical exaggeration of an inherent tendency of our political reality, or is he, through his play, pointing out current facts? Perhaps the nightmare images of Pinter's dramas are not so separated from reality. As I write, deep into the administration of the second President Bush, it appears to many that dissent from ruling ideas has been rendered unpatriotic, deviant, beyond the pale. Bush has "used his wartime aura to silence critics . . . and suppress civil liberties," writes journalist Anthony Lewis (2003, 4). Even before September 11, 2001, the *New Republic* stated that senators who opposed Administration foreign policy were anti-American; afterward, the *Washington Post* opined that anti-globalization protestors had been "exposed by the suicide bombers" (2002, 10). One commentator in England labeled Pinter's anti-Americanism a provocation of such violence: "No amount of bon mots can quite distance him morally from what took place" on September 11 (qtd. in Cohen 2002, 10). "Postmodern relativism" in particular—the attitude that moral judgments are complex and cannot be answered exclusively through tradition and religion—was pernicious and quasi-traitorous, commentators such as Bill Bennett argued, and should be replaced by "moral clarity."[10]

If one embodies moral clarity, by implication, of course, one's opponents are morally tainted. Presently, that is, conservatives disallow the notion that anyone could differ from them and still be honestly, honorably mistaken: "It is one thing to believe, and believe fervently, that someone has got something wrong; it is quite another to believe that the someone you think to be wrong is by virtue of that error unpatriotic, devoted to lies, and downright evil" (Fish 2002, 39). For a species of politicians, however, a difference in political opinions is always a moral error, not an intellectual one. If opposing ideas are treasonous or evil, they need not be engaged with, only denounced. President Bush proclaims openly that "Either you're with us or against us," and it appears he means exactly this: that anyone who disagrees with him is treasonous, on the side of terror. In the aftermath of the most recent war in Iraq, it seems, also, that the decision makers in a number of "democratic" countries—such as Tony Blair's Britain as well as George Bush's America—have disconnected themselves from what a significant number of their citizens believe. This marginalization of oppositional ideas, while it may differ from the outwardly violent destruction of dissent in *Party Time*, nevertheless aims to ensure that all dissent is perceived under the sign of a morally deviant Otherness.

If Pinter succeeds in dramatizing an effectively propagandized and one-dimensional society, one that has subsumed principles and metaphors of change, the question of his method as a political playwright again comes into focus. The use of satire to denounce impregnable power calls into question the efficacy of dissent—in both the world of the play and our world. In some political theater, the ways of power are demystified with clarity. Demystification is spoken of as "bringing light to" and can thus be seen as punningly evoking the Enlightenment task of philosophical and political maturity. In *Party Time*, the theme of demystification as enlightenment is built through use of theatrical lighting; Pinter foreshadows the entrance of a potentially disruptive usurper by several times showing a light streaming into the privileged space of the party. This light encourages expectation that an exposing counterforce will enlighten us, exposing the nature of power. However, this expectation is subverted and made ironic, as the play of light and darkness resolves into an imagistic triumph of darkness. In his and the play's final speech, Jimmy, the defeated, defiled (if not already dead) protestor asserts, "The dark is in my mouth and I suck it. It's the only thing I have." (Isaiah 6:5, "I am a man of unclean lips," is evoked by Jimmy's words [New American Bible].) Light is promised but none is shed, and the character equated with light (enlightenment) is only a prisoner of darkness. Just as Stanley has nothing to say in his own ultimate defense, never specifying the principles of his cause, so too does Jimmy decline to state the motivation for his dissidence. As the abject Jimmy is left sucking the dark, our hopes for a transformative perspective dissolve. By portraying the uselessness of demystification, *Party Time* seems to question the very roots of Enlightenment itself, to suggest that we are not so much beyond Enlightenment as always prior to it, never capable of achieving it.

From both dramaturgical and political points of view, Pinter risks tautology and anticlimax in the resolution of his plot. In the previous overtly political plays, the audience was privy to at least some portion of the process by which dissenters are marginalized. In *Party Time*, repression is marked by its invisibility, a theme underscored by references to invisibility and disappearance in Jimmy's speech. The defeat of the committed, oppositional character occurs out of sight. It all happened, to allude to Hamm's assertion of bad faith in *Endgame*, without us (Beckett 1958, 74)—we can almost claim to be in the dark about it if we choose, extending the ignorance or pretended ignorance of political suffering of which Pinter has accused his audience. Indifference begins the loss of civil liberties; history is beyond spectators.

Second, to satirize the language of groups such as the Moral Majority is to attack a rather obvious, easy target. To this, it might be responded that merely because a target is intellectually easy game does not mean it is not worth attacking. It is the actual force and effect of political ideas in the world that are at stake here. Also, Pinter cunningly takes beliefs that many people might see as normal and reasonable—that one's society is substantially right and just, that it has enemies that must be defended against—and shows the effect the purest version of these beliefs will produce. The relevant differences here between the society of *Party Time* and our own may be merely a matter of degree.

And while the assertion that social and cultural systems of advanced Western democracies are unchanging and reproductive of themselves, whether through ossification, repressive tolerance, or co-optation, is not a novel idea, the triumphalism Pinter depicts in this play has historical specificity. It relates directly to its political moment just after the final collapse of the Communist regimes. This political development authorized a sense in the West that the bourgeois liberal democratic model represents the culmination and solution of all problems in world history. The West is reasonable, placid, a political ideal translated from the realm of political philosophy to solid actuality. Political problems had disappeared, or did not need to be thought about— you don't have to think about anything, or do anything, or believe anything, just enjoy the party, is Terry's expression of this view (*PT*, 8). Seldom in history has any one group so conceived of itself as without the need for change or improvement, as so perfect. The complacency of the privileged society of *Party Time* illustrates a particular moment within Western self-perceptions. (There is reason to believe that this complacency extends though the post-Cold-War period to today. In considering the relationship of so-called Third World and Arab nations to the West, and the problem of fanaticism and terrorism against the West, novelist Orhan Pamuk captures one aspect of this dynamic: "[A]t no other time have the world's rich and powerful societies been so clearly right, and 'reasonable'" [2001, 12]. This "reasonability" drives the feeling of humiliation that feeds hatred of the West.)

Artistically as well as politically, Pinter's language in the climax of the play achieves specificity so as to meet the challenge of predictability. The play's concluding speech is a charged, condensed account of depersonalization, a core theme in Pinter's career. The threat that one can be unmade or unmanned, psychologically deprived of one's self and substance, underpins Pinter's oeuvre. Uniquely in *Party Time*, however, the grounds for this deprivation are explicitly political. Although no one articulates this truth, Jimmy's words suggest a fully achieved dual process of exclusion and destruction:

Sometimes a door bangs, I hear voices, then it stops. . . . It all stops. It all closes. It closes down. It shuts. It all shuts. It shuts down. It shuts. I see nothing at any time any more. I sit sucking the dark.

It's what I have. The dark is in my mouth and I suck it. It's the only thing I have. It's mine. It's my own. I suck it. (*PT*, 47)

The utter banality of these repetitions makes the point that Jimmy and his ilk have been deprived of a vocabulary in which to articulate, even to have, experience. It may not be regarded as coincidental that the character bears the same name as the original Angry Young Man, Jimmy Porter from Osborne's *Look Back in Anger*. The reimposition of traditional forms of social and moral authority equals the complete loss of individualism. Jimmy is no longer a self, a name, or a person. He speaks, paradoxically, only to tell us he has no words and no existence, as Pinter comes as close as possible to creating a voice for the disappearance of voice.

Jimmy's final words have an ambivalent effect in terms of the play's function as political theater. The fact that Jimmy speaks at all can be taken to indicate the surviving presence of an oppositional principle, however tenuous. (Martin Regal, however, sees Jimmy as dead at this moment [1995, 125]; the *Macbeth* reference in Dusty's name —a thousand candles lighting the way to dusty death—suggests she may well be marked out for imminent execution.) Power may need subversion, that is, simply to justify its repression, but this implicitly licensed subversion may transcend the limits placed on it (or so it is possible to hope). Or, it might be argued that there is a rich poetry, and thus perhaps a kind of consolatory power, in this speech. Perhaps Jimmy's loss of self acquires Beckettian overtones, as a minimal survival is endorsed as the only available form of heroism in a bleak, unforgiving world.

Experienced readers of Pinter's plays know to be wary of sentimentalism. A sharp antisentimentalism has been recognized as a central principle of the playwright's method (Knowles 1995a, 7). The plays seek to avoid evoking those positive feelings (warmheartedness, optimism, sentimental approval of central characters) that characterize melodrama and popular art. There is no reason not to see antisentimentalism in Pinter's political plays. In the case of *Party Time*, sentimental reactions may be provoked by Jimmy's appearance and words as the index of his symbolic survival. (Compare his image of sucking the dark to the topic Gavin and Terry discuss in the first scene—burning out blackheads.) If such an image is not enough to discourage sentimentalism here, let us recall that it is a fundamental political problem that compassion and empathy are limited resources— Pinter in fact frequently indicts his audiences for not caring about or ignoring political evil. (Beckett captures the fragility of empathy with great economy in *Not I*, in which a woman's tale of abuse and suffering is met by a Listener who shrugs sympathetically four times—each gesture less emphatic than the last until even the minimal response disappears by the end of the play.) To see Jimmy's appearance as the enduring or undying presence of opposition, subdued by force but now surfacing to be articulated, is a sentimental reaction that overreads the available evidence of the play and overrates our general social practice of empathy. Jimmy speaks only to index his own disappearance from the realms of public speech and existence; it is a marginal form of speaking that charts the vanishing distance between Jimmy and absolute nonexistence. Jimmy's last words should not be reacted to solely with sympathy; if the audience does so, it exempts itself from the play's critical metaphor comparing its audience to its characters.

A draft version of Jimmy's speech is relevant to these questions of tone and effect. This early version is rather more specific than the final one about the causes of Jimmy's plight. Here, Jimmy's situation is explicitly political and material:

Sometimes I hear things. Then it is quiet.

I had a name.
People called me Jimmy. That was my name. My name was Jimmy. People called me that.
Sometimes I hear things. Then everything is quiet. When everything is quiet, it is then I hear my heart.
When the terrible noise comes I can't hear anything at all.
Can't hear can't see don't breathe don't see can't hear don't
Then everything is so quiet. It is a silence. I hear some quiet breath somewhere, some heartbeat.
It is probably not my heartbeat. It probably is someone else's heartbeat.

Somewhere in this place there are many people. Bad people. People who are wrong.
Like me. I am a bad person. I must be. I must be a bad person. I must be. Why else would I be in this place?

Am I a bad person? What am I?

Sometimes a door bangs, I hear steps, I hear metal then it goes. Then in a deep silence & I sit sucking the dark.

The dark is in my mouth & I suck it. It's what I have. It's mine. The darkness is my breath. (PA, Box 44)

This draft makes clear that Jimmy's question "What am I?" is primarily material and actual, not existential and rhetorical. The Voice here is evidently imprisoned—the door that bangs is not that to Gavin's apartment, but a set of prison bars. Jimmy's dispossession and capture by power are rendered explicitly here, but the relative lack of such specificity in the final version should not prevent us from perceiving, between the lines, the material basis and crushing nature of Jimmy's destruction in the published version. While the draft's Keatsian phrase "quiet breath" glances toward a suicide wish, the Voice significantly accepts its own designation as inferior and other: "I must be a bad person."

The sense of shame Jimmy describes is a crucial aspect of the play's pessimistic politics. Even as the final draft of the play lightens the specificity of Jimmy's investment in his worthlessness, the play ultimately illustrates by implication the painful phenomenon of internalized degradation. This sense of shame, born out of inferiority and powerlessness, substitutes for outward violence in the control by the powerful of those who seek to resist power. These feelings of shame, visible in both draft and finished versions of Jimmy's speech, interfere in the (hoped-for) process of delegitimizing power. If power could be seen rationally, "the perception of [power's] illegitimacy would eventually erode the strength seen in . . . authority" and thus lead to revolt and liberation (Sennett 1980, 46). But this does not happen because, though reigning power may be seen as unjustified, an individual's feelings about power involve shame over one's vulnerability and weakness in regard to established authority (94–95). Pinter's political plays dare to feature these feelings of vulnerability and shame that inhibit active political resistance. Jimmy's plaintive assertion that he is a bad person—an assertion that can be read between the lines of the finished speech—shows that even victims of repression may subscribe to the "just-world theory." An individual's basic desire to survive can always be exploited by the powers that be (Butler 1997, 7); victims of power would rather be bad people than nonpeople. In fact, they may well believe in the fundamental fairness of the world that tortures them, so that they, not their oppressors, are in the wrong.

Jimmy's disappearance, reported in what could be termed a language of disappearance, or a disappearing language, is Pinter's way of indicting our society for its all-pervasive quietism and triumphalism. The play does not expose an articulated critique of the political conditions it represents. Where the conventions of political theater lead us to expect subversive critique, there is only absence. This absence implies a complacent society that has dispensed with critical self-awareness. As far as dissent goes, the party really is over, and silence, a lasting silence that denies the possibility of conversation, is all there is.

At this point the Beckettian mode of Pinter's politics becomess ultimately clear and acutely painful. There is no hope for dissent or subversion, only the need for it—as Kafka once said, there is no end of subversion, only not for us now. Or perhaps it is wrong to deny the possibility of oppositional hope: there may be such hope, but it must be of a sort that is, paradoxically, grounded in its own impossibility. I am aware that certain readers may be accusing my reading of this play of "presentism," the notion that that present conditions will extend indefinitely into the future—this is held to be a bad and mistaken thing to believe if you are on the political left. I'm cognizant too of the idea that one should embrace, the leftist phrase goes, pessimism of the intellect but optimism of the will (in other words that you should act as if what you know is true isn't true). What *Party Time* does is to insist, against such nostrums of leftist hope, is that there is no honest way to gainsay or minimize the silencing, repressive force of a murderous, cunning, well-established, naturalized, and self-satisfied status quo.

However, the accurate portrayal of complacency, of a society without opposition, is at best an ambivalent strategy for the kind of political art that, as traditionally defined, wishes to alter audience behavior or belief. This commitment to representing reactionary indifference reinforces how Pinter diverges from prominent models of political drama. Pinter's style of political theater in *Party Time* is powerfully bleak and maximally self-questioning. Small wonder, perhaps, that when Pinter returned to representing the political cruelty and shallowness of the rich, he did so in the mode of comedy.

Pinter returns to the theme of the rich at play in *Celebration* (1999), a play that reiterates *Party Time*'s motif of a protected zone of power excluding a social "other." Here Pinter specifically aims at the nouveau riche, whose vulgar ways are not obscured by their copious wealth. The author's direction of the play in 2001 emphasized this class position, as the male characters had rough-sounding East End accents. The characters in *Celebration* are perhaps even more depthless and superficial than those in *Party Time*—here they can't even remember what they ordered or if they were just at the opera or the theater. Women are degraded in this play, quite casually as they are also in *Party Time*, as pieces of flesh to adorn the successful male. The role of the unwanted interlocutor in *Celebration* is taken by the Waiter, whose attempts to converse with the diners emphasize his social powerlessness.

There is a sense, however, that in the world of *Celebration* power relations have inverted, with women as well as men capable of exercising power and using force. "The woman always wins," says Julie (*C*, 62) (though saying doesn't make it so). Prue recalls how "when we were babies . . . we used to lie in the nursery and hear mummy beating the shit out of daddy" (21). In another inversion of customary power relationships, while Russell boasts of his prowess and accomplishments, he complains of being manipulated by his secretary: "They're all the same, these secretaries, these scrubbers. They're like politicians. They love power. They've got a bit of power, they use it. They go home, they get on the phone, they tell their girlfriends, they have a good laugh" (7).

Here Pinter shows how empowered elites see themselves: not as secure but as constantly imperiled by those below them. Not only do these people want to control the world; they want us to pity them for the difficulty of being who they are.[11] These inversions of power suggest a mobility within social hierarchy: it is as if these formerly working or middle-class members have attained the power of the rich, while women have inherited the power of men. The men even apologize—or seem to—for some of their cruel, insensitive, stereotypically male behavior. Russell and Matt seem eager to demonstrate sensitivity, emotionality, and compassion (*C*, 29, 47), while Lambert vows to be reincarnated as a more "civilised, gentler, nicer person" than he is currently (56). But the fact of abusive power and its violence has not altered; only the specific identities of dominators and the dominated have become unpredictable. Furthermore, despite the power assumed by women at local levels of social interaction—marriage, the family, business—there is an overarching form of male power whose existence suggests that power has been redistributed only superficially. If the rulers have sometimes ceased to rule—to act unapologetically as dominator—the slaves are still slaves. Hierarchy endures. This is still a male-dominated society in which coercive power persists and is controlled by men.

Money remains in the service of entrenched power, and the brothers in the play are "strategy consultants" whose jobs involve force and violence (arms dealers, perhaps). It might even be suggested (by someone truly cynical) that male acknowledgments of insufficiency and tolerance of female force represent, for the truly powerful, a small price to pay to preserve their status and control. It is tempting but inaccurate to equate the comic power inversions of the social behavior in *Celebration* with lasting change in larger political structures.

Beyond such witty reversals of power, the comic dynamic of *Celebration* includes the social pretensions of the major characters, our laughter at the woman characters, Prue and Julie, who are overdressed floozies, and, especially, our bemusement at the Waiter's implausible stories about his grandfather. The Waiter delivers three monologues, which he calls "interjections," in the play. These speeches revolve around his grandfather's improbable connections to luminaries of modern art and politics. It is the Waiter who is fated for expulsion from this privileged zone, left forlornly alone at the end of the play as the diners return to the world they dominate. His treatment suggests that he is the sacrifice this celebration (Mass or Eucharist) requires.

The waiter obsessively points to a realm of cultural achievement (both modernist and popular) in stark contrast to the present:

> He knew them all in fact, Ezra Pound, W. H. Auden, C. Day Lewis, Louis MacNeice, Stephen Spender, George Barker, Dylan Thomas and if you go back a few years he was a bit of a . . . companion of D. H. Lawrence, Joseph Conrad, Ford Maddox Ford, W. B. Yeats, Aldous Huxley, Virginia Woolf and Thomas Hardy in his dotage. (*C*, 31)
>
> He used to knock about with Clark Gable and Elisha Cook Jr and he was one of the very few native-born Englishmen to have had it off with Hedy Lamarr. (49)

The Waiter comically mistakes varieties of social difference, describing his grandfather's connection with Hollywood's "Irish mafia": "Al Capone and Victor Mature for example. They were both Irish. Then there was John Dillinger the celebrated gangster and Gary Cooper the celebrated film star. They were Jewish" (50). All instances of outsiderdom are apparently equivalent. Later, the grandfather's acquaintances extend to major figures of twentieth-century political history:

> Well it's just that I heard all these people talking about the Austro-Hungarian Empire a little while ago and I wondered if they'd ever

heard about my grandfather. He was an incredibly close friend of the
Archduke himself and he once had a cup of tea with Benito Mussolini. They all played poker together, Winston Churchill included.
(65)

Here Pinter uses the comic figure of the Waiter to invoke the
bloody history of our war-ravaged century, cleverly linking
World Wars I and II, thus suggesting war as the persistent, characterizing fact of the twentieth century.

If the Waiter's speeches bring all of twentieth century history
into play, the relationship between the Waiter and his customers
bespeaks a highly contemporary form of oppression. The restaurant as workplace embodies a capitalist oppression legible in
psychological terms as sadomasochism. Workers who need their
job for survival are made "excessively and symbiotically dependent" (Chancer 1992, 94) upon their employers in a way that parallels the dependence of a masochist upon his or her sadist
partner. Though such feelings are the norm for many laborers,
they are nevertheless quite extreme and debilitating: workers
live in a state of "endemic insecurity" poised above "a chasm of
fear that gapes beneath the surface" of their consciousnesses.
They know that if they rock the boat or show displeasure they
can be thrown out into the cold (C, 96). If the diners, in this era
of postmodern egalitarianism, seem to accept the Waiter's interjections—he even sits down with Russell and Suki once, in Pinter's direction of the play—this does not mean that these
consumers want actual subversion of their position, but only a
simulacrum of it. When the Waiter truly transgresses, the diners
ignore and abandon him. The Waiter appears to personify the
masochistic feelings of dependency and fear created within capitalist hierarchy. He even describes how he is symbiotically tied
to the restaurant. When Russell not so obliquely threatens to get
the Waiter fired, he reacts with fear: "Are you suggesting that
I'm about to get the boot? . . . To be brutally honest, I don't think
I'd recover if they did a thing like that. This place is like a womb
to me. I prefer to stay in my womb. I strongly prefer that to being
born" (32–33).[12]

The Waiter's final speech converts such mordant comedy into
something much darker. Although the Waiter is not thrown out
into the cold, he is nevertheless sharply excluded from the world
controlled by the diners. As they go out into that real world, the
restaurant's doors clang shut several times as if in an echo, soni-
cally underlining the Waiter's isolation. Then we see the defeat

of the Waiter's attempts to engage in the act of articulation. The Waiter's confusion and sadness illustrate what Hegel saw as the poignant tragedy of social dominance: the subordinated are left to their own devices to make sense of what power is. He tries *and fails* to continue speaking: "And I'd like to make one further interjection. *He stands still. Slow fade*" (*C*, 72). Even given that the limits of the Waiter's language seem both imposed from without and accepted from within, his final silence poignantly illustrates his ultimate dispossession. The limits of one's language are the limits of one's world (2003, 119), as Wittgenstein remarks in section 5.6 of the *Tractatus*: in the brutal politics of Pinter's dramas, what you say is what you get.

This silence is strongly dispiriting; as Robert Gordon describes, this moment was "surprisingly moving, expressing the shared incomprehension of the audience and the waiter, implicated in a cultural moment from which there appears to be no escape" (2000, 71). The deflated nature of this dramatic moment should at least temporarily prevent us from interpreting this "appearance" of circumscription as mere seeming which, upon closer inspection, would yield to a deeper reality in which escape is possible. Appearance here is reality; there is, for the moment, nothing else. This lack of depth, this lack of ironic reversal, is itself a kind of silence, just as the play finds a way to emphasize silence, finality, and absence in its final moments. That is, given the broad humor of the Waiter's speeches, one waits eagerly to hear more of his words. What the play focuses on is precisely the lack of these desired words. The Waiter's silence is literally a silence beyond echo, taking place after the echo of the doors closing underlines his isolation. It is another consuming silence that characterizes dystopian representation of power in these political plays.

The seemingly perpetual nature of contemporary inequities of power is indicated by the diners' prediction of "Plenty of celebrations to come. Rest assured" (*C*, 69). The eternally closed and enclosing system of power in which the Waiter is entrapped can be illustrated through Herbert Marcuse's ideas about bourgeois society. Marcuse famously claimed that bourgeois society needs the critique of art but has so institutionalized it so that art's liberatory or transformative potential will never be realized. Countercultural tendencies are given space in discourse but simultaneously neutralized. This dynamic—being allowed to speak but ending in inefficacy and silence—characterizes the Waiter in *Celebration*. The sense that he is being lethally enclosed is underlined by a draft version of the play's final lines. Pinter handwrote these lines and then deleted them: "My grandfather introduced me to the mystery of life & that's where I still am. I can't find the door to get out of it. The mystery of life is like the ambiance of a good restaurant. . . . It takes you by the throat and it gradually strangles you" (PA, Box 74).[13] (This passage clarifies what is more implicit in the final version: even vis-à-vis the grandfather, the Waiter feels himself incapable, weakened.) Even without this rather explicit line, the close of the play suggests that the Waiter will be eternally isolated—once again Pinter stages the circumscribed, paradoxical, vanishing space granted to voices that counter the status quo.

Celebration's posh restaurant setting may seem far removed from the torture sites of *One for the Road* and *Mountain Language*. But the Waiter's penultimate speech links the world of the diners to the brutal realities of worldwide torture. These are the words that finally provoke the diners to silence the Waiter:

> He [the grandfather] loved the society of his fellows, W. B. Yeats, T.S. Eliot, Igor Stravinsky, Picasso, Ezra Pound, Bertholt Brecht, Don Bradman, the Beverley Sisters, the Inkspots, Franz Kafka and the Three Stooges. He knew these people where they were isolated, where they were alone, where they fought against pitiless and savage odds, where they suffered vast wounds to their bodies, their bellies, their legs, their trunks, their eyes, their throats, their breasts, their balls— (C, 66)

The wounds the Waiter enumerates evoke the effects of torture. One of the fundamental facts about torture is how easy it is to produce crippling pain in a body under one's control, a fact that the Waiter's anatomical precision brings home to the diners and the audience. The diners interrupt this unpleasant reminder of political pain. Pinter is playing a double game in this passage, equating torture victims with cultural icons. The Waiter mentions not victims of political oppression, but artists, whose "isolation" was more a matter of iconoclastic unpopularity or modernist alienation than material oppression (excepting perhaps Brecht, who spent long periods in exile). Not only does Pinter remind the audience of expulsion and torture; he also imagistically merges the suffering, marginalized artist with the suffering, marginalized victim of political violence.

The allusion to political violence in the Waiter's speech here is made even more obvious in Pinter's early drafts. During his process of revising his drafts into the final published version, Pinter effaces a number of precise political references that, despite their ultimate absence from the finished play, indicate how Pinter conceived of the character's contribution to the play. The draft reveals the author's emotional inspiration:[14]

> He knew these people where they were isolated, where they were utterly alone, people like Sacco and Vanzetti, Paul Robeson, Tom Joad, Oscar Romero, Ernesto Cardenal, he knew these people when they fought against pitiless, savage odds, people like Augusto Sandino who said "No, I will not surrender, A free country or death," Pablo Neruda, Che Guevara, Salvador Allende, Nazim Hikmer, Jorge Ellacuria, he knew them all where they suffered vast wounds in their bodies, their bellies, their legs, their trunks, (their eyes, their throats), their balls, their breasts and where they said No no no no no **Fuck you**. (PA, Box 74)

This list of names is again wildly various, mixing the fictional with the real, artists with politicians. But the concentration on victims of political struggles, and their bodily suffering, is unmistakable and vivid. So too is the explicit sympathy for those who actively resist the gigantic power of the status quo.[15] The reasons that Pinter effaced these specific details—including matters such as Central America that he has spoken publicly about with great passion—can only be speculated upon. One factor might be the playwright's persistent concern for not letting his characters speak more than they know (*VV*, 19).

Or perhaps Pinter came to feel that being so specific would demean the intelligence and interpretive ability of his audience, making the play similar to those unsubtle political plays he disliked in the 1960s. His audience could and should be trusted to link the Waiter's references to the widely available (if widely ignored) facts of torture as practiced across the globe. There are large issues here as to how to proceed with political theater. One wonders if this unspecificity and ambiguity, characteristic of all Pinter's theater including, as Batty notes (2001, 113), the "political" plays, may not dilute the intended political focus of those works. John McGrath and Edward Bond criticized *Party Time* specifically for lacking context, as they put it—for not supplying or pointing to the information necessary to a properly political interpretation (Billington 1996, 333–34). If *Celebration*'s spectators do not link the Waiter's references to international torture, the regimes it is used by, and the inequities of power it symbolizes, have they evaded a central political thrust of the play?

Pinter's latest play, *Press Conference* (2002), like *Celebration*, invokes both torture and the fragile, circumscribed existence of dissent. Pinter writes the part of a government Minister, formerly head of the Secret Police and now the Minister of Culture, a part he acted when the play premiered. The sketch consists of the Minister's vicious, outrageous answers to sycophantic press queries. This piece shows what happens after the silencing of dissent: the powerful can say whatever they wish, with a frightening honesty.

In one example of the Minister's discourse, he brazenly announces that the government is kidnapping and killing the children of dissident families as well as raping their mothers. As in *One for the Road*, *Mountain Language*, *The Hothouse*, and *Party Time*, the state sees the family as a threat, evidently because it inculcates destabilizing, antisocial values. "We abducted them and brought them up properly or we killed them," the Minister says of "subversive" children. As for the women, "We raped them. It was all part of an educational process, you see. A cultural process" (*PC*; the script has no page numbers). The Minister's forthright manner shows the inversion of language that takes place when power operates. Violence, murder, oppression express humane values: "What was the nature of the culture you were proposing?" the Press asks. The reply: "A culture based on respect and the rule of law" (*PC*). This society, like the others in Pinter's political works, preaches moral values and kills in their name.

In this sketch Pinter draws attention to another political deployment of language, the purposes to which the term "subversion" has been put. "As head of Secret Police," says the Minister, "it was my responsibility, specifically, to protect and to safeguard our cultural inheritance against forces which were intent upon subverting it" (*PC*). The political process referred to is the creation of the so-called "doctrine of national security" in South America. With the sponsorship and instruction of the American military, South American governments evolved this doctrine, holding that using the military to strengthen political institutions against so-called internal enemies was more important than defending against traditionally defined external enemies. Armies thus became instruments of social and political policy aimed at enforcing uniformity of opinion; in practice, these powers led to widespread State-sponsored torture of enemies of the ruling class. Subversion was defined by the Uruguayan Army, for example, as "actions . . . with ultimate purposes of a political nature . . . whose aims are perceived as not convenient for the overall political system"; as Lawrence Wechsler notes, this definition is so large that, according to it, subversion is the same thing as democracy (1990, 121). These military and governmental policies were established and aided by a number of U.S. administrations.

The horror of the Minister's pronouncements is due not merely to their content of murderous repression but to the forthright, undisguised manner in which they are delivered. What distinguishes this play's treatment of how society justifies repression is the way in which the alibis of order and social perfection fail to occlude the practiced facts of rape, torture, and murder. Everything is out in the open; acts of murder and rape need not be euphemized. The visibility of these propagandistic words should detract from their ability to whitewash unpleasant political reality. In a sense, this regime does not need to justify itself or provide effective rhetorics of legitimation. It is so powerful it needn't bother with such gestures, except in a pro forma sense—such rationalizations exist as residues of established propagandistic habits—or simply for the fun of parading oppression in the faces of those whose function is supposedly to protest it. The clarity of the Minister's cruelty is significantly complemented by the lack of outrage with which his ugly words are received. The Press's obsequiousness—the softball questions and their laughter as the Minister threatens them—abets the Minister's oppression. This subservience goes even beyond the acquiescence to power of Jimmy in *Party Time* or Stephen in *Precisely*. The Minister's openness about his "principles" measures the extent of his power. This is a government that can do and say whatever it wants without fear of contradiction or reprisal.

This lack of fear with regard to contradiction extends into an outright embrace of disjunction between act and justification, between appearance and reality. This disjunction reminds us of one more irony about the power systems of Pinter's political dramas. While the regimes in plays such as *Party Time* and *Press Conference* urge the establishment of "authority" and "values," they also conduct a brilliant manipulation of images and what is presented as substantive reality. *Press Conference* underlines government and media collusion in misrepresenting reality. Pinter's regimes make use of both these seemingly contradictory techniques of premodernism in the form of transcendental values, while in postmodern fashion playing with images, language, and reality. This syncretic combination must be seen not as a disabling internal contradiction but as the greatest strength of the fascist states Pinter dramatizes.

This regime's hegemony over public articulation allows the Minister one final, powerfully offensive comment. "Under our philosophy," the Minister promises, "he that is lost is found. Thank you!" (PC). The evangelical language implies that this Minister is in the business of saving people's souls (the title "Minister" has governmental and religious meanings, thus becoming another political pun). That is, people are killed, raped, and brutalized for their own good. If the bureaucrats of *Precisely* imagined their opponents as deserving the punishment due to king killers, the Minister sees himself as above the level of royalty. Not merely portraying himself as ruling by divine right, the Minister depicts himself as God, a savior who offers redemption to all.

If nothing the government does need be hidden, this triumph of power frees dissent so that, officially, it need not be banished. It is in this context that *Press Conference* engages the issue of how critical dissent can exist at all. This issue connects to Pinter's own life. Pinter has noted the contradictory elements of his current life: he is a member of established society, by virtue of his fame and artistic career, at the same time as he relentlessly criticizes that establishment. Pinter's opponents in the press often assert that as a privileged member of society and as an artist he has no right to make political statements—as a "Bollinger Bolshevik," or in American terms a "champagne socialist," his political positions are inauthentic and worthless. Pinter's involvement in the June 20 movement of left-wing writers was roundly denounced on this basis in the British press (Billington 1996, 307).

Obviously, Pinter does not agree with such arguments, regarding them as an Establishment device to marginalize protest. He has theorized that such attacks are part of a tradition of mockery against the artists in his country, and at other times he has speculated that something like a governmental-media conspiracy attacks those who criticize society (Riddell 1999). However, Pinter does see the potential paradox in his position as a privileged citizen of a country he consistently opposes. He is an "outsider in society because I simply use my critical intelligence," but simultaneously is "very much part of the world in which [he] live[s]" (Pinter 2001). "I'm a CBE for God's sake," Pinter remarked in another interview. "Slightly preposterous, isn't it, but

I haven't sent it back. There are certain inconsistencies in the way one conducts one's life" (Riddell 1999).

One such inconsistency relates to the paradox of dissent: if the status quo is as starkly repressive as Pinter's plays depict, one might ask, why is he or anyone like him allowed to speak at all? The Minister has an answer:

> MINISTER. Critical dissent is acceptable—if it is left at home. My advice is—leave it at home. Keep it under the bed. With the piss pot.
> *He laughs.*
> Where it belongs.
> PRESS. Did you say *in* the piss pot?
> MINISTER. I'll put your head in the piss pot if you're not careful.
> *He laughs. They laugh.*
> Let me make myself quite clear. We need critical dissent because it keeps us on our toes. But we don't want to see it in the market place or on the avenues and piazzas of our great cities. . . . We are happy for it to remain at home, which means we can pop in at any time and read what is kept under the bed, discuss it with the writer, pat him or her on the head, shake him by his hand, give him perhaps a minor kick up the arse or in the balls and set fire to the whole she-bang. By this method we keep our society free from infection. (*PC*)

The suggestion is that "dissent" is allowed only because it is, in a metaphorical sense, domesticated. (The metaphor is amusingly made literal in the Minister's words.) Society permits critical thought to the extent that it can be circumscribed and made futile. Marcuse's notion of affirmative culture suggests that art has the ability to offer alternative critiques on reigning political structures. Criticism provides a kind of utopian framework for society ("it keeps us on our toes"), but it is not to interfere in public life, especially economic life ("the market place"). In his political commentaries, Pinter often nominates economic pressure as inhibiting free expression of the truth (*VV*, 198). Art, free thought, and dissent are tolerated, though also they are threatened with imprisonment. Writers are tolerated and their works permitted; they may even be congratulated, ostensibly admired, used as figureheads of cultural sophistication, but this approval shades off, in practice, into oppression. It's all the same, as the Minister indicates, whether the writer or social critic gets a pat on the back or a kick in the arse: either way the actual operations of power are immune from any possibility of criticism. Critical thinkers, and the press, may not be literally silent, but, reduced to impotence, they have been effectively silenced nevertheless.

Dissent that has been imprisoned, marginalized, and effectively silenced is the subject of *The New World Order* (1991), a work that distills the worldview of Pinter's expressly political plays. In this sketch, two men, Lionel and Des, chat before commencing torture upon a blindfolded man. The victim's silence is emphasized: he remains without speaking or making a sound throughout the play, more phenomenological object than mimetic character. To amuse themselves, the torturers mockingly banter about what their victim knows about his fate. After disagreeing over this and other questions, including the "theological aspirations" of women, they ecstatically congratulate each other for performing the moral duty of "keeping the world clean for democracy" (*NWO*, 60). In closing, Des casually mentions that their victim will soon be grateful to his torturers. "I'm going to shake you by the hand," he promises Lionel, and then Des *"gestures to the man in the chair with his thumb."* "And so will he . . . *(he looks at his watch)* . . . in about thirty-five minutes" (60). The audience is left to realize that after this glib flippancy, physical torture is about to commence.

The New World Order conjoins verbal antagonism, insult, and interrogation as prelude to torture. Des and Lionel's sense of leisure and relaxation, before their strictly physical duties begins, implies their invulnerability. They act and chat without haste, not driven by uncontrollable emotions or spontaneity. This psychological security parallels the poise of Nicolas and the depthless one-dimensionality of Terry, two predecessors to Lionel and Des. In *The New World Order*, this psychological stability has an objective political cause glanced at indirectly when the two discuss the nature of their victim:

> LIONEL. Who is this cunt anyway? What is he, some kind of peasant—or a lecturer in theology?
> DES. He's a lecturer in fucking peasant theology. (*NWO*, 55)

In referring to class differences and to spirituality, Pinter highlights two foundations for critiques of Western politics: class-based theories (socialism and Communism) and organized religion.[16] As they are made fodder for absurdist language games, class politics and religion verge on nonexistence. The world being dramatized here has completely lost these two traditional sources for opposing the status quo.

The play, in the classic manner of the theater of the absurd, deals with the gap between reality and language. Language and logic do not represent reality but instead obfuscate it. The logical distinctions promised by definitional language are absent, so that opposed terms describe the same thing. The blindfolded man is therefore, illogically, both a cunt and a prick, and "not finishing" with someone is the same as "not having begun" with him (NWO, 58–59). This double-talk anticipates the play's ultimate linguistic inversion, when Des describes the basis of Lionel's "purity": "Because you're keeping the world clean for democracy" (60). The real meaning of such politically loaded language can, again, only be understood by inversion.

The atmosphere of violence in The New World Order is all the more powerful because it is so restrained. The bizarre behavior and emotional deadness of Lionel and Des is an interesting strategy in the play. Unlike One for the Road, there are no colorful, flamboyant archvillains here; these villains do not boast of their power over life and death as, for example, does Nicolas. By not showing these characters sadistically glorying over their victim in typical ways, an easy response of moral outrage at them is subverted. The audience is left looking for a place to deposit its moral shock. Since what these torturers do is confined to the linguistic realm, the audience has difficulty responding appropriately to their behavior. Pinter abstracts physical menace from the situation of torture (he strikes from a typescript draft one of the characters kicking their victim to the ground [PA, Box 36]), positing verbal harassment as synecdochical with corporal abuse. Every word the audience hears is intuited as the displaced expression of actual violence: words become tokens of fleshly punishments. The result is to capture with remarkable force the terror that torture provokes.

This terror is not so much the consequence of tangible mistreatment as of the atmosphere of tension and unpredictability that characterizes torture in practice. The play seems in performance to last far longer than the ten or twelve minutes it actually does (as Robert Cushman notes in the section on The New World Order on Pinter's website, http://www.haroldpinter.org). Torture distorts the experience of time by foregrounding the absolute asymmetry of power between victim and torturer. Marcelo Vignar, a victim of the Uruguayan military authorities, describes his experience:

> If I'd known in advance that they'd be keeping me just those two months, well, that would have been easier to endure. But instead it

seemed like forever, with every second permeated by fear, by dread anticipation. *L'etat de menace*: that's what makes you crazy—it's not just what they do to you but the terror of what they might do to you next, at any moment, at *every* moment. (qtd. in Weschler 1990, 85)

Des and Lionel note in similar terms the fear they inspire: "He hasn't got any idea at all about any one of the number of things that we might do to him." "That we will do to him." "That we will" (*NWO*, 53). What are these "things"? Not only is there no need to enumerate them, but there is a need served by not specifying them. Torture works by implication, by inconclusive hints, by the threat of open-endedness.[17]

The threat of terror in this play is conducted through words. Disconcertingly, Lionel and Des speak in a style that self-consciously acknowledges their status as Pinter characters:

> DES. You called him a cunt last time. Now you call him a prick. How many times do I have to tell you? You've got to learn to define your terms and stick to them. You can't call him a cunt in one breath and a prick in the next. The terms are mutually contradictory. You'd lose face in any linguistic discussion group, take my tip.
> LIONEL. Christ, would I?
> DES. Definitely. And you know what it means to you. You know what language means to you.
> LIONEL. Yes, I do know. (*NWO*, 57–58)

Here again the arrested joke asserts itself; in Pinter's political tragicomedy, the state of the world is "past a joke." We laugh but then stop ourselves when we realize what that laughter is complicit with. The contrast between Des's scrupulous sense of logic and the scatological violence that logic underwrites might well be comic—were not the facts the play refers to so severe and shocking.

Contrasting *The New World Order* with *The Birthday Party* demonstrates the bleak severity of Pinter's political vision and illustrates how his political theater deals, as Esslin puts it, in concrete facts rather than rich metaphors. In *The Birthday Party*, Goldberg and McCann at least try to lure Stanley back into his societal obligations, mentioning duties to wife, religion, and country, as Charles Carpenter mentions (1979, 106–7). If Stanley needs to be brought back into mainstream public life, or the "organization" Goldberg and McCann represent, that society or organization sees potential value in Stanley. In opposition,

Des and Lionel have nothing but contempt and hatred for their victim, whose individuality they do not engage with at all. Stanley can both hear and respond to his interlocutors, while the victim in *The New World Order* is nearly catatonic. He does not participate in what happens to him; he has been rendered an object, nevermore to be a political subject. (Des's assertion that the man will thank them later is merely an ironic, smirking joke.) The audience of *The Birthday Party* does not know what, if anything, Stanley has done wrong, but both Stanley and Goldberg seem to have knowledge about this issue. Des, however, proclaims that the specific crimes of *New World Order*'s unnamed transgressor are irrelevant—there is no effort to ascertain them or to convince the victim of his wrongdoing:

> DES. . . . Look at this man here, for example. . . . Before he came in here he was a big shot, he never stopped shooting his mouth off, he never stopped questioning received ideas. Now—because he's apprehensive about what's about to happen to him—he's stopped all that, he's got nothing more to say, he's more or less called it a day. (*NWO*, 58)

Des and his regime are provoked simply by the fact of opposition, mere difference per se, and it is this fact that authorizes their torture.

Despite the presence of this difference, Lionel is so convinced of his own correctness in dealing with political transgression that he weeps out of the sheer joy of being on the right side of morality and history. His crying evidences existential fullness—the moment is ecstatic self-fulfillment. As such, this behavior is opposite to Goldberg's breakdown in *The Birthday Party*, which signals a temporary sense of incompleteness. Goldberg falters because of inner emptiness caused by the arbitrary, rickety nature of his personal philosophy; Des cries because of his utter belief in his self-justifying politics and their fulfillment in the world he and his cohorts create. The thought that Goldberg's faltering shadows Des's outburst is consoling but false. The magnitude of what contemporary opponents of the status quo are up against permits no such untruthful comfort. So too of the silences that characterize the early works and the later ones: the silence that Kullus subverts to gain power is existentially and politically different than the enforced silences in which the political plays end.[18]

The violence in plays such as *The New World Order* and the

other plays analyzed in this chapter takes place in secret, hidden places, out of public sight. Repressive governments rely on the fact that we may have difficulty imagining the suffering of distant others. Pinter asks us to admit historical suffering into our consciousness—we must imagine it and accept its reality without whitewashing it with reference to ideals such as stability or security or "democracy." We have to imagine or deduce the activities these plays allude to, even as governments everywhere attempt to hide their crimes or mask them under empty idealistic language, or rely on our own apathy to minimize them. Both during and after writing the plays analyzed in this chapter, Pinter explored the dilemmas of how individuals may attempt to assimilate and confront historical suffering and political violence —themes of his screenplay *Reunion*, dealing with a life altered by Nazi power, and *Ashes to Ashes*, in which an Englishwoman tries to imagine herself as a victim of political violence. The shock ending of *The New World Order* implicitly challenges its audience to use its imagination to apprehend political terror. However, it is this very same audience whose resistance to such acknowledgment allows oppression its long and happy life.

5

Pinter at the Movies: *The Comfort of Strangers* and *Victory*

PINTER'S POLITICAL CONSCIENCE, INTEGRAL TO HIS ARTISTIC IMAGI-nation, shows itself throughout his recent work, including his screenplays. The themes in screenplays after *The French Lieutenant's Woman* (1981) complement those of the dramas from the '80s and later: *The Heat of the Day* (1989), based on a novel by Elizabeth Bowen, involves political and private betrayals in World War II Britain, and *Reunion* (1989), from a novella by Fred Uhlman, concerns political and social conditions in Germany at the beginning of the Nazi era. And although Pinter wrote only part of the final script for Margaret Atwood's *The Handmaid's Tale* (1990)—in which a fundamentalist theocracy perpetuates itself via the systematic rape of the female population—his participation suggests his protest against the misogyny and "family values" of the New Right.[1] Similarly, Pinter's adaptation of Ian McEwan's *The Comfort of Strangers* (1990) presents a thematic along the lines of his recent drama—an authoritarianism that would crush political and personal freedom in emulation of the powerful father. Pinter has also returned to classic modernist texts: the Pinteresque and the Kafkaesque merge in the 1992 adaptation of *The Trial* (1922); *Victory*, an unfilmed adaptation (1982) of Joseph Conrad's 1915 novel, features sexual politics as it dramatizes the protagonist's movement from private isolation into public obligations and conflict.

Pinter's screenplays, no less than his plays, concern the forces that constitute the self at the same time as they constitute society. Running through the plays is the dream—usually frustrated—of escape from a conflict-ridden world or, indeed, from various forms of imprisonment: a wish shared by characters such as Teddy in *The Homecoming*, Stanley in *The Birthday Party*, Rose in *The Room*. When this outer world does intrude into the realms of the self, from which it was only ever notion-

144

ally separated, it has profound and traumatic effects upon the individual. Simply, the world is objectively too strong, too overwhelming for the self to handle, even if it does gain profound knowledge of that outer world and the forces that shape it. Thus, whereas Brecht, say, imagines political drama as effecting social change, Pinter's political works seem to illustrate the scale of inequities inherent in the everyday functioning of the world.

Pinter's method as an adapter respects the integrity of his sources; his aim, clearly, is to preserve the author's particular vision and extend its expression to the medium of cinema. Still, translation from text to screen is necessarily a co-authoring, permitting if not requiring interpretive shadings and outright changes on the part of the adaptor. For example, Pinter's interpolations sometimes add topical or political edge to his sources. This chapter considers Pinter's treatment of the political and the personal, the public and the private, in two screenplays, *The Comfort of Stranger*, from the end of the '80s, and *Victory*, from the beginning of Pinter's "turn" to the political.

THE COMFORT OF STRANGERS:
POLITICS AND SEXUAL POLITICS

With his work on McEwan's *The Comfort of Strangers*, Pinter highlights the notion that relations between males and females form the main ground of social and political conflict in the late twentieth century. Whereas in *Party Time* female behavior apes the viciousness associated with the masculine, *The Comfort of Strangers* presents through its antagonist Robert the traditional ideal that male and female roles are to be kept scrupulously distinct. Behavior is markedly gendered, with violence and domination codified as male, masochism and submission as female (interestingly, these distinctions even appear in the narrator's language in addition to that of his characters). Mary and Colin are led to destruction by their failure to recognize fanatic sexism when they encounter it—in spite of their "advanced" awareness of gender stereotypes. Like the late drama—*Party Time, Moonlight, Ashes to Ashes* —*The Comfort of Strangers* uses gender conflict to demonstrate the frightening nature of power in its purest form. McEwan's novel and Pinter's adaptation suggest, indeed, that the battle between the sexes has reached an impasse: with communication nearly impossible, with language itself imperiled, men and women live out the legacy of institutionalized sexism without recourse to generally accepted new understandings, institutions, or roles. As gender conflict persists, the brutal realities and consequences of domination appear inextricable with what is called civilized life.

In McEwan's novel the mise-en-scéne is not named, though clearly it is Venice, that most historic, romantic, and literary of cities, one that exemplifies civilization as well as the foreign, the dangerous, the strange. The novel inevitably suggests a post-modern response to Mann's *Death in Venice,* the locus classicus in modernist literature on the intertwined themes of desire, death, and illicit passion. Self-knowledge, sex, and self-destruction intertwine in this thematic, one that also runs through *The Comfort of Strangers.* McEwan's setting recalls Pinter's *The Homecoming* and *Betrayal,* both of which associate Venice with romantic adventure and danger. Like *The Homecoming, The Comfort of Strangers* links sexuality and violence without clearly signaling how the combination should be responded to. And, as with *The Homecoming,* some reviews of *The Comfort of Strangers* registered outrage: the novel was termed "morally annoying," "definitely diseased," and "hateful" (qtd. in Slay 1996, 72).

McEwan suggests the sexual-political burden of his text with an epigraph from Adrienne Rich: "Now we dwelt in two worlds / the daughters and the mothers / in the kingdom of the sons." Venice represents the kingdom of the sons, the patriarchy founded on the male violence pervading everyday life. With its ominous atmosphere of violence emerging from banal circumstances and its sexual-political thematic, McEwan's short novel is an inviting vehicle for Pinter's adaptation. His screenplay follows McEwan's feminist impulse by delineating the twisted power of Robert's adherence to patriarchal order and a chauvinist past supposedly more certain and harmonious than the present.

In the novel male violence is inscribed in the romantic, honeymoon world of Venice: "The narrow passageway had brought them onto a large, flatly lit square, a plain of cobbles, in the center of which stood a war memorial of massive, rough-hewn granite blocks assembled to form a gigantic cube, topped by a soldier casting away his rifle. This was familiar, this was the starting point for nearly all their expeditions" (McEwan 1981, 20). The wry comment on male violence as Mary's and Colin's "familiar . . . starting point" hints ominously at their limitations: their self-congratulatory awareness of gender oppression exists as comfortable cliché—a fact concerning history and society that allows for enlightened discussion without, however, challenging them personally. "When they talked of the politics of sex, which they did sometimes, they did not talk of themselves" (17). The metapolitical thrust of the novel and screenplay is that both investigate how a certain kind of fashionable political awareness both inhibits and provokes a more robust sense of the truly vile political opponents the world provides. Colin and Mary are aware and progressively inclined, but they fail to translate the political ideology of patriarchal violence, visible subtly in the landscape and exaggeratedly in the person of Robert, into their lives—a failure which costs Colin his.

The "starting point" of male domination, overt or threatened, shapes both culture and history, which is to say that it operates through the actions and language of human beings—but not the "advanced," very liberal Mary and Colin. Mary and Colin's sexual-political "awareness" is treated satirically, as in the following excerpt:

> Their talk turned to orgasms, and to whether men and women experience a similar, or radically different, sensation; radically different, they agreed, but was this difference culturally induced? Colin said that he had long envied women's orgasms, and that there were times when he felt an aching emptiness, close to desire, between his scrotum and his anus; he thought this might be an approximation of womanly desire. Mary described, and they both derided, an experiment reported by a newspaper, the purpose of which was to answer this very question, did men and women feel the same. Volunteers of both sexes were given a list of two hundred phrases, adjectives and adverbs, and asked to circle the ten that best described their experience of orgasm. A second group was asked to look at the results and guess the sex of each volunteer, and since they made as many correct as incorrect identifications, it was concluded that men and women feel the same. They moved on, inevitably, to the politics of sex and talked, as they had many times before, of patriarchy which, Mary said, was the most powerful single principle of organization shaping institutions and individual lives. Colin argued, as he always did, that class dominance was more fundamental. Mary shook her head, but they battled to find common ground. (McEwan 1981, 79–80)

This language mocks the speakers, but in a light way.[2] Colin and Mary analyze the world with some intelligence—their language is fairly up-to-date and progressive. They are not immature or hidebound in their opinions, though McEwan's narrative voice suggests their political beliefs have an element of cliché to them—and therefore that they serve as a source of comfort and familiarity.

What truly mocks the characters' awareness of the gender and power issues they discuss is their inability to see Robert as a danger. (An additional irony is Mary and Colin's sexual relationship revives after they meet Robert and Caroline—as if there is something attractive and vital about the latter couple.) They are unable to recognize what they describe, even when a threatening adherent of patriarchy is staring them in the face.[3] Their debates about the priority of gender over class critique look pale and ineffective besides the monstrous enemy that is Robert. The unrestrained destructiveness he allows himself makes him an extreme, severe opponent, whose essence cannot be predicted through the polite, rational arguments of civilized beings. The real enemy out there, Pinter loves to suggest, is more vicious and powerful than it is comfortable to imagine. "[M]eet the opposition" (McEwan 1981, 27), says Colin aptly when he first meets Robert (a message Colin fails to heed), and it is a phrase that in the roughest shorthand evokes a central impulse of Pinter's politics: the need not to underestimate the unrestrained nature of power.[4]

Besides the satire on the characters' theoretical "knowledge," the passage about gender and orgasm hints at another of the book's central themes. The "open" but basically empty talk conceals a genuinely unfamiliar and unsettling challenge—namely, sexual ambiguity (Colin feels "an aching emptiness, close to desire, between his scrotum and his anus"). And while the Venetian cityscape records male domination, McEwan's Venice is also a world where male and female are strangely mixed and indistinct. The narrator remarks of a kiosk near the war memorial: "Inside . . . sat the vendor, barely visible through the tiny hatch, and in virtual darkness. It was possible to buy cigarettes here and not know whether it was a man or a woman who sold them" (19). The vaginal and phallic imagery, hermaphroditically mixed, suggests a danger that the sexually emancipated couple is not equipped to meet, and androgyny, rather than symbolizing mutuality or equality as some varieties of feminism hold, threatens breakdown, dissolution.

Colin's supposedly advanced awareness of sexual indeterminacy ironically prefigures the confrontation with Robert, whose complex desire of and hatred for womanliness, integral to his fanatical sexism, makes him one of Pinter's powerful representations of fear of sexual ambiguity (Billington 1996, 317). Yet, perhaps inevitably, Robert's attempts to privilege stereotypical masculinity does not excise the feminine and the homosexual realms: his father often used a mascara brush, "such as ladies use," on his mustache (*CS*, 3), and Robert owns what looks like a gay bar, or else a place that supports male intimacy. Like Robert's fear of sexual indeterminacy, his emulation of his powerful father illustrates a recurrent thematic in Pinter; Robert's father, like Max in *The Homecoming*, like the father in *Family Voices*, or the "father of the country" in *One for the Road*, is one of Pinter's representations of the powerful father.[5] The father, in all of these cases, is looked up to for his personal and social authority and serves to protect the son against emotional insecurity and ambivalence. The father provides judgments that ground personal and political life—he provides "standards," a word that is invoked by many of Pinter's political villains (as in *Party Time* and *Celebration*).

The familial roots of Robert's sexual fanaticism are underscored in both novel and screenplay. Robert talks of his father to Mary and Colin repeatedly and at length; Pinter emphasizes the account by interspersing partial narrations throughout the screenplay, whereas McEwan has Robert tell it only once, as Burkman notes (1993, 39). Throughout his life, Robert has idolized his father, "a very big man," for his strength and authority (*CS*, 1, 15, 61). He also sees his father, an ambassador, as an important man in the world, and in terms of adherence to traditional standards—a reminder of a time when men were men and women were women. Yet, intriguingly, Robert was fascinated by the mascara his father used to color his mustache black (1, 16, 51). As a child Robert competed with his sisters for his father's affection, believing himself the favorite. Once, he revealed his sisters' misbehavior and caused them to be punished by their father; they avenged themselves grotesquely by causing him to gorge on drugged snacks, then locking him in his father's study, which he defiled with vomit and excrement. With this kind of baggage—Robert's past sounds like a satire of a Freudian case study—Robert becomes, as a man, obsessed with exercising male authority, with punishing females, and with living up to the standards of a powerful father whose displeasure he can never forget or erase. The screenplay preserves, perhaps furthers, McEwan's emphasis on the Father who brooks no dissent, sexual or otherwise.

While he highlights McEwan's connection between patriarchy and violence, Pinter also uses his position as adapter to dramatize issues not explicit in the novel. Pinter also adds incidents and dialogue into the script that clearly reveal his own political investments, such as in this conversation:

> MARY: Did I ever tell you the terrible thing that happened to me when I was a little girl, the worst thing that ever happened to me?
> COLIN: You never told me.
> MARY: Well, I was about seven—or eight—and I was part of a gang of kids—boys and girls—and we were this gang . . .
> COLIN: Uh-huh?
> MARY: And one day some of them said, "One member of this gang isn't really good enough to be a member of this gang and does everyone agree that we should throw that person out?" And I said, "Yes! Yes!" I clapped—
> COLIN: You clapped?
> MARY: Yes. I clapped. And I said, "Yes—throw this person out!" And you know who that person was?
>   COLIN *stares at her.*
> COLIN: You.
> MARY: Yes.
>   *He stares at her.*
> COLIN: God. That's a terrible story. (*CS*, 9)

This dialogue is Pinter's own invention, minimally suggested by the novel (though McEwan has several of the couple's conversations include childhood references.) In Pinter's imagination, exclusion is a political motif, perhaps the one in which his entire statement about politics might be condensed. To exercise power is to exercise the power of exclusion; groups integrate (to use that word from *The Birthday Party*) themselves by defining some of their members as unworthy. To banish is a primal urge, and to be banished is an unforgettable experience. The tendency to form groups, with their innate desire to produce conformity and exclusion, is a central manifestation of human cruelty. Thus the pattern of exclusion running through Pinter's work (*The Dumb Waiter, A Slight Ache, The Hothouse, The Homecoming, Party Time*) has meaning on both psychological and political levels. This characterization of group dynamics accords with the emphasis Pinter puts in discussions of his own political activity on the value of the lone, isolated individual.

Also for Pinter, the feeling of social exclusion drives political quietism. Such a feeling is admittedly "immature," evoking the perspectives of childhood we would like to believe we have, as adults, outgrown. Pinter suggests, in an interview with David Edwards, that we haven't (Pinter 2001). The playwright recalls getting letters in response to his political pronouncements from people who agreed with his stances but felt "lonely" in a society where few, if any, shared these sentiments. Pinter floats this idea: "a lot of intelligent people, who can't miss what's happening in this bloody world, just like being part of the establishment." They do not speak out against this establishment because of a need to belong and a fear of being an outsider. As if evoking Mary's "terrible" story of exclusion, Pinter concludes, "I think that with some people there's a terrible fear of being unpopular" that keeps them from openly contradicting the status quo (2001).[6] This explanation suggests a deep psychological cause for political indifference—a cause that has to do with rooted drives and fears, and thus not necessarily correctible through intellectual or rational means.

This negative portrait of groups raises other issues about Pinter's politics. Mark Batty points out how Pinter's groups legitimize themselves by declaring their devotion to shared assumptions, thus allowing communication and social cohesion (2001, 117), quoting for instance the question to Lamb in *The Hothouse* "Do you ever feel you would like to join a group of people in which group common assumptions are shared and common principles observed?" (*H*, 56) and Nicolas's "I feel a link, you see, a bond. I share a commonwealth of interest. I am not alone" (*One*, 51). Batty observes:

> The seemingly innocent desire to belong to a group and play one's part in an ordered society can never be wholly free of political exploitation, and . . . the impulse to participate and the comfort of sharing ethical values can easily degenerate into the rejection and castigation of those who dare to question the motives behind that participation and the basis of those ethical values. (118)

For an individual to succumb to such a desire for social inclusion, however, is not necessarily only a matter of personal weakness. To exist outside such a group is to deprive oneself of the capacity to communicate and to have the company of other human beings ("society" in an older definition). Furthermore, Batty sees a desire for commonality and ethics as causing exclusion as a by-product or as a cover story to legitimate anger toward nonconformists. But perhaps the truth is even more dire.

In Mary's story, her banishment is not given any sort of pretext or rationale. Anger and exclusion here seem to exist on their own and for their own sake; the cover story of ethical commonality is not necessary to cause or justify exclusion. The communal bond exists purely to produce repression. Sartre assesses a society marked by anti-Semitism in just these terms: "The social bond is anger; the collectivity has no other goal than to exercise over certain individuals a diffused repressive sanction" (1995, 30). His point could be applied to any society that permits oppression—which is to say, any society.

The question of how society defines difference as sanctionable deviance shapes a significant interpolation from novel to screenplay. In the following conversation, the couples debate the concept of freedom:

> ROBERT: So how is England? Lovely dear old England? Hampshire! Wiltshire! Cumberland! Yorkshire! Harrods! Such a beautiful country. Such beautiful traditions.
> MARY: It's not quite so beautiful. Is it, Colin?
> *COLIN does not respond.*
> Colin? Are you feeling all right?
> COLIN: *(quietly)*: Sure.
> ROBERT: In what way? In what way not beautiful?
> MARY: Oh, I don't know—freedom . . . you know . . .
> ROBERT: Freedom? What kind of freedom? Freedom to do what?
> MARY: Freedom to be free!
> ROBERT: You want to be free? *(He laughs.)* Free to do what?
> MARY: You don't believe in it?
> ROBERT: Sure I believe in it. But sometimes a few rules—you know—they're not a bad thing. First and foremost society has to be protected from perverts. Everybody knows that. My philosophical position is simple—put them all up against a wall and shoot them. What society needs to do is purify itself. The English government is going in the right direction. In Italy we could learn a lot of lessons from the English government.
> COLIN: Well I'm an Englishman and I disagree violently with what you've just said. I think it's shit.
> ROBERT: I respect you as an Englishman but not if you're a communist poof. You're not a poof are you? That's the right word, no? Or is it "fruit"? Talking about fruit, it's time for coffee. (*CS*, 292–93)[7]

The novel does not so clearly link Robert with a specific right-wing agenda.[8] "By foregrounding timely sociopolitical issues . . . Pinter . . . [makes] the screenplay less general, more immediate, more urgent than the novel" writes Burkman (1993, 51). Robert's dialogue about "freedom" invokes the theme of civil rights being eroded in 1980s Britain. His references to "perverts" and "poofs" point specifically to Clause 28. This was a proposed British government plan to forbid public authorities, including schools, "to promote homosexuality" or to advocate "the acceptance of homosexuality as a pretended family relationship" (Billington 1996, 307). Similar laws were proposed in America at approximately the same time; while always portrayed as efforts to deny homosexuals special rights or to preserve the family, such legislation was often seen simply as discrimination and hatred with a legalistic facade.

The scene points to one specific aspect of Pinter's quarrel with Thatcherism. Even so, without Pinter's public discussions of Clause 28 around 1988, one might not connect Robert's conversation with this particular proposal: Pinter is topical, that is, but not fully and explicitly so. Further, in one of his mentions of this Clause, he equates it to the beginnings of Nazi anti-Jewish legislation, designed to mark out one social group to be deprived of civil rights: "I really think it's reminiscent of the Jews in the 30's in Germany" (Gussow 1994, 69). Pinter makes a contemporary reference but sees it as having much in common with a past situation. Again Pinter visualizes discrimination as continuous and recurrent—oppression is an historical constant.

Seeking to illustrate recurrent impulses to oppression, Pinter is thus led to examine politics in the light of psychology or human nature. Through the character of Robert, whose erotic fascination with Colin hints he might be one of the "poofs" he detests, Pinter shows that sexual insecurity correlates with authoritarian urges. Once again, as in plays such as *One for the Road* and *Party Time*, Pinter draws an equivalence between suppressing civil liberties and an attitude that violently fears and castigates anyone who transgresses socially enforced binary distinctions. In this political perspective, crucially, violence replaces irrelevant reason: "My philosophical position is simple— put them up against a wall and shoot them." The enemy does not offer anything that attains the status of an idea; hatred and fear are the true basis for relating to the social other (even as the oppressor offers a moralizing discourse). Given this tendency to violence, opposing social oppression becomes nearly tantamount to self-sacrifice. The notion of sacrifice is hinted at by this action of purifying society that Robert espouses and that is echoed in the fascistic societies of Pinter's works. In these societies, the outsider is not only marginalized, but must be additionally expelled, sacrificed, killed.

The Comfort of Strangers and *Victory* feature tragic paradigms of political awakening, showing characters who come to a proper understanding of their worlds, but too late to allow for actions that might personally save them. Mary's awakening is to the depth of gender conflict and oppression in her world. However, there are ambiguities in Pinter's conclusion, as Ann C. Hall insightfully notes (2001, 97). One of these ambiguities has to do with the structure of the ideas the novel offers about female and male behaviors. McEwan seems invested in an essentialist theory of male violence and female submission, a theme visible in the novel's penultimate paragraph:

> [Mary] was in the mood for explanation . . . she was going to explain it all to him [Colin], tell him her theory, tentative at this stage, of course, which explained how the imagination, the sexual imagination, men's ancient dreams of hurting, and women's of being hurt, embodied and declared a powerful single organizing principle, which distorted all relations, all truth. (McEwan 1981, 126)

This passage's placement near the end of the novel suggests its importance. Mary's "theory" oddly echoes Robert's own suggestion in the novel that "Whatever they might say they believe, women love aggression and strength and power in men. It's deep in their minds. . . . It is the world that shapes people's minds. It is men who have shaped the world. So women's minds are shaped by men" (71). The similarity of Robert's beliefs and the quasi-thematic statement the narrator ascribes to Mary demands explanation.

Both sets of ideas are essentialist in describing certain behaviors as definitively male or female. A passage from McEwan's libretto for *Or Shall We Die?*, a piece protesting nuclear weaponry, defines maleness in terms of objectivity, factuality, and clarity, and womanliness in terms of flux, interdependency, and cooperation, ending "'Shall there be womanly times, or shall we die?' I believe the options to be as stark as that" (1983, 19). The scope of gender problems is huge, verging on irreparability, an emphasis that parallels the apparent impulse in Pinter's political theater to assert that solutions to major sociopolitical problems are (currently, or permanently?) unavailable. The problems McEwan insightfully identifies are of such scale that he is led to large, generalizing solutions. His distinction between male and female consciousness is an essentialism aiming to solve contemporary problems, but it is essentialism nonetheless. Given how patriarchy assimilates essentialism for discriminatory purposes, one wonders if a benign, positive version is possible. But Robert's invocation of the shaping of minds hints at the issue of social construction: people's psyches and drives are historically conditioned. The novel thus combines a political feminism with a psychological investigation into sex, domination, and pleasure. McEwan states that he wanted to do more than "talk about men and women in social terms"; he also wanted to explore "how the unconscious is shaped . . . there might be desires—masochism in women, sadism in men—which act out the oppression of woman . . . but which have actually become related to sources of pleasure" (Slay 1996, 87). This aim is extremely broad and extremely provocative. Accounts of how power works in society, as Judith Butler points out, often ignore its psychological dimensions (1997, 5); however, saying anything about the nature of the unconscious is bound to be problematic.

Before making this intriguing and contentious analysis of sexism, McEwan has Mary deny that she was married to Colin, or that she ever would (perhaps recognizing his insufficiency as a person—he appears infantilized in the narrative, called a "silly boy"—or perceiving the insufficiency of their relationship). The screenplay features an interpolated scene that dramatizes Mary's disconnection from Colin's rather grudging offer of cohabitation, and another scene that amusingly turns the tables on Colin as he discusses male objectification of the female body (CS, 39–40, 33–35). These scenes point to a feminist thematic in the screenplay, demonstrating the limiting, insufficient nature of male perspectives and behaviors. However, Pinter's screenplay has Mary state that she was planning to marry Colin (50) while in the novel she denies this. It is possible to wonder if Mary's declaration about Colin here complicates, or even vitiates, the screenplay's feminist agenda. "It would appear that in the novel Mary resists stereotypical characterization by the patriarchy while in the Pinter screenplay she accepts it" (Hall 2001, 97). A draft variant showed Mary happily back with her children, a scene that seems to move even further away from her feminist awareness (Gale and Hudgins 1996, 111–12). This softer ending could also be seen as suggesting a functioning, sane world not destroyed by Robert's violent patriarchal attitudes.

While Pinter does not afford Mary a chance to express any conclusive realization, he does, as Hall notes, end the film with

Robert reciting his story again, in explanation or self-justification. McEwan's novel allows the inference that Robert's actions represent a death wish, but Pinter brings Robert, vampiric, back to life. Opposed to the fragility of progressive forces is the self-assured, self-perpetuating presence of power in the form of male chauvinism. We meet the political enemy once more. The film thus demonstrates the "violent and oppressive" nature of such chauvinistic self-assurance (Hall 2001, 97), of course, through the screenplay's narrative (assuming we didn't know it before).[9] Pinter challenges us by asserting just how socially and politically entrenched is such offensive certitude.

The dominant sense for both McEwan and Pinter is that social problems springing from sexism's hierarchies are massive and overwhelming. While Mary embodies a feminist awareness, she is unable to counter the presence of sexism, and her story, in both McEwan and Pinter's versions, emphasizes her insufficiency compared to the forces she opposes: "She alone is unable to turn the tide" (Slay 1996, 83). Once again, Pinter's political works demonstrate the destruction of those who combat the status quo. The strength of that status quo, and its viciousness, suggest both the absolute need for it to be opposed—in this sense the book and screenplay are not negative but (re)constructive in tone and effect—as well as the likely costs for doing so. The specific manifestations of deadly power the novel and screenplay critique form the contours of everyday social and sexual relationships. Authentic communication between the sexes is nearly impossible; males and females are unable to understand each other or bring their needs in line; the legacy of institutionalized sexism persistently troubles and damages personal relationships; language is a barrier to understanding rather than a means of it—these ideas characterize many of Pinter's late works even as they may seem to describe the problems of contemporary gender relationships. Works such as *Party Time, The Comfort of Strangers, Ashes to Ashes*, in addition to the less obviously "political" *Moonlight*, reflect the contemporary sense that the divide between men and women has opened into a chasm.

VICTORY: ISOLATION AND ENGAGEMENT

Joseph Conrad's novel *Victory*, with its large-scale action and exotic setting, seems an unlikely vehicle for Pinter, whose imagination is more typically minimalist. Nevertheless, the novel's conflicts and themes have clear parallels in Pinter's work as a playwright and screenplay author. As does *The Comfort of Strangers, Victory* investigates the sources of male power, the relationship between family dynamics and social and political forces, and the dream of escape from a conflict-ridden world.

Pinter's 1982 screenplay was never filmed, due to financial difficulties in the company that was to produce it.[10] The screenplay is remarkably faithful to Conrad—it preserves the major plot events and characters and either replicates or closely follows Conrad's dialogue—and thus a synopsis of the novel will be helpful. Axel Heyst is friend and business partner of one Morrison; together they invest in a coal mine on a remote island. When the business falls through, Heyst is blamed. Belatedly following his father's advice—"he who forms a tie is lost" (Conrad 1924, 199–200)—Heyst lives in isolation on the island. The crisis of the novel follows a visit to a neighboring island, during which Heyst forms another "connection," one whose consequences ultimately prove fatal. Out of a complex mix of compassion, duty, pity, and romantic ardor, he defends the vulnerable young woman Lena against the villainous Schomberg. He takes Lena to live with him on his island, where, in spite of her distrust of men and his own emotional reserve, the two form a deep relationship across the barriers of temperament, gender (and class also, more particularly in the novel) between them. Heyst's sexual feelings are so repressed and encased in guilt that when he acts upon them, the encounter, though Lena does not object to it, has the violence of a rape (189–90).

Schomberg meanwhile fosters his hatred for Heyst, finally inventing a tale that Heyst is hiding money on his island. Consequently, a trio of henchmen—Jones, Ricardo, and Pedro—invades the island; their pursuit of Heyst is complicated by desires and fears centering on the one female character of Lena. The criminal duo of Jones and Ricardo is broken up when Jones, effeminate and misogynist, shoots Ricardo after the latter begins making love to Lena. She tries to make Heyst understand she acted strategically in order to steal Ricardo's knife to attack him, and thus that she truly loves Heyst and is willing to sacrifice her own safety for him. Curiously indifferent to his own survival— "His very will seemed dead of weariness" (Conrad 1924, 390)— Heyst recognizes his defeat by Jones but also his attainment of true love with Lena. Knowing he has been loved, he sets fire to himself and Lena in their cottage. Though Conrad hints that

Jones kills himself, at the end of Pinter's screenplay we see only Jones looking forlornly at Heyst's burning cottage (evoking the ending of the *Comfort* screenplay which similarly concludes with an image of a revivified enemy).

As in works such as *The Homecoming*, *The Birthday Party*, and even *Accident*, Pinter sets different masculinities in opposition to each other—one critic terms the novel an "open-ended exploration of 'masculinity'" (Hampson 1992, 237). Male types include the fortitudinous Heyst, the dandyish Jones, the animalistic Ricardo; male attributes feature stoic independence and ascetism in Heyst, misogyny in Jones, animalistic aggressiveness and energy in Ricardo and Pedro. By contrast, "It was the very essence of [Heyst's] life to be a solitary achievement"; detachment makes him "invulnerable because elusive" (Conrad 1924, 90). Heyst eventually discovers that his duty-bound, quasi-chivalric, stoic version of masculinity as invulnerability is inadequate.

Like Stanley's in *The Birthday Party*, Heyst's withdrawal from conflict is a conflict-ridden and impracticable choice; each fails to understand that, despite the distance they put between themselves and others, their "appearances in the world will, nevertheless, be interpreted by others" (Hampson 1992, 233). It is impossible to live without being drawn into community or society—yet to be observed at all is painful, the basis of oppression, just as it is (though in different forms) in *The Dumb Waiter*, *The Comfort of Strangers*, and *The Birthday Party*. Christopher C. Hudgins observes striking similarities between the characters in *Victory* and *The Birthday Party*, with Jones and Ricardo echoing Goldberg and McCann, and Heyst paralleling Stanley (1991, 23). Although Stanley is an artist and Heyst an intellectual, both evince sexual and emotional underdevelopment along with a wish to hide from the world, understood to be a vulgar place. Both have been ill served, it seems, by distant and judgmental fathers. Additional parallels link Conrad's characters to Pinter's. When Jones says he has come to pay Heyst a "visit"—"I am the world itself, come to pay you a visit" (Conrad 1924, 379)—the language evokes Meg's question to Stanley: "Did you pay a visit this morning?" (*BP*, 23) (this is Meg's euphemistic way of asking after his digestion). When Jones speaks of his attack upon Heyst as a "test," "a delicate mission" (Conrad 1924, 208), he echoes Goldberg's bland, bureaucratic characterization of his and McCann's task: "I can assure you that the assignment will be carried out and the mission accomplished with no excessive aggravation to you or myself" (*BP*, 30). Jones and Goldberg both seem to represent "the real world," which pulls in those who believe themselves above the fray of human struggles and compromises.

But "the real world" is inescapable—there is, as Stanley wisely tells Lulu, nowhere else to go (*BP*, 26). Disconnection from the world and one's obligations to it are illusory goals, as Pinter illustrates through the fate of Rose in *The Room*, his first play, in addition to *The Birthday Party*. The plot whereby attempts at personal isolation are frustrated runs through Pinter's works. In both *Victory* and *The Comfort of Strangers*, the protagonist's attempts to create a private world are defeated by insistent intrusions from the wider social world, what we might call, for lack of a better world, reality.[11] Jones clarifies that this world has no affection for those who try to withdraw from it: he is, as Conrad puts it, the "world itself come to pay you a visit . . . a sort of fate—the retribution that waits its time" (1924, 379).

Similarly, one's self is inescapable, for the self is constituted by the very forces that constitute the world. The social world replicates the familial, its patterns of power and dominance, an echoing of forms of power that also characterizes *The Comfort of Strangers* with its exploration of patriarchal power. Pinter's repeated use of the powerful father illustrates the deep, personal roots of societal power. The image of father as guarantor and embodiment of all law and right appears in *The Homecoming* and *Moonlight;* it looms off-stage in *The Birthday Party* (Stanley's father), *One for the Road* (Gila's father as well as the "father" of the unnamed country), and *Ashes to Ashes* (the older man whom Rebecca refers to); and its presence is felt powerfully in *The Comfort of Strangers* (Robert's father) and in *Victory*.

Not surprisingly given the prevalence of such fathers in Pinter's work, his screenplay emphasizes more than does Conrad's novel the psychic burden Heyst inherits from his father. Heyst's father was a "thinker, a stylist, and man of the world" (Conrad 1924, 91) who turned into a "bitter contemner of life" (175). In the novel Heyst blames his downfall on fate and on his initial connection with Morrison ("he who forms a tie is lost" [199–200]), whereas the screenplay's Heyst assigns pointed responsibility to the father's influence. Pointing to his father's portrait, Pinter's Heyst says, "He is responsible. The night he died I asked him for guidance. He said, 'Look on. Make no sound.' This is what I have done all my life" (*V*, 216). In the novel, by contrast, the character Davidson says, more vaguely, "His father seems to have been a crank, and to have upset his head when he was young" (Conrad 1924, 409). To emphasize this fatherly influence, the screenplay invents Jones quoting the aphorism of Heyst's father as Ricardo is kissing Lena: "Look on. Make no sound. Mud souls, obscene. Mud bodies. . . . Look at it" (V, 223).

If Pinter uses *Victory* to further explore a central motif of patriarchal authority, his portrayal of Lena's femininity augments his valuation of female agency and power. Indeed, Pinter seems once again to enjoy the sardonic joke that while males pretend to stoic detachment—the ability to operate on things, not in things, as Teddy phrases it in *The Homecoming* (Pinter 1965, 61), females achieve this self-control and capability far more efficiently. Pinter in general makes Lena as female power stronger than Conrad does (Hudgins 1991, 23). Lena's instinctualism is significantly more effective than Heyst's intellectualism. In Conrad's novel, the reader is always aware that Lena loves Heyst and is on his side: "She no longer wondered at that bitter riddle [of her existence], since her heart found its solution in a blinding, hot glow of passionate purpose" towards Heyst (1924, 367). This sense of love gives her the courage to protect Heyst. Pinter makes the final physical confrontation between Lena and the desirous Ricardo, in which she apparently accepts his advances in order to steal his knife, more extensive and sexually explicit than does Conrad (V, 223; Conrad 1924, 391). This scene, which initially tempts the viewer into perceiving Lena as acceding to Ricardo, develops to underscore her true purpose—she brandishes the knife. The screenplay also makes Heyst's initial response to Lena's action more accusatory than it is in the novel—he sarcastically asks her, "And it amused you . . . to charm him. Didn't it?" (V, 224; Conrad 1924, 404).[12] This reaction is a "damnable misperception" of Lena's bravery (Hudgins 1991, 29). Heyst's behavior here emphasizes the thematic contrast between the usefulness of Lena's instinctual emotions of love and self-preservation and the uselessness of Heyst's intellectual detachment. It is possible to see in this contrast a consonance with Pinter's political awareness, an awareness that is born out of passionate moral observation of the world and its horrors, rather than an intellectual commitment to a systematized ideology.

Pinter underscores that Heyst's prejudice that "he does not want to dirty his hands with life" is morally false (Hudgins 1991, 28) and pretentious. His habits of detachment and coldness, his preference for inactivity and contemplation, are represented as leading to an evasion of necessary duties. The screenplay condemns Heyst for his passivity and fastidious detachment, his disdain for action, more harshly than does the novel. It is interesting to note that Pinter, already moving into his explicitly political period, treats this aspect of Heyst more coldly than does Conrad, as if Pinter has even less patience than Conrad for this habit of privacy, isolation, and disconnection.[13] However, while Pinter pessimistically treats Heyst's capability to act and suggests that Lena's love for him is less clearly redemptive than in Conrad (Hudgins 1991, 23), Pinter nevertheless accords with the novel in presenting Heyst's suicide as morally worthy. Heyst is never able to utter a "cry of love" (Conrad 1924, 406) to Lena as she is to him—but nevertheless Heyst is at least allowed to know what it is to be loved, to perceive what his false ideas about life led him to miss. The screenplay emphasizes the one action Heyst undertakes—suicide—by moving directly from the acknowledgment of Lena's love to the setting of the fire (Hudgins 1991, 28), which then seems a fulfillment of Lena's ethic of love as sacrifice as well as a symbol of redemption.

In addition to themes of gender, love, and identity, Conrad also offers an irony about how the world is run that seems to accord with Pinter's view of a power elite that oppresses intellectuals, writers, and those who think differently. In Pinter's world, psychological interiority is a matter for disdain and alarm; just as Lenny mocks Teddy in *The Homecoming* for being a remote intellectual, "a bit inner" (64), Ricardo is enraged by Heyst's depth and by his "doing a think" (Conrad 1924, 269, 262).[14] In *The Dreaming Child*, Pinter invents a scene in which townschildren accuse the title character of being too contemplative; he replies, "I don't think I'm thinking"—ironically revealing the truth of what he is denying (Pinter 2000b, 452). Conrad writes of Heyst and his father: "It is not the clear-sighted who rule the world. Great achievements are accomplished in a blessed, warm mental fog, which the pitiless cold blasts of the father's analysis had blown away from the son" (1924, 174). This line supports Pinter's view of an unreflective, anti-intellectual elite ruling the world, free of the incapacitating doubt that burdens the psyches of the contemplative. It is the unthinking who get things done, who undertake action (Dusty's words in *Party Time* seem to echo the converse of this statement—those who do think never do anything because they never stop thinking: "I don't know what to believe" she says [*PT*, 7]). This emphasis accords with Conrad's "Author's Note": "Thinking is the great enemy of perfection. The habit of profound reflection . . . is the most pernicious of all the habits formed by the civilised man" (1924, xi). (A central character in Conrad's *Nostromo* is described thus: "If Gould thought too deeply about his policies, he could not have put them into action." It may not be too much of a stretch here to invoke Adolf Eichmann as described by Arendt's theory of the banality of evil, its unthinkingness— Eichmann performed evil precisely because he was not able to think deeply about his actions.) Just as when Nicolas gloats over the defeated dissident Victor, here again a kind of intellectualism is snuffed out, as it were, by forces of unsubtle (though far from uncivilized) savagery.

Victory is the story of the external and internal pressures put on Axel Heyst to overcome the intellectual habit of "detachment" founded on his father's commands to "Look on—make no sound." Heyst must move from a private world of meaning to reconcile himself to the demands of the outer world and its definitions of meaning. Pinter's reawakened interest in Heyst in the early 1980s might be read in autobiographical terms. If Pinter in the early phases of his career appeared to be skeptical about the traditional authorial function of supplying referential meaning, if he seemed singularly "elusive" and "invulnerable" in this regard, his later work as writer and activist embraces the necessity of confronting and entering into the world as it is— with its aspects of contingency and compromise. Reality is so pressing it must be confronted directly.[15] In this way, the screenplay analogously resembles the story of Pinter himself, who chose to enter a more overt engagement with the world and his responsibilities to it. He has allowed himself, to use Conrad's language about Heyst, to be "tempted into action" (1924, 54). This parallel tempers the distinctive pessimism of Pinter's political theater with the possibility of tragic triumph. Conrad's complex ideas of human nature include the possibility of moral greatness (Philips 1995, 130), and Pinter at this point in his career, a year before his self-identification as a political artist, seems to subscribe in *Victory* to a modernist vision of the human heroic possibility that our postmodern era in general discounts. Also, the language of morality remains at least potentially redemptive in *Victory*, although in Pinter's works that directly followed it, morality is almost always used only by oppressors to disguise and falsify their victimization of others. Heyst's decision to act, finally, on his sympathetic instincts ironically leads to his death but also, in a tragic paradox, to a

new awareness of love and life. If he had not left human connections until too late, perhaps he would not have been destroyed.
It almost seems as if Pinter's nearly constant political activities
as writer and citizen are motivated by a similar feeling of belatedness—an impulse not to leave engagement with the world
until too late.

6

Pinter and the Politics of Fascism: *Reunion, Taking Sides,* and *The Trojan War Will Not Take Place*

Pinter lived through World War II in London and its environs. He has testified to the fact that he was, by the close of the war, cognizant of the Nazi assault on the Jews and struck by its singularity: "I was a boy in the war, and near the end of the war, I did learn what had happened, what was happening to the Jews in Europe. So that left a *very, very* considerable impact on me" (Pinter 2002a, 32). "I was about fifteen when the war ended; I could listen and hear and add two and two, so these images of horror and man's inhumanity to man were very strong in my mind as a young man" he noted in 1996 (*VV*, 64). Though widespread historical consciousness of what came to be called the Holocaust did not arise until a number of years after the events, Pinter notes that he was never unaware of the genocide. After the war, he witnessed renewed fascist activity in Britain and had occasional run-ins with anti-Semites in London's East End. In numerous interviews he makes clear how he sees Nazism in universal fashion, in terms of good and evil and in terms of fascist politics in general: anyone can be a fascist, including Jews. Consider, for instance, Goldberg, the terroristic Jew in *The Birthday Party*, or Pinter's directing of Robert Shaw's *The Man in the Glass Booth*, in which a Jew poses as a Nazi (British premiere 1967, American 1968). Elements of Nazism's war on the Jews and of the European response to that war —the definition of social otherness as a crime, the evasions of responsibility and knowledge, the supposedly exculpatory defense of "following orders"—typify the social order as such, which rests on violence or its threat and on ignoring or whitewashing human suffering.

Pinter's investigation of fascism, and its implications for contemporary society and morality, has taken several forms. The vexed question of how the past may be properly remembered links these works. In his screenplay for *Reunion*, the short novel by Fred Uhlman, Pinter depicts Germany during the rise of Nazism and in the present: how, he asks, did fascism take root, and how are its crimes remembered, or forgotten? As director of Jean Giraudoux's *The Trojan War Will Not Take Place* (1935), he considers whether any moral distinction can be made between warring countries (Pinter directed the play in 1983). And in directing the premiere of *Taking Sides*, a 1995 play by his friend Ronald Harwood, Pinter examines the relationship between fascism and culture, asking whether and how fascism in the past can be remembered and judged in the present.

REUNION: HISTORY, REMEMBRANCE, AND TRAUMA

The Holocaust has figured paradoxically in Harold Pinter's work—obliquely yet centrally. Pinter's artistic involvement with the Holocaust includes a number of works. In addition to his 1995 direction of Ronald Harwood's *Taking Sides*, about the "denazification" of conductor Lionel Furtwängler, to be discussed later in this chapter, in 1968 he directed *The Man in the Glass Booth*, Robert Shaw's play inspired by the trial of Adolf Eichmann. Pinter adapted Elizabeth Bowen's World War II novel *The Heat of the Day* for the screen. He acted alongside Peter O'Toole in the film *Rogue Male*, about an assassination plot against Hitler. In other works, the genocide can be seen in the background, an indirect yet inescapable reference. *The Birthday Party* puts its audience in the position of those who tolerate Nazi terror, according to Ronald Knowles (1995a, 38). Diverse references in that play reveal an historical connection to the mechanics of that terror, as I argued in a previous chapter. Rosette C. Lamont interprets *The Hothouse* as a parable of the Holocaust (1993, 71), and D. Keith Peacock connects *The Dumb Waiter* to the Nuremberg War Crime trials (1997). The threat of arbitrary punishment and unspecified guilt link *The Birthday Party* to later plays such as *Mountain Language*.

Harold Pinter is not, however, a "Holocaust author" in Alvin Rosenfeld's sense of one whose work centers on Hitler's genocide (1980, 7), nor does he identify himself as a writer whose work focuses on Jewishness: his own Jewishness, he has said, amounts to an identification with "Jewish suffering" in history (Knowles 1995a, 169). About the legacy of the Holocaust, Pinter has remarked, "The distinction between then and now is that then, in 1957, the concentration camps were still an open wound which it was impossible to ignore, whereas now it's only too easy to ignore the horror of what's going on around us. There's too much of it" (1986b, 9). Humankind forgets the painful facts of its violent history, even (or especially) when the present begins to resemble the horrifying past. The postwar era, Pinter further implies, is even more horrible than the Holocaust itself—worse in that the horror is easier to ignore, or in that the lessons of the Holocaust, despite their airing in both high culture (Washington, D.C.'s Holocaust Museum) and popular (Spielberg's *Schindler's List*) have been unlearned. Pinter's view here diverges from historiography that argues for the historical uniqueness of the Holocaust, instead interpreting the Nazi era in generalizing, universalist fashion. Elements of the Nazi genocide and the ways in which it was abided by other European countries —the definition of social otherness as a crime, the evasions of responsibility and knowledge, the widely proffered rationalizations that oppressors were simply "following orders"—are central features of how all societies operate. The impulse to exclude unwanted others is abetted by an inability to recognize and to remember—to properly witness—cruelty, oppression, and violence.

The screenplay adaptation of Fred Uhlman's 1977 novella *Reunion* is the most historically direct of Pinter's works bearing on the Holocaust. Born in Stuttgart, Germany, like his narrator in *Reunion*, Uhlman became a lawyer, opposed the Nazis, and immigrated to England in 1933, where he became a painter, an art collector, and a writer. In his introduction to the English edition, Arthur Koestler calls this novella a "minor masterpiece" (1977, 7), while George Steiner wrote about it in *The New Yorker* respectfully, but not so approvingly as Koestler.

The novella, set in Germany in 1932, is recounted decades later (Pinter extends the interval from some thirty years to fifty-five years; the present in the screenplay is 1987—also the year he began its writing). An American lawyer, Henry, struggles with the German heritage he has "tried to forget" (Uhlman 1971, 107), with the memory of himself as Hans Schwartz and his friendship with a gentile schoolmate, Count Konradin von Hohenfels. The friends share coin collections, discuss German poetry, bicycle through the countryside. But then anti-Semitism endangers and finally ends the friendship. At the opera with his parents, Konradin snubs Hans. Konradin explains that his mother is "afraid of [Jews] though she has never met one" (86–87). Hans's parents send their son to America and commit suicide by gassing themselves. Konradin embraces Hitler as Germany's best hope, though he believes that "within a year or two" desirable Jews will be accepted back into Germany (103). Now, in the novella's present, Hans/Henry receives a letter from his old school asking for a donation to a war memorial, and he discovers—in the final words of the book—that Konradin was executed for plotting Hitler's assassination.

Pinter said in an interview about the film "I did more research on this script than I have ever done in my life" (Pinter 1989b, 21). As revealed in the Pinter Archives, Pinter consulted William Shirer's *The Rise and the Fall of the Third Reich* for historical details of Nazi electoral campaigns and propaganda techniques, the historian Saul Friedlander on issues of remembrance and attempted Jewish assimilation, and Bernt Engelmann's *In Hitler's Germany: Everyday Life in the Third Reich* to learn how the Nazi period felt to those who lived through it. Pinter aimed for historical accuracy and specificity. His use of Shirer produces, for one example, a borrowing of the historian's language to describe the Nazi election triumph of July 31, 1932 ("a resounding victory": Shirer 1960, 166; *R*, 82).[1] During the drafting process, Pinter contemplated using Hitler's speeches in voice-over and inserting newsreel and documentary footage of the July 20, 1944, assassination plot trials to portray the specific reality of the Nazis, a goal also carried out through descriptions of Nazi rallies and violence that were, ultimately, written into the screenplay (86).

It is not only in terms of Germany's Nazi past that the screenplay examines German history and society. Pinter made one major structural change to Uhlman's novella, bringing Henry back to contemporary Germany to confront his past and learn about his friend's fate. With this double time frame, Pinter can address the question of the Nazi legacy in Germany, comparing fascist horrors and the postwar legacy. By adding considerable historical detail and by pointedly juxtaposing the Nazi and postwar periods, Pinter engages controversial and sensitive issues surrounding Germany and the Holocaust. His screenplay becomes an investigation of contemporary Germany—its sense of responsibility or lack of responsibility, the moral necessity of remembering and the social process of forgetting:

> What is left of the Nazi past is tangible in some respects, shadowy in others, possible in yet other respects, or simply nonexistent

among some of the young. But on the whole, I don't think they have really managed to overthrow the past. Because let's face it, it's probably the *strongest* imaginable in the impact on the consciousness of the people. No wonder it can't be erased too easily. (Pinter 1989b, 21)

Four historical issues concern Pinter and Uhlman's use of the past in their versions of *Reunion*. First, Pinter's research into Nazi Germany yielded information about the Nazi judge Roland Freisler that Pinter found meaningful enough to include in his screenplay. Second, the thematic use both Uhlman and Pinter make of the Resistance conflicts with some historical estimates of its moral worth and legacy, aligning the screenplay with a view of the Resistance that others see as partial, elitist, and romanticized. In the process of drafting and revising the screenplay, Pinter invented plot elements and motifs for Uhlman's novella in order to illustrate important historical analyses of how the Nazis were able to convert a civilized nation to their doctrines. He uses his characters to illustrate the notion that the Nazis succeeded in converting their nation into an instrument of evil by secularizing theological into political needs and by manipulating language. Last, though the screenplay's positive depiction of the anti-Hitler conspiracy signifies how Germany can and has transcended its past, Pinter's script also suggests that Germany's taint of evil persists into the present. The contemporary Germany pictured in Pinter's *Reunion* has little or no interest in honestly acknowledging its Nazi past. The strength of Pinter's commitment to the notion of an unrepentant Germany emerges especially clearly from an inspection of the various screenplay drafts he produced from September 1987 to February 1988.

Upon Henry's arrival in Stuttgart, he comes across a TV documentary in which a German announcer compares Laurence Olivier acting Henry V to a figure the script names as Judge Freisler. Here we see one significant example of Pinter dramatizing his historical research, as Roland Freisler—not mentioned in Uhlman's book—was the judge in charge of trying the circle of conspirators who plotted Hitler's death. The attempt was led by Lt. Col. Claus von Stauffenberg and is known by its date, July 20, 1944. Crucially, however, Pinter introduces this specific information about Freisler and the assassination trial within the context of its remembrance and use by present-day Germany, a context that may be tainted by present German needs for easy self-absolution. Here is the scene:

PRESENTER: *(Voice over)* Henry the Fifth actually feels very uncertain indeed about the battle ahead but is able to hide this uncertainty by putting on a mask—by acting! Now here is a quite different case. Or is it?
> Suddenly the voice of *JUDGE FREISLER* screaming. HENRY stops unpacking and, suddenly riveted, stares into the mirror. He goes into the other room.

. . .

PRESENTER: *(Voice over)* Now that man—is he an actor? Is he acting? Is he simply playing the part of a cruel and sadistic judge? Or is he real? Is he the real thing?
> HENRY switches the television set off abruptly. (R, 59)[2]

Freisler was a high-ranking jurist instrumental in the Nazi perversion of the German justice system. Along with many other German jurists, he was responsible for the breakdown in German legal ethics in the early Nazi era, instituting the principle of *Gesinnungsstrafrecht*, according to which criminals were punished not for individual deeds but for their essential personality as degenerate or anti-*Volk*. He helped redesign German courts so that "German judges in reaching their decisions should always put themselves in the shoes of the fuehrer" (Davidson 1997, 319). Presiding over the White Rose trial and the Stauffenberg trials as head of the so-called "People's Court" (*Volksgerichtshof*), his savage interrogations and rabid manner earned him the sobriquet "Raving Roland." Freisler ordered the pants braces of defendant Erwin von Witzleben removed and then berated him for holding up his trousers, a detail Pinter alludes to twice in his screenplay (R, 55, 96). Even amid general approval of the trials, some, according to Eugene Davidson, "said that Roland Freisler . . . behaved in a way unbecoming to the highest court in Germany" (1997, 326); Martin Bormann, Hitler's secretary, noted how distasteful were Freisler's antics. The "guilty" were strung up, according to Hitler's instructions, on chicken wire suspended from butcher's hooks.[3] Pinter ends his screenplay with this image, which evidently stayed with him, as he reuses it in *Moonlight*. Jake and Fred discuss their father: "He knew his beer and possessed the classic formula for dealing with troublemakers." "What was that?" "A butcher's hook" (M, 62).

As Pinter's TV announcer notes, the judge acts almost too stereotypically like a fanatic. The implication of the announcer is that Freisler is somehow not genuine, not what he seems to be. Is he "faking it," acting under compulsion, merely following orders, according to the famous postwar German defense? This seems an unlikely, or intellectually dishonest, defense of a figure Shirer calls "the most sinister and bloodthirsty Nazi in the Third Reich after [Reinhard] Heydrich" (1960, 1023), whom the Nuremberg Trials ranked with the most heinous of Nazi criminals and who declared at the July 20 trials: "Only in one respect does National Socialism resemble Christianity: we demand the whole man" (Rothfels 1962, 113–14). Ultimately, the either/or choice presented by the announcer about Freisler's "realness" or authenticity is a spurious (and offensive) question, amounting to a distinction without a difference. While it may matter in terms of history, it certainly does not matter from the viewpoint of its victims whether Freisler's sadism is a matter of pretense or not, whether he is an actor or the real thing. Pinter frames the announcer's idea as meretricious, an effort to render uncertain something that should not be ambiguous. The intellect here produces a rationalization that covers over a memory of extreme violence and oppression. The announcer's argument that even a person so full of apparent conviction as Freisler may have been only acting or pretending is superficially coherent but morally repugnant. Perhaps Henry's clicking off the program suggests irritation at this bogus line of inquiry as well as his desire not to engage with the past.

Henry's visit to Germany (as well as Pinter's initial work on the script, both in 1987) follows upon a contemporary controversy having to do with the interpretation of the Nazi past, the "historians' conflict" which began in 1986 and continued into 1987. In this conflict, Ernst Nolte, a conservative West German historian, attempted to revise understanding of the Holocaust as a "unique event" by comparing it to other twentieth-century atrocities, notably the murderous excesses of Communist rule. Nolte also argued, on thin evidence, that Hitler might have conceived his "Final Solution" as a response to a perceived threat of annihilation by the Russians, thus crediting the genocide with a preemptive logic and justification. Jürgen Habermas, among others, sharply criticized the way in which this brand of historical explanation so easily shaded off into the excusal of atrocity. Habermas argued that Nolte's position was, in fact, designed to exempt present-day Germany from any obligation to remember its horrific past.[4] The controversy revealed a German desire to announce that enough time had elapsed to allow the country to "erase" the memory of its Nazi past.

Pinter's *Reunion* clearly counters this exculpatory wish, just as it clearly intends a historically informed record. The film is at odds with itself, however, when, following the novel, it qualifies German anti-Semitism by romanticizing the resistance to Hitler. The surprise ending of both the novel and the film, revealing Konradin to have been one of the conspirators in the July 20, 1944, assassination plot, has the effect of mitigating German guilt for Hitler's atrocities. The question could be asked: why do Jews in the Germany of the Holocaust seem to have more and nobler defenders in novels and films than they had in real life?[5]

Certainly in *Reunion* Pinter commits himself to accurate representation. In fairness, it should be stressed when judging Pinter's use of history that historians present divergent views (and that their views change). After the work of Primo Levi, anyone must be cautious about recognizing the existence of a "gray zone" of actions that resist simple moral classification; moreover, as Pinter himself goes on to explore in *Taking Sides*, forming moral judgments after the fact can be problematic, as it may merely be vanity to apply current ethics to prior conduct. Additionally, it should never be forgotten that to resist in such conditions as Nazi totalitarianism requires a crazy, desperate, unusual courage. Still, it is probably fair that the best history on this issue would deem Pinter's and Uhlman's use of the Resistance to be less than impartial. In this light, novels and films, including *Reunion*, could be said to absolve Germany at the expense of historical fact.[6]

There is a salient historical irony about the Resistance that is painful but necessary to recount in any consideration of it, even if this irony cannot be fairly used to indict those who gave their life to destroy Hitler's regime. Nearly five million Germans were killed from mid-1944 to the end of the war, a period that was arguably shortened by the Resistance's actions. But by mid-1944, five million of the approximately six million killed by the Nazis had already perished. The Resistance may have saved many Germans from the terrible effects of war, but it did not alter the fate of the preponderance of Jews in the Holocaust.

Organized German resistance to Hitler—the resistance of Stauffenberg and the fictional Konradin—was, in historical fact, generally scattered, uncoordinated, and ineffective. Historians define several groups: first, the largest and most organized, was what became known as the 20 July group, with Stauffenberg as leader, and most of its members middle- or high-ranking military officers, often of Prussian ancestry. Due to its access to power, this was the effort with the most potential to eliminate

Hitler. Other resistance groups were the Kreisau circle and a socially conservative group centered on Carl Goerdeler, former mayor of Leipzig and Ludwig Beck, a former army chief of staff. The Kreisau circle was headed by Count Helmuth von Moltke and animated by its members' Christian socialism. Both within the 20 July group and between it and the Kreisau and the Goerdeler-Beck circles, disagreements reigned over practical matters, the shape of a post-Nazi society, and especially the moral questions of whether it was right to take Hitler's life. Such action represented treason to one's country, and the conspirators spent much time pondering whether the loyalty oaths they had sworn to Hitler, the regime, and Germany bound them to eternal fidelity. (These last debates, which took place at great length, are especially frustrating for non-Germans to read.)

The July 20, 1944, assassination plot carried out by Stauffenberg and his cohorts is often featured in such arguments about how Germany has transcended and can transcend its Nazi past, in order to be viewed simply as one country among others, rather than always being seen in connection to the Nazi era.[7] In 1995, Daniel Goldhagen's *Hitler's Willing Executioners: Ordinary Germans and the Holocaust* reactivated debates about how widespread was German knowledge of and complicity in Nazi atrocities. This powerful book, which Pinter discusses admiringly (*VV*, 65), documents many instances of German joy at oppression of the Jews. Goldhagen argues that "millions of Germans" knew about the mass slaughter of Jews (1995, 111) and that perfectly ordinary, unideologized, non-Nazi Germans took willing parts in this slaughter. The sometimes virulent attacks upon the book often adduced German opposition to Hitler, most prominently the Stauffenberg plot, as sufficient disproof of Goldhagen's thesis of generalized German guilt. In *Reunion*, the surprise ending that reveals Konradin to have been a conspirator, as Ronald Knowles writes, tends to qualify and lessen German guilt for Hitler: "A somber and pitiful sense of waste prevails, but there is a degree of mitigation in Konradin's act. His sacrifice not only atones for the betrayal of friendship but also symbolically atones for the larger self-betrayal of Germany" (1995a, 171). The audience is invited by the example of Konradin's self-sacrifice to have faith in human possibility even in light of the moral perversion represented by the Holocaust.

The issue of the Resistance to Hitler, like others surrounding the era, remains psychologically charged and historically controversial. Many historians have suggested that the German Resistance that culminated in the July 20 attempt on Hitler's life is not deserving of an heroic reputation and does not prove the existence of widespread, or even significant, internal opposition to Hitler's anti-Semitic goals. In *Eichmann in Jerusalem*, Hannah Arendt, a writer Pinter has read and appreciated, writes that the Resistance was impelled not by morality or conscience but primarily by nationalistic pride: "No doubt these men who opposed Hitler, however belatedly, paid with their lives. . . . [Their] courage . . . was not inspired by moral indignation or by what they knew other people had been made to suffer; they were motivated almost exclusively by their conviction of the coming defeat and ruin of Germany" (1977, 100). "What had sparked their opposition had not been the Jewish question but the fact that Hitler was preparing war, and the endless conflicts and crises of conscience under which they labored hinged almost exclusively on the problem of . . . the violation of their loyalty oath to Hitler" (98). She maintains that these conspirators were distinct from the few opponents of Nazism who truly apprehended the vast moral disaster around them (99).

The July 20 conspirators have been interpreted historically in widely varying ways. Hans Rothfels, author of *The German Opposition to Hitler* (1962), sees the resistors as thorough moral exemplars, avatars of West German values of democracy and freedom, while Arendt's interpretation typifies those who deny moral validity to the July 20 conspirators. In a recent and outwardly impartial book, *On the Road to the Wolf's Lair: German Resistance to Hitler*, Theodore S. Hamerow suggests that a need to idealize Stauffenberg and the military resistance makes sober historical judgment of their actions difficult (1997, 372). Hamerow, a respected historian of generally conservative political bent, attempts to present the Resistance as heroically motivated, yet his thoroughness leads him to echo Arendt on many points. He describes how some of the anti-Hitler plotters came to repent their roles in the conspiracy (374). Both Hamerow and Davidson point out that many conspirators were led into opposition by their distaste at what the Nazis became in practice, not the original beliefs of National Socialism (Hamerow 1997, 377), and one conspirator said afterward, "I still approve of National Socialism as we understood it and as it was taught to us during the years of struggle for power" (Davidson 1997, 327). Hamerow does note that several of the conspirators were shocked by how the German regime treated Jews and minorities in the conquered territories and how the army waged war in Russia (1997, 315).

However, he finally nears concurrence with Goldhagen, Arendt, and Steiner that the conspirators mostly turned against Hitler "owing to disagreement over policy or method rather than proclaimed principle" (14) and primarily out of the desire to "protect the fatherland against the consequences of military defeat" (319).[8]

Yet Hamerow does not end where Arendt and Steiner do, with condemnation of the conspirators. He concludes his book:

> Their motives may have been mixed, parochial and universal, expedient and selfless, patriotic and humanitarian, mean and noble. But in the end they risked and lost their lives fighting a brutal and tyrannical political system. Is that not enough? Posterity has perhaps no more right to demand more from those it decides to anoint as its martyrs and heroes. (1997, 405)

The ambivalent, contested, still indeterminate nature of the Resistance's legacy is captured by the "perhaps" in Hamerow's concluding sentence above.[9]

In the screenplay as ultimately filmed and published, Pinter privileges Konradin's gesture of martyrdom through placement—by ending his screenplay with the news of Konradin's fate, just as Uhlman does in his book. Thus Pinter seems to agree with Uhlman that within the Nazi era, courageous and moral dissent occurred on a scale sufficient to represent some sort of counterbalance to the disaster of the Holocaust. As late as the fourth draft of the screenplay, however, Pinter wrote an alternate ending, never filmed, that contextualizes the surprise of Konradin's unexpected anti-Nazism and lessens its exculpatory force. In this ending, Henry is on his flight away from Germany, drinking and contemplating the coin he recovered from his family's possessions (this scene exists in two slightly different forms, scene 117 in the typed fourth draft, and a handwritten version also found in PA, Box 50; see Gale and Hudgins 1996, 133). The film's last images show Henry first considering the Corinthian coin Konradin and Hans once shared, and then "look[ing] at Germany disappear below." By bringing us back to the present, this version of the screenplay would have begun to problematize the film's view of Konradin's actions by forcing us to contemplate not just what Konradin did but what his country as a whole did (and did not do) both during and after the Nazi era. The materials in the Archives did not reveal why this ending was excluded from the film. It is possible to see the filmed ending, with its revelation of Konradin's resistance, as being "stronger" in the sense that it offers a sharp surprise to viewers, and a more positive one, as opposed to the muted conclusion in which Henry reflects upon his (broken) friendship with Konradin.

The contemplation of Germany and German conduct as a whole, suggested in the image of the country "disappearing" below Henry as that film ending had it, is a prime concern of the screenplay. Pinter wishes to analyze both contemporary Germany and the perennial question of how Weimar Germany fell under Nazi rule. As Pinter conceives, drafts, and revises it, his screenplay presents with ever-greater clarity themes that are echoed in historical, political, and sociological explanations of how the German nation could have allowed the Nazi rise to power. How, it is repeatedly asked, could an apparently civilized society succumb to such irrationality? Two such interpolations, in central scenes between Hans and Konradin, exemplify prominent theories used to answer these perplexing questions.

In *Reunion*, Pinter reminds us that the choice for Nazism in Germany was not a choice between obeying a fascist government versus facing death. The choices and rationale for the behavior of Germans in 1932 are of a different sort. The choice to embrace Nazi anti-Semitism is less constrained than many people find it customary to believe. "Even the most educated Germans," writes Robert Gellately, "found reasons for supporting the system, and were less regimented, cajoled, or forced than we often assume" (2002, 257). The clichéd excuse of "just following orders," in addition to being morally odious, fits the facts far less than its frequent invocation would suggest. It is this idea about German choice that Goldhagen pursues in such horrifying detail in *Hitler's Willing Executioners*. Both Pinter and Uhlman show how the Nazi program gained credence and followers by offering a vision of a rejuvenated, purified, and remoralized Germany, and how cultural theories of Aryan superiority attracted an audience eager to believe in its own, supposedly historically predestined, eminence. Pinter challenges us to disentangle his screenplay's material from the usual ways we have of interpreting Nazi Germany. He makes us attend to the birth of atrocity out of innocence.

Pinter diverges from Uhlman's source material to illustrate an idea about the kinds of people who are attracted to the Nazi ideology and to fascist movements in general. He ends a colloquy about belief in God between the two boys in a way that foreshadows Konradin's conversion to Hitlerism, an allegiance that is founded upon Konradin's need for transcendent authority. Hans denies a benevolent God, while Konradin asserts that moral goodness does exist:

KONRADIN: But there is good . . . in the world . . .
HANS: I know. But somehow . . .
KONRADIN: What?
HANS: There's no one in charge. There's no one in control. Is there?
Pause.
KONRADIN: There must be. (R, 80)

This dialogue is one of the few allusions to religious experience in Pinter's works. Its thrust bears out a supposition that in religious terms Pinter might be seen as a Sartrean atheistic existentialist (King 2001, 251). Orthodox religious belief seems a crutch for those who cannot deal with the complexities of interpreting the world and facing up to their ethical responsibilities in it. Faced with contradiction and flux, the immature thinker leans on definitive answers that preclude debate and thoughtful analysis. Truth, that "thing of indefinite approximation," is guaranteed by a divine presence (Sartre 1995, 19).[10] That is, Konradin's final line admits of two meanings, one metaphysical and the other reductively prosaic. The concept of who, exactly, is in control of this universe means two different things in this conversation. The first meaning is a benevolent, caretaker God (Hans's idea), while the second (which Konradin hints at) has to do with a secular leader conceived of as divine: with transcendent authority, deserving of absolute trust. Konradin uses the concept of God to anchor a sense that the world is controllable. Unsurprisingly, Konradin views this God not merely as guaranteeing the stability of the world but also as supporting Konradin's own partisan, real-world ambitions.

Such a conflation of the spiritual with the secular underlined Nazi success, as Alvin H. Rosenfeld writes: "That National Socialism theologized politics and secularized theology in order to politicize it cannot be overstressed" (1980, 133). Pinter connects and contrasts religious yearnings with a secular desire for order and implies that Konradin's religious doubt, as far as it goes, becomes a need satisfied by Hitler's political promise of a rejuvenated Germany. Those who see their leaders as divine—the sociological term is "numenification"—lack self-esteem, a stable identity, and the "assurance that . . . the world is a predictable place" (Bailey 1988, 95). The problem of obedience to tyranny involves a craving for order and a defense against a threatening vision of a disordered, chaotic, decentered world—one without a guarantee or guarantor of meaning.[11] Those who perceive such a vision as personally endangering, those who cannot cope with doubt, are liable to participate in authoritarian abuses of power. The anxieties of internal doubt about inherited belief structures drive the need for unthinking group identity, an adherence that tends to play out through oppressing those defined as outside this group.

Pinter makes a similar point about individual moral responsibility as Uhlman, a theme visible when Hans and Konradin discuss their embattled friendship:

KONRADIN: Anyway, he [Konradin's father] thinks the Jewish problem is bound to be resolved, sooner or later. He thinks it'll resolve itself.
HANS: How?
KONRADIN: I don't know.
HANS: But what is the Jewish problem exactly?
    They stare at each other.
KONRADIN: Oh, don't look at me like that! Am I to blame for all this? Am I responsible for my parents? Am I to blame for the world? Why don't you grow up and face the facts? Face reality.
    Pause.
Look. I should have told you all this before but I'm a coward. I couldn't bear to hurt you. Try to understand.
HANS: *(Slowly)* Yes. You're right. We have to face reality. (R, 85)

Konradin intends "Am I to blame for the world?" as a rhetorical question with only a negative answer possible. From our perspective, we perceive the true answer as "Yes," as Pinter proclaims we must take moral responsibility for what happens around us. This theme of moral responsibility, which Pinter goes on to explore in *Ashes to Ashes*, is political as well as ethical. Pinter's distaste for the idea that one must grow up and accept reality—that is, stop trying to change it for the better—is strong. One is reminded of the terrible cliché that a conservative is a liberal who has, similarly, "grown up."

To this scene, Pinter adds an idea not found in Uhlman. Hans pointedly denies that there is such a thing as a "Jewish problem." Berel Lang connects the derivation of the term "*Endlosung*," or "Final Solution," with the phrase the "Jewish question" or "Jewish problem," which were not inventions of Nazi ideology or of anti-Semitic rhetoric: "The 'Jewish Question' . . . was in fact a conventional locution, used by non-Jew-ish—and anti-Jewish—writers, but also by Jewish and philo-Jewish writers" (1990, 86). Lang notes that designating some-thing a problem is a political act leading inevitably to action: "[P]hrases such as 'The Jewish Question' or 'The Jewish Prob-lem,' even in formulations well disposed toward the 'question,' anticipate responses in the form of 'solutions'" (87). Addition-ally, since the more thorough a solution is, the better, an inter-nal logic leads to a preference for a *final* solution over a mere solution: "Given the reasonable corollary, moreover, that if a problem is to be solved, it is best solved once and for all, an *End-losung* is desirable in a way that provisional or incomplete solu-tions are not" (87). Language use, as Hans in his own way tries to point out, has not only the capacity to describe reality but the power to alter it, perhaps in horrifying ways.

Contemporary accounts of discussions of the "Jewish Ques-tion" show that, in historical fact, this ostensibly intellectual matter was socially used as prelude to and instrument of anti-Semitic attitudes. Sebastian Haffner, who lived through the early days of Nazification, writes of how Germans and Nazis in-terpreted the very existence of a so-called "Jewish Question" to further separate Jews from mainstream German life. He de-scribes how public reactions to *Kristallnacht* debated not the abuse of Nazi power, but rather the provocative presence of Jews in Germany:

Apart from the terror, the unsettling and depressing aspect of this first murderous declaration of intent was that it triggered a flood of arguments and discussions all over Germany, not about anti-Semi-tism but about the "Jewish question." This is a trick the Nazis have since successfully repeated many times on other "questions" and in international affairs. By publicly threatening a person, an ethnic group, a nation, or a region with death and destruction, they provoke a general discussion not about their own [that is, the Nazis'] exis-tence, but about the right of their victims to exist. In this way that right is put in question.

Suddenly everyone felt justified, and indeed required, to have an opinion about the Jews, and to state it publicly. Distinctions were made between "decent" Jews and the others. If some pointed to the achievements of Jewish scientists, artists, and doctors to justify the Jews (justify? what for? against what?), others would counter that they were a detrimental "foreign influence" in these spheres. (2000, 142)

This recollection is another reminder of how simple it is to blame the victims of oppression for their suffering—and how rational-sounding ideas become a façade for deadly prejudice and hatred. The use of language complements and aids physical oppression.

Pinter's screenplay extends German guilt from the war and prewar era into contemporary times. As he told Ciment, Pinter is curious about the legacy of the Holocaust in terms of the memory of everyday Germans. In the latter third of the screenplay, Pinter interpolates a number of scenes in which Henry meets ordinary Germans (R, 92–93). These ordinary Germans are forbidding and strange, apparently concealing complicitous memory. For example, Pinter reanimates the character of Gertrud, the Graefin von Zeilarn und Lizen, Konradin's cousin who adored the Hitler Youth—Henry visits her in contemporary Germany. When Henry encounters Gertrud, she feigns ignorance of Konradin and his fate, and icily refuses to discuss the subject with Henry. In a key line in the scene, she characterizes her experience of the Nazi era as "wonderful" (R, 94). Here Pinter drew from a story recollected in Engelmann's *In Hitler's Germany*. Decades after the war Engelmann visits Marga, a childhood friend. Her memories of the Nazi era concern only the pleasures of her own life. The one thing that stuck in her memory about *Kristallnacht* was that her engagement dinner was held on that night—and she was forced to wear delicate formal shoes on the glass-littered streets. The texture of ordinary life makes it easy to forget or not to see the atrocities surrounding us. She bids goodbye to Engelmann: "I really enjoyed talking about old times. There are so many things one forgets, and then suddenly it all comes back . . . All in all, we had a wonderful, carefree youth, didn't we?" (Engelmann 1986, 34).[12] This last sentence is quoted in Pinter's reading notes (PA, Box 49), and it appears in the screenplay when the Graefin contentedly labels her youth "Wonderful years" (R, 94).

In the draft marked "corrected September 1, 1987" (PA, Box 49; Gale and Hudgins 1996, 130), Henry's encounter with Gertrud is granted more importance than in the filmed version. The scene is split up, so it appears directly before the story of the two boys, then reappears near the end of the draft. The next-to-last scene in this script contains shots of Hans's parents committing suicide, and the final scene is Gertrud dismissing Henry curtly, ending with a shot of Henry looking after her. Such an ending would have certainly allowed an amount of skepticism about the morality of contemporary Germany to dilute Konradin's example. Later in Engelmann's book, readers discover a startling fact about Marga that again parallels her to Gertrud. Marga's husband was one of the conspirators against Hitler—yet Marga went through her subsequent life hiding this fact. Like the fictional Gertrud, Marga was apparently ashamed of being related to a Resistance member. Half a century after World War II, many Germans still believe the anti-Hitler conspirators were traitors who dishonorably broke their oath (Maier 1988, 22; Fest 1997, 3; Hamerow 1997, 394).

Moments after this encounter with the past in the form of Gertrud, Henry, in the final screenplay, erupts in anger against a German cabdriver. The driver, identified by Pinter as a man in his sixties (thus of age during the Nazi era), mutters about being sick of driving American Jews around Stuttgart—a line that does not appear in the published screenplay:

> HENRY: . . . That was my house. My parents died there. You understand?
>   *The TAXI DRIVER turns his head.*
> TAXI DRIVER: *(In German)* What?
> HENRY: Do you understand?
> TAXI DRIVER: Nein.
> HENRY: My parents died there. They killed themselves there.
> TAXI DRIVER: *(In German)* I don't understand.
> HENRY: My father fought for Germany. But he was a Jew. They died of despair. Do you understand?
> TAXI DRIVER: Nein.
> HENRY: What do you mean? What do you mean, nein? *(Savagely, in German)* What do you mean, nein? Of course you understand! You understand perfectly well! You bastard!
> TAXI DRIVER: *(In German)* You get out.
>   *He opens Henry's door. HENRY gets out.* (R, 95–96)[13]

This outburst suggests the expansion, not the amelioration, of guilt. In this cathartic outburst Henry gives voice to the wish that the past should live in the memory of other Germans the way it does in his own. The scene suggests that all Germans of a certain age bear some moral responsibility for the Holocaust or, failing that, at least a special and lasting duty to remember and acknowledge it. However, this average German has apparently managed very well to "erase" the Nazi past; he comes from a Germany that wants to forget, and is forgetting, if it weren't for intrusive and obnoxious reminders such as Henry. The emotional weight of this confrontation is strengthened by means of a long, extremely tight close-up on Henry's face. Having just learned the extent of Henry's suffering through his enforced exile, Jason Robards's agonized face directly expresses the interior currents of Henry's psyche, creating an intense empathetic bond between character and audience (see Plantinga 1999, 251–53 on cinematic empathy). Speaking "savagely in German," as Pinter puts it, Henry attempts to force remembrance onto the gentile German, to reforge his boyhood kinship with Germany, with Konradin, and with his parents. But it is also a cry of despair. This "bastard," this country, won't adequately remember the past, choosing instead to believe in an illusorily absolute separation between then and now.

Previous drafts of Pinter's screenplay contained even more denial of the Nazi past, comparable to the cabdriver's anger and his "You get out" (with its echo of "*Juden raus!*"). In response to Henry's inquiries about the Lohenburgs (hence about the past), a tax official says,

> I understand very well what you are saying. But I believe it to be entirely impertinent. I think you must learn not to walk into people's offices without an appointment. But perhaps they don't teach you that in New York. I am an Inspector of Taxes. I am not a Professor of History. As you see, I am working. I do not care to be interrupted. (PA, Box 50; see Gale and Hudgins 1986, 134, item 8)

This caricature of officialdom seems less frightening than ridiculous—or more frightening because ridiculous. Like a Gogol character, he invites mockery when he uses his status and duties as an "Inspector of Taxes" to deny moral obligations as a person. His manner, no less brutal for being refined, recognizes but inhumanly frustrates Henry's total personal involvement. The notion that the Lohenburgs' house has become a tax office alludes to Germany's postwar "economic miracle" (*Wirtschaftswunder*), which has been suggested as one of the conditions making it easy for Germany to forget (ignore? repress?) the enormity of its past. The passage hints too at lasting German anti-Semitism, inasmuch as New York is stereotyped as a Jewish city. (This stereotype is referenced in the September 1 draft, in which another German taxi driver says he moved back to his homeland from New York because New York was too noisy.)

In that early draft Henry yells at a hotel maid ("savagely in German"), "My room hasn't been made up." The maid responds,

"I am sorry. We are late. I am sorry" (PA, Box 49). This seemingly banal exchange manages to hint at deep questions about remembrance and forgiveness: will it always be too late (or too early) for an apology from Germany in regard to its past? Henry's yelling in German, his "savagery," here as in the cabdriver scene, hints at the gutter German of the camps, the lunatic ravings of Hitler or Freisler. Henry's wrath illustrates again his frustration at finding no place for himself in Germany, at being considered less than fully German (or human), and the brutalization he feels (and it is a wrath which, ironically, brings out in him the savagery his interlocutors are unwilling to acknowledge). But it is too late (or perhaps too early) for Germany, represented by a driver, a tax official, or a hotel maid, to respond; Germany is incapable of summoning up the humanity to respond. The past, too troubling to face, continues in the present so that contemporary Germany in effect remains Nazi Germany.

In two early drafts, Hans again expresses direct anger. After Konradin has explained that he has become a Nazi and that the Fuehrer will eventually distinguish between "the good Jewish elements and the . . . undesirable Jewish elements," a line that is retained in the screenplay (Pinter 1990, 90), Hans in the drafts of September 1 and of September 2 says "Alright. Now fuck off" (PA, Boxes 49 and 50). Pinter wrote this line twice and crossed it out each time. There is a drama inherent in the revision process, visible here. Presumably, Pinter saw such a profane utterance as too anachronistic, too unrefined, and also too prescient for the young Hans. But one can see an immense, passionate, unreserved—and certainly justifiable—moral wrath within Pinter himself, as human being and writer, which he is struggling to express in a fictively appropriate way through his characters.

In choosing to restrict Henry's anger as he ultimately revised, Pinter is able to emphasize how such a reaction has been building in Henry for years. The explosion at the taxi driver is "the accumulation of all the resentment built up in the fifty-five years since he [Henry] left Germany" (Pinter 1989c, 26; my translation). This reaction represents an outpouring of repressed emotion, behavior indicative of trauma. Traumatic reactions possess a truth outside that of logic and reasoning; as Cathy Caruth writes, "trauma . . . seems to evoke the difficult truth of a history that is constituted by the very incomprehensibility of its occurrence" (1995, 153). Henry's impossible desire that the incomprehensible be rendered understandable—understanding is a repeated word in the exchange with the cabdriver—defines his being. That frustrated desire is what history has reduced him to. The repetition of this impossible goal of understanding reminds us that the Holocaust represents a kind of historical trauma, an event which, as Elie Wiesel, Claude Lanzmann, and many others have said, cannot usefully be approached with our usual rational desires for historical comprehension. When dealing with the history behind Uhlman's *Reunion*, Pinter paradoxically illustrates both the amelioration and the persistence of German guilt and leaves us to grapple with this enduring contradiction.

Taking Sides: Dilemmas of Remembrance and Judgment

In directing *Taking Sides* in 1995, a play by his friend Ronald Harwood, Pinter again examines the legacy of the Nazi genocide. By doing so, he engages with issues through his directing that he would later explore as a playwright; *Ashes to Ashes* premiered in September 1996, a little over a year after the premiere of *Taking Sides* in July 1995. Pinter read Gitta Sereny's biography of Albert Speer, who is mentioned several times in Harwood's play, in the winter of 1995 (Billington 1996, 374). This experience, Pinter recounted, led him to write *Ashes to Ashes*.[14] Harwood's play addresses the personal behavior of Wilhelm Furtwängler, the noted conductor, and examines how that behavior can be seen in a public, political context.

Furtwängler (1886–1954) was a great German conductor who remained in Germany throughout the Nazi era despite the fact that many other artists were forced out or left in protest. The play dramatizes the American prosecution team—Major Arnold, a former insurance investigator, and Captain Wills, young and idealistic—that tried to ascertain for the Denazification Tribunal of 1946 whether Furtwängler served the Nazi regime. The play asks whether history can ever be adequately clarified, whether anyone's behavior in extreme historical circumstances can be appropriately judged after the fact. If everyone has normal human frailties, who can judge anyone else? Would ordinary people have acted substantially differently when faced with equivalent historical extremities? Wills puts this point most succinctly in the final scene: "I wonder how I would have behaved in his position? I'm not certain I'd have 'acted courageously.' And what about you, Major? I have a feeling we might just have followed orders" (Harwood 1995, 59). Through Wills's

analysis—that no one is morally privileged and all are in potential equally corruptible—is allowed the idea that it was only a
quirk of fate that rendered Germany into victimizers; it might
have been anyone else selected by fate to be historical villains.
Anyone can be a fascist; all you have to do is be in the wrong
spot at the wrong time—again, the fact that Goldberg fulfills the
role of a Gestapo agent in relation to Stanley in *The Birthday
Party* illustrates this point. The political import of this thesis
about universal human villainy is ambiguous. It is, at first
glance, a corrosive point of view, offering a negative if not cynical take on human nature (or the way in which human behavior
is conditioned by social forces). On the other hand, if we are all
capable of becoming Nazis or mini-Hitlers, does this lessen our
resolve to condemn the Nazis and their specific deeds? Given
this dilemma about interpreting historical behavior, the irony of
Harwood's title becomes clear. While the moral issues involved
make an audience adopt a definite position, the play's vision of
human moral fragility makes taking sides problematic.

Arnold and Wills emerge as opposites in the play: Arnold eager
and Wills cautious about judging Furtwängler, Arnold a gentile
and Wills a German-born Jew; Arnold a philistine and Wills a
music-lover. Harwood also has the two characters stand for opposite approaches to historical memory and thus judgment.
Wills wants to be a history teacher after his army service, a thematic embodiment of the necessity to accommodate the historical past with the future. However, Arnold is obsessed with the
past, particularly with the misdeeds of the past, an attitude that
has served him well during his career as an insurance investigator. He attempts to position this quality as necessary to the investigation of history. Arnold challenges Wills by asserting a
photographic memory: "Me, I've got a terrific memory. I've been
examined by psychologists. Because of my memory, nothing
else. I've got what they call 'total recall.' I remember everything.
It's a curse" (Harwood 1995, 7). Without this kind of memory,
Harwood suggests, our relationship with history will be incomplete, just as it will also be incomplete without Wills's sense of
proportion and caution. There is a double bind here. Historical
understanding involves a necessary compromise between two
opposite conditions, a detailed remembrance of the past and the
pressures of the present to make practical use of that remembrance.[15]

Through Harwood's play, Pinter once again puts a special

focus on hypocrisy, on the pretense of moral status. Arnold tells this story of postwar Austria:

> last month I was in Vienna. I had with me an Austrian driver, Max his name was, he'd done time in the camps. We were looking at these Viennese cleaning up the bomb damage, scavenging for rotting food, butt ends, anything. I said, "To think, a million of these people came out to welcome Adolf on the day he entered the city, a million of them, and now look at 'em." And Max said, "Oh not these people, Major. These people were all at home hiding Jews in their attics." You get the point . . . ? The point is they're all full of shit. (1995, 18)

Hypocrisy disgusts character and director. The theme of moral equivalency meets its conceptual opposite. No matter what anyone might have done in a sort of moral thought experiment, things were done which need to be accurately accounted for. The actions performed in the past exert their own moral pull on the present. If we admit that making retrospective moral judgments is problematic, it is still the case that despite this intellectual reservation, we go ahead making these judgments. Harwood dramatizes the theme of false heroism, as Emmi Straube, a "good German" secretary to Arnold, reveals that her father, reputed a hero, joined the plot to kill Hitler only after he realized the war could not be won. (This version of the July 20 plot conflicts with the more positive image of it in Pinter's *Reunion* screenplay.)

Arnold and Wills acknowledge in the course of the play that there is no legal case to be made against Furtwängler. The investigators discover that Furtwängler may have stayed for personal reasons—he was afraid of losing his position as preeminent conductor to Herbert von Karajan (who did join the Nazis), he was well supplied with women, and he had the backing of Hitler. There is, however, no clear proof of collusion with or service to the Nazi regime. His many anti-Semitic comments and attitudes do not add up to political crimes, while his instances of help to Jews are numerous and real. He is acquitted at the Denazification Tribunal.

Though the legal case disappears, there is nevertheless a desire to see justice done in moral terms, to see truth unearthed. This desire to pierce through moral pretense is the basis of Arnold's appeal as a character. Arnold, however, continues to smear Furtwängler through disinformation in the press, an action that will disappoint spectators who would identify Arnold with a strict desire to expose the truth and do justice.[16] The play here raises a fundamental issue of justice. Justice privileges the deliberative will against the passions—judgment always takes place well after the events being judged. Does "justice" lose something by dispensing with passionate reactions of outrage? Harwood's play also has contemporary political resonance about the vagaries of post hoc judgment. The play warns us not to expect accurate justice from the "truth commissions" and other projects to investigate the history of totalitarian regimes, even as we desire that justice be served and hypocrisy exposed.

Taking Sides also debates the issue of the political role of the artist in a way that underlines how Pinter has emphasized his public power. If language and music can preserve political values, then Pinter is committed to using all the aspects of his theatrical creativity to argue for the values he sees as crucial to civilized conduct. Through the character of Furtwängler, *Taking Sides* argues that art is never truly separate from the social circumstances in which it arises. In act 2, Furtwängler concedes that the artist's extrasocial role exists alongside his social one. "[A]n artist cannot be entirely apolitical. He must have some political convictions because he is, after all, a human being. As a citizen, it is an artist's duty to express these convictions," Furtwängler concludes (Harwood 1995, 57) in words that parallel Pinter's own desire to be heard as a public citizen, to make use of his voice. Through its voicing of this theme, Harwood's play can be considered an apologia for Pinter's public stance since the early 1980s. This directing project illuminates Pinter's predilection for stressing the horrors of war and his interest in the moral judgment of historical behavior as well as in the complexities of such judgment.

THE TROJAN WAR WILL NOT TAKE PLACE AND NATO IN SERBIA: PACIFIST DRAMA, PACIFIST POLITICS

Pinter's work as a theatrical director remains an underanalyzed dimension of his artistic and political career. Since 1983, when he directed Jean Giraudoux's *The Trojan War Will Not Take Place* (1935) for the National Theatre in London, Pinter has more frequently directed plays, his own and others, mostly involving himself in explicitly political projects. His role as director is the opposite of his earlier persona as a playwright-artist aloof from his works' meanings. As director, Pinter identifies himself with the plays as theatrical experiences. Also, by controlling initial productions, he affects the interpretations of his own later works, such as *One for the Road*, *Party Time*, and *Ashes to Ashes*. Pinter has added to his role as political dramatist by acting as a dissident intellectual, debating international politics in newspapers and on television.

The Trojan War represents an attractive vehicle for Pinter as director and as pacifist. With unambiguous pacifism, the play recasts the story of Helen and Paris in a mode of ironic fatalism. Like *Precisely*, Giraudoux's play addresses how a militarist context shapes discourse such that war is portrayed as desirable or inevitable, and it exposes the moral blindness of unquestioning devotion to "glory" and country. The timing of the production, just after the British conquest of the Falklands, must also have appealed to Pinter.

The central debate in the play is between Demokos, a Trojan poet, and the warrior Hector. Demokos, together with the old men of Troy, argues in favor of war by appealing to the memory of those who have already died—their sacrifice mandates ours. Only the battle-weary Hector objects to warfare. Hector directly addresses these same dead with opposite intention, inverting Demokos's popular viewpoint that remembrance should lead to further battle. Hector's speech counters the abstract justifications for war by which the grave becomes, supposedly, "a reward for the living." War is, instead, simply and only a waste of human life, and any responsibility we have in the present is simply to the perpetuation of life:

> But what I have to say to you today is that war seems to me the most sordid, hypocritical way of making all men equal: and I accept death neither as a punishment or expiation for the coward, nor as a reward to the living. So, whatever you may be, absent, forgotten, purposeless, unresting, without existence, one thing is certain . . . we must ask you to forgive us, we, the deserters who survive you, who feel we have stolen two great privileges, I hope the sound of their names will never reach you: the warmth of the living body, and the sky. (Giraudoux 1955, 48)

Nothing justifies war, is Giraudoux's point, and Pinter's. (It is a phrase that gained resonance and publicity during the buildup to the 2003 war in Iraq.) Hector's dissent in the play, his rejection of his society's widely held and loudly proclaimed assumptions, reflects Pinter's own publicly avowed antimilitarism.

The sometimes-scathing reviews of the play mentioned the predictability and rhetorical style of the script, a slowness in the production, and what some saw as the naiveté of Giraudoux's theme. A number of critics were skeptical of the play's pacifism (*London Theatre Record*, 1983, 362–66). That is, when the existence of evil is stipulated, countering this evil may well be a valid reason for deploying force or making war.

This criticism anticipates one given to Pinter about his position about the 1999 NATO military actions in Serbia: in the face of actual evil, can a stance of pacifism be useful? Thus, the play's often-negative reviews anticipated objections to Pinter's strong critiques of the NATO bombing of Serbia. The directing of *The Trojan War Will Not Take Place*, like Pinter's other writing and directing projects of the 1980s and 1990s, is illuminated by his forays into the wider political arena. Whatever the efficacy or inefficacy of political theater, Pinter's work as a dissident intellectual reflects concerns similar to those he presents on stage, and even though Pinter's theatrical work strongly suggests the odds against dissent by illustrating the links among power, repression, and retribution, Pinter himself *does* dissent.

In history, as opposed to Giraudoux's play, the Trojan War does take place, again and again, as war and military violence recur, as they have in Afghanistan in 2001 and Iraq in 2003. Akin to Hector in the play, Pinter strongly protested NATO's attack upon Slobodan Milosevic's forces in Serbia. He did so even though the professed aim of the bombing was to interrupt Serbia's systematic "ethnic cleansing" of Muslims from the city of Kosovo, arguably the worst humanitarian crisis in Europe since World War II. Milosevic, as of 2003 being tried as a war criminal by the International Tribunal at The Hague, led sweeps of ethnic cleansing motivated by a reactionary brand of ethnic nationalism. The bombings aimed at derailing continued ethnic cleansing by Milosevic's forces in Kosovo. (The fact that Milosevic is now out of power and on trial might be construed as a result of NATO's actions.)[17] Pinter spoke against NATO's actions on BBC 2 in 1999; he elaborated these themes at the Committee for Peace in the Balkans Conference in London the next year; he expanded on these views in the "Unthinkable Thoughts" interview with David Edwards; and he reiterated his positions in his talk with Mel Gussow at the 2001 Pinter Festival.

Given American involvement in destructive actions abroad, Pinter insists over and over again, no pretense to a special American morality could withstand scrutiny. In 2001, Pinter noted at the Pinter Festival at Lincoln Center that the bombing of the marketplace in the Serbian town of Nis during the NATO action was a "criminal act" (2002a, 25). A year earlier he claimed that the bombing of this marketplace was not an accidental error as NATO claimed, and he provided graphic descriptions of the death and destruction these bombs caused to innocent civilians. Pinter again noted the hypocrisy of the United States claiming to be moral while committing evil and destructive deeds. The "actions of successive US administrations . . . I think are really open to question and cannot masquerade *any longer*, as they have been doing for many, many years, under moral stances, because the moral stances no longer *work*" (2002a, 26). Pinter has continued this line of attack on America's morality in reference to the 2003 war in Iraq led by President Bush and Prime Minister Tony Blair. On the occasion of Bush's state visit to Britain in November 2003, Pinter wrote in an open letter in the *Guardian*: "Dear President Bush, I'm sure you'll be having a nice little tea party with your fellow war criminal, Tony Blair. Please wash the cucumber sandwiches down with a glass of blood."[18]

In 1998 and 1999 the left was split over how to combat Milosevic and the excessiveness of Serbian nationalism—some embraced the use of "force" (that is, violence) to prevent deportations, murders, and other atrocities, while others questioned whether military force could be used for moral good. Pinter, in ringing tones, assessed NATO's bombings as atrocities in themselves. They were a display of "deplorable machismo" whose real purpose was to divert attention from the scandals in the Clinton Administration and to enhance NATO's standing and credibility. Pinter has noted that as a public citizen he determines what is and is not fact in a different way than as an artist (http//www.haroldpinter.org). It is interesting to note that a writer so given to complicating the question of motivation is, speaking as a public citizen, so certain about it. His central argument was that the bombings lacked a moral basis:

When they said "We had to do something," I said "Who is this 'we' exactly . . . ? . . . Under what heading do 'we' act, under what law?" . . . The notion that this "we" has the right to act . . . presupposes a moral authority of which this "we" possesses not a jot! It doesn't exist! (Pinter 2001)

This "we" is the United States, with NATO following along. Pinter's argument rejects the moralism in which American imperialism cloaks itself. Thus his anti-Americanism fits with his view of language as molded by power, nullifying and misappropriating moral concerns. Pinter alleged that "the United States was determined to wage war against Serbia for one reason and one reason only—to assert its domination over Europe," and he derided Prime Minister Tony Blair for going along with U.S. policy (2000a, 2). He objected, too, to the invocation of "genocide" as an illegitimate usage that fostered warmongering, claiming that "only" 2,000 people had been killed in the year before NATO's military actions (2001). (Here he is perhaps forgetting that by definition genocide is not a matter of numbers but of the *intent* to destroy totally or in part a certain ethnic group.)

The only serious response to Pinter's position, as he noted, was a May 4, 1999, article in the *Independent* by historian Timothy Garton Ash. While Ash praised Pinter's moral vigor and his courage, he argued that Pinter relied on "a distortion of reality far more extreme than any of those he attacked" (1999, 4). He noted that while Pinter described Milosevic's actions as a "standard counter-insurgency," provoked more or less understandably by Kosovo Albanian military forces, he severely understated the extent and cruelty of Milosevic's campaign of ethnic cleansing. American complicity in the expulsion of the Serbs from Krajina—an abuse Pinter had pointed to—did not disallow America from doing good at another time and place:

> [Pinter] is correct, for example, that the US condoned the largest single ethnic cleansing in former Yugoslavia until now. . . . But that is all the more reason not to condone it now, when it happens in Kosovo. It's also true, as Pinter insisted, that the West has done far too little to stop repression of the Kurds by our Nato ally, Turkey. But if we are wrong to allow Turks to kill Kurds, then surely we are right to try to stop Serbs killing Kosovars. (1999, 4–5)

This critique seems to strike at the core of Pinter's objections to NATO's actions. The issue is one of moral perfectionism. In the real world, are not all actions taken by people who are, by definition, morally compromised? If one makes absolute moral cleanliness a prerequisite for action, one has instead made a permanent case for inaction.[19]

Pinter published a brief letter a week later in the *Independent* responding to Ash's critique. He conceded the blandness of characterizing Milosevic's campaign to drive out of Kosovo a quarter-million Albanians as a "standard counter-insurgency."

However, Pinter tried to deny Ash's allegation that this blandness was meant to be exculpatory. "The reason I did not specify
the Serbian atrocities which lay behind the term was because
this is done every day of the week by others on television and in
the press. But nothing I said in the programme could suggest that
I condone these atrocities" (1999, 2).

But Pinter seems on a slippery slope here. By articulating Serbian violence in such bland language, one might say Pinter is indeed trying to draw attention away from it, not toward it. One
might wonder if Pinter is investigating this matter partially, in
the sense that any opponent of the United States, which Pinter
sees as ultimate evil, gets something of a free moral pass. Furthermore, even granted the partiality of what the media airs, and
the collusion between media and reigning governments, does
there in fact exist some limit at which atrocities have been suf-
ficiently publicized? This seems to be Pinter's assumption in declaring that Milosevic's murderous actions (and abettings) had
been adequately reported. Rather it seems an axiom of Pinter's
politics, as we derive them from his art, that all suffering, regard-
less of the abstractions that cause or rationalize it, mandates
equal and concentrated attention. All oppression is an assault on
human dignity.

Pinter's letter goes on to invoke the irony that in order to prevent Serbian murder of innocent Kosovars, it proved necessary
to kill innocent Serbians. He underlined again that NATO's
bombing of the Belgrade TV station was an unlawful attack upon
civilians, identifiable simply as an act of mass murder. This
truth, in Pinter's mind, belies NATO's characterization of its
program as "humanitarian intervention," a phrase he has often
ridiculed.[20] By defining NATO's campaign as murder, Pinter
aims to obviate the question of whether NATO's ends were
worth its chosen means—if the means are murder, they are absolutely wrong. Here, Pinter shows astonishing consistency in
making the argument that murder is never morally justifiable.
In 1949, at just nineteen years of age, Pinter read a statement to
a British court in defense of his status as a conscientious objector. In it he spells out his reasoning and indicts what armies do,
dispelling all conventional justifications for war: "To join an organisation whose main purpose is mass murder . . . and whose
result and indeed ambition is to destroy the world's very, very
precious life, is completely beyond my human understanding
and my moral conception. And finally, to take one human life is
completely alien to my moral code" (Knowles 2000, 187).

However, Ash uses the very consistency of Pinter's conception of the United States to critique Pinter's anti-NATO stance in 1999: Pinter "has been blinded in one eye by his longstanding, vehement hatred of what he sees as America's hypocritical, militaristic, imperialist policies" (5). The word "hatred" seems well chosen, pointing to the notion that Pinter's politics are instinctive or reactive, based in a reaction of moral outrage (which is not to say they are without intellectual merit). He is expert at exposing lies and half-truths and moral pretensions. Yet this debunking strategy, no matter how well executed, left those who shared Pinter's stance without a way to challenge the inhuman actions of ethnic cleansing. The one thing Pinter's side could not offer was a way to stop Milosevic's campaign.[21] Here there is a logical gap in the thinking that America is monolithically immoral. Merely because a certain party may have no extant "moral authority," as Pinter asserts often, it does not follow that every action that party undertakes in the future will be immoral. There may well exist a situation in which our choice may well be between the lesser of two evils (to adopt that admittedly horrible-sounding cliché of mainstream political discourse), or between one party of dubious or hypocritical morality versus another of evident evil. Even such a figure as former Czech President Václav Havel favored military action in Serbia in 1999 (and earlier) and against Saddam Hussein's Iraq in 2003 on the grounds that evil must be countered.[22] Human rights advocate Aryeh Neier's view is that the NATO campaign was a "just war unjustly carried out" (Urquhart 2003, 41). In the matter of Serbia and NATO, Pinter may have arrived at a problematic position by virtue of too vigorously applying one of his core political beliefs, the notion of U.S. imperialist hypocrisy, and not considering evidence and ideas that suggested to others, at least, that in Kosovo the United States may have acted for constructive as opposed to imperialist motivations.

To Ash, Pinter's distortions resulted from his opposition to the U.S. and its ongoing imperialist conduct. Pinter's view of America as hypocritical and murderous is one he has expressed with increased vehemence in recent years. While it is often said that after the events of September 11, 2001, world politics has changed forever, American foreign policy after September 11 has only sharpened Pinter's resolve to attack the essential moral falsity of the United States. The wars against Afghanistan and Iraq initiated by President Bush have only reinforced (not that reinforcement was needed) Pinter's opinion about American power and its evil. In 1988's "Language and Lies" Pinter indicts U.S. conduct: "US foreign policy is a classic case of a depraved moral position—where, while maintaining a stance of moral rectitude it instigates or abets murderous acts and modes of behavior; where, while demanding recognition as 'Peacemaker' or the true 'Force for Good,' the child of eight is raped and her head cut off" (1988a, 2). In late 2001 he declared: "The United States has in fact—since the end of the Second World War—pursued a brilliant, even witty, strategy. It has exercised a sustained, systematic, remorseless and quite clinical manipulation of power worldwide, while masquerading as a force for universal good" (2002c, 67–68). If anything, even this pretense of moral values has vanished, Pinter feels, in light of America's war against the Taliban in Afghanistan. The United States "has—without thought, without pause for reflection, without a moment of doubt, let alone shame—confirmed that it is a fully-fledged, award-winning, gold-plated monster" (2002c, 68–69). Beginning in the spring of 2003, news reports suggested that the promised American commitment to rebuild Afghanistan is weak—the security promised for the entire country does not even extend to the whole of its capital Kabul, for instance. If these charges are true, the military campaign against the Taliban might well appear simply as extravagant, high-tech revenge. (By early 2003, similar charges of lack of planning with regard to postwar Iraq began to coalesce into conventional wisdom—see the *New York Times Magazine*, June 1, for instance [Bearak 2003]). At the core of Pinter's anti-Americanism is his resentment of American "exceptionalism"—the notion that America is uniquely blessed, that its interests and its wars are always moral. Given that the war in Iraq has led to the torture of Iraquis by U.S. soldiers, American exceptionalism seems exposed as either an illusion or a fraud.

It may be that in recent years, Pinter risks allowing his political voice to be interpreted solely as a matter of anti-Americanism. Of course, anti-Americanism is now sharply prominent among the British and European left, so Pinter is hardly alone in this political emphasis. It is often said that such anti-Americanism mistakes America's leaders for the whole of America, failing to note that many Americans do not agree with those leaders and their actions. (To this, Pinter might conceivably reply that all Americans are morally responsible for what is done in the name of America.) As political battles contemporarily focus on the issue of globalization, a political development intimately connected to that of American power, anti-Americanism will most likely continue to feature in progressive politics, so that Pinter's denunciations of the United States are merely the crest of a future wave. Nevertheless, in terms of the arc of Pinter's stated political opinions over his career, what had been a denunciation of power, hypocrisy, self-righteousness in general may now seem an attack only on American power, hypocrisy, and self-righteousness. The plays' deliberately unspecific locations of oppression yield to a concept of evil in unambiguous terms of a local habitation and a specific name.

Whether this shift from the general to the particular sharpens or reduces the impact of Pinter's politics is an open question. Nor should this be an easy question, for there is no neutral space from which to answer it. The moral challenge of the political plays for Pinter's audiences involves seeing ourselves as the agents of moral and political catastrophe: the enemy is not out there, it is us; we, the democratic West, must see ourselves as morally equivalent to those whom we define as our enemies.

7

Ashes to Ashes: Morality and Politics after the Holocaust

ASHES TO ASHES IS BOTH A SUMMARY AND A CROWNING ACHIEVE-ment of Harold Pinter's theater. The play merges the diverse strands of Pinter's political and private dramas. Its atmosphere of fascist interrogation links it to *One for the Road* and *Mountain Language;* its commingling of bourgeois comfort and violence evokes *Party Time;* its battles over memory, truth, and sexual fidelity recall *Old Times* and *Betrayal;* its depiction of a sensitive outsider struggling for a working identity in the world connects it to *The Birthday Party, The Dwarfs,* and *Landscape.* In its dramatization of the conditions and dangers of confronting issues of violence and political suffering, of accepting the necessity of engagement and living with political awareness, it alludes to *The Dumb Waiter* and *The Dreaming Child.* Furthermore, *Ashes to Ashes* reveals the Holocaust to be at the root of Pinter's contemplations of politics and power. The play emerges from those of his works that indirectly evoke the Nazi genocide, positing it as unavoidable background, such as *The Birthday Party, The Dumb Waiter, The Hothouse,* and *Mountain Language,* and those that feature Holocaust history, such as *The Man in the Glass Booth, Taking Sides,* and *Reunion.* Though this play brings the characteristic twentieth-century fact of genocide to the dramatic fore, it nevertheless and paradoxically presents this reality indirectly, through allusion and as the traces of unreliable personal memory rather than through direct reference or representation. Past and present, there and here, self and other merge inextricably, as political violence is located within the space of private life.

Ever since Theodor Adorno's famous, though often misunderstood, injunction against writing poetry after Auschwitz, the propriety of depicting Holocaust through art has been fiercely debated (1977, 188).[1] It has often been argued that any writing about the Holocaust, either as history or art, results in falsification. As Emily Miller Budick claims, "To survivors and nonsurvivors alike, the Holocaust has always seemed to be beyond our ability to know it and therefore to represent it. Writing about the Holocaust . . . has seemed . . . not simply to miss it but to violate it: to distort or trivialize or even to deny it" (1998, 329–30). Efraim Sicher notes that current Holocaust remembrance "once more stir[s] up the questions Theodor Adorno and Elie Wiesel raised about legitimacy and authenticity" (1998b, 7). The so-called historical "uniqueness" of the Shoah, often adduced as a cause of its inability to be interpreted or represented, may not stand up to historical scrutiny, given the genocidal impulses of the twentieth century. Yet there lingers a sense of the Holocaust's uniqueness as a horrific crime against human morality and dignity. The sheer scale of the Nazis' crimes, their deliberate nature, and the unprecedented means of genocidal murder they invented render the Holocaust "intransigent" to "puny human interpretation" (Clendinnen 1999, 18). What happens, then, when artists try to imagine and to represent horrors and crimes that have been forcefully termed unimaginable, inexpressible, and unrepresentable?

The idea that the Holocaust should not be the subject of art has hardly prevented writers and artists from attempting to represent it. In recent years, critics of Holocaust literature have described artistic qualities necessary to avoid the dangers of illegitimacy and inauthenticity first described by Adorno. One such criterion is a kind of indirection that frequently takes the form of allusiveness. "The most effective imagined evocations of the Holocaust seem to proceed either by invocation . . . or by indirection," observes Clendinnen aptly (1999, 165). Another element in "successful" Holocaust writing is a metadiscourse that declares and confronts its inherent paradoxes and difficulties. Sicher believes that authentic Holocaust literature "succeeds in showing the impossibility of [its] representation. . . . [N]o account claiming to have found words to express the truth can be genuine" (1998a, 321). Berel Lang argues that any writing of the Holocaust must question our "presumption of illumination" (1990, 145), that is, our desire for increased knowledge or comprehension. Equally important to nonreductive Holocaust art is an ability to contemplate atrocity without allowing one to escape such bleakness by constructing positive or redemptive meanings that lead away from genocide's deep depravity and evil. Lawrence Langer is a persuasive advocate of this idea, arguing in *Holocaust Testimonies* (1991) and *Admitting the Holocaust* (1995) that the deepest, most authentic engagement with the Holocaust is also the most dangerous, the most psychologically self-wounding.

In *Ashes to Ashes*, Harold Pinter presents history allusively in the register of memory. Highlighting the impossibility of verifying what may or may not be historically accurate, he employs a style of indirection, referring, for example, to specifics of the career of the war criminal Albert Speer, Hitler's architect and arms minister, without detailing names, places, or dates. *Ashes to Ashes* invokes Holocaust history but never shows Nazi criminal behavior or uses the words "Nazi" and "Jew." Pinter investigates his own artistic medium through this play, showing how sustained empathy with the legacy of atrocity is made problematic by the circumstances of bourgeois comfort and by the social and temporal distances between the events of the genocide and his audience. Budick claims that "increasing temporal distance has made speaking about the Holocaust that much more precarious and forgetting it all that much easier" (1998, 330). *Ashes to Ashes* dramatizes this precariousness, the uncertain place that authentic commemoration of the past is granted in contemporary society.

Ashes to Ashes dramatizes the difficulty of bearing witness to the Holocaust, suggesting that a self-conscious witness, aware of its own distance from the Holocaust, is the only kind now possible. Pinter emphasizes the forces—internal and external, psychological and social—that operate to silence this witness. As Pinter's play underlines the challenge of moral engagement, it urges us to transvalue our perceptions of what is real and unreal in our daily lives and in the constitution of our moral selves. For Rebecca, the embattled protagonist of *Ashes to Ashes*, life's most familiar moments—going to the movies, a marital spat, children growing up—seem foreign, even alienating, while at the same time also trivial and clichéd. The Shoah somehow has the power to render contemporary life banal and scant of meaning. Pinter wants us to see the events of Rebecca's life as she does— tiredly familiar and horribly alien. Thus, he depicts her attempts to confront the Holocaust as far more profound than anything associated with her domestic roles. Haunting the play is the premise that normal life is drained of moral substance, while conversely it seems as if compassionate contemplation of the Holocaust makes it too profound, too big, for our everyday lives.

This moral paradox, which amounts to the impossibility of "thinking" the Holocaust, is the dilemma with which the play confronts us.

In her narrative, Rebecca recounts a sexual affair with a man who took part in an "atrocity" reminiscent of Nazi genocide. Her description of ritualized abuse at the hands of this "lover" suggests perhaps she was raped (*AA*, 13). The enormity of these events is dressed in everyday terms, however, as she quite factually describes her lover as a "courier" for a travel agency and then as a "guide" (19, 21). In her second story, the man takes her to a factory where the workers show him elaborate deference, "doff[ing] their caps" (23). Rebecca next tells a story, apparently from a different time, when she witnessed a mass suicide as guides led fur-coated refugees into the waters off Dorset. Later, she recounts what seem like normal events: a movie matinee, a visit to her sister. Devlin, both jealous and concerned, seeks to clarify these references to a man in his wife's past and attempts through a combination of flattery, reassurance, and anger to talk Rebecca back into the quotidian life from which she is so radically alienated. However, near the end of the play, Devlin attempts briefly to emulate the violence Rebecca accepted from her lover. In her final story, which takes place on a train platform, Rebecca tries to rescue a baby by disguising it as a bundle but gives the baby up to her lover, now a guard. She then denies she has abandoned the baby. An echo repeats her phrases. Once she reaches the point in her narrative in which she once again has failed to have impact, she steps out of the story, repeating its final line: "I don't know of any baby." Pinter uses this moment to emphasize the disjunction of history, memory, and conscience, and after a "[l]ong silence," the play ends (85).

Ashes to Ashes, like *Old Times*, is a play "about" an unhappy marriage, but also, perhaps more importantly, it enacts a debate about historical knowledge. As the play ends, we are confronted with questions. In regard to Rebecca's historical allusions, we might wonder what parts of her stories could truly have happened to her or to others whom she may or may not have known. What is the meaning of these stories if they are not grounded in (her) experience? Asserting the interpersonal meaning human experience should provide, Arthur Miller described his play *All My Sons* as an assault upon "the fortress of unrelatedness," the idea that our lives have no necessary connection one to another, that we have no responsibility for each other (1978, 131). Rebecca's fabric of being is a battle against this prevailing unrelatedness.

In analogous fashion to Miller, Pinter's *Ashes to Ashes* raises what might be termed "pastlessness," the idea that the past has nothing to do with the present. Through Rebecca's stories, Pinter critiques our definition of knowledge and questions our opportunities for confronting, or evading, history. In a discussion of the play after a 1996 reading,[2] Pinter commented that intellectual understanding exists alongside emotive or intuitive knowledge. Rebecca assumes that human knowing cannot be solely rational, nor that it can properly be ahistorical. Jumping the gap between reflection and immediate experience, she seeks to relieve "cognitive unknowing," caused by distance in time from the events themselves, with a kind of "emotional knowing" (Horowitz 1998, 290) prompted by the fact that as the Holocaust recedes into the past, into "history," those who would reflect upon it must do so indirectly, generations after the events. Rebecca tells her stories as a way to test her own moral-imaginative capacity to apprehend history in the present. "Nothing has ever happened to me" (*AA*, 41), she admits under Devlin's interrogation of her conduct; thus, narrative becomes her only entry into the past and imagination her only route to moral engagement.

By linking historical truth with inventive and emotive memory, Pinter undermines conventional distinctions between history as factual record and history in more subjective, allegedly less "verifiable" forms. From the viewpoint of Holocaust historians, identification with the subjects of history is not a guarantee of knowledge. Eva Hoffman points to the importance of the separation between an event and its historical perception: "[T]he distance between ourselves and that event needs to be taken account of in the ways we remember it. The gulf cannot be closed by insistence on 'identification'" (2000, 22). Even sympathetic people may be "unable to identify intellectually or to experience vicariously the feelings, thoughts, and attitudes of the victims," not to mention those of the perpetrators of genocide or of their passive or approving bystanders (Magurshak 1988, 424). The inherent difficulty of Rebecca's attempts at empathy is made clearer by these cautionary statements. Finally, Rebecca's difficulties in communication lead to problematic relationships with her husband in the play and (according to some reviewers) with the audience watching it. Through these difficulties and through her final isolated silence, Pinter raises the possibility that imaginative, emotive knowledge of history may be so personally consuming as to end in stalemate and futility.

Pinter uses the character of Devlin, who is apparently a scholar or professor, to introduce one aspect of the theme of knowledge:

> You understand why I'm asking you these questions. Don't you? Put yourself in my place. I'm compelled to ask you questions. There are so many things I don't know. I know nothing . . . about any of this. Nothing. I'm in the dark. I need light. Or do you think my questions are illegitimate? (*AA*, 11)

Here the clear knowledge Devlin hopes for, enlightenment in the traditional sense, equates to light, while ignorance is symbolically paired with darkness. In voicing rational curiosity about Rebecca's stories, Devlin is a proxy for the audience, which also desires to assess her truthfulness. Her refusal to enter the discussion on Devlin's terms—"What questions?" she asks—threatens to leave us in the dark. Pinter specifies the stage lighting to supplement the play's concern with defining knowledge. He writes: "*The room darkens during the course of the play. The lamplight intensifies.*" Pinter insists on this contradiction: "*By the end of the play. . . . [t]he lamplight has become very bright but does not illumine the room*" (*AA*, 1). The ability of darkness to overcome light suggests that darkness is not just an absence of light but an encroaching, positive force in itself, phenomenologically prior to light. The lasting power of darkness echoes Berel Lang's phrase that any act of writing the Holocaust must call into question the "presumption of illumination" (1990, 145), that is, the expectation for increased understanding of "the truth" that we bring to any representation of history. The moral symbolism of light and darkness is also relevant here: how Pinter lights his play seems a metaphorical illustration of the triumph of evil (darkness) over goodness (light), a triumph suggesting that ideals of morality may never overcome evil.

According to Billington's biography, the playwright began writing *Ashes to Ashes* after reading Gitta Sereny's *Albert Speer: His Battle with Truth* (1995), which recounts an affair Speer had with a young German woman in his last years.[3] Speer's liaison suggested to Pinter Rebecca's connection with an older man who may be a war criminal (Billington 1996, 373). Additionally, Pinter, who often traces his impulse to write his plays to a particular visual image, was inspired to write *Ashes to Ashes* by a

specific moment in Sereny's book. Rebecca's story about a visit
to her lover's factory is born out of Speer's 1943 visit to a secret
work camp called Dora—a successor facility to Peenemunde established to build V-2 rockets and supplied with slave labor from
the Buchenwald concentration camp and European deportees.
Thus, Pinter's play dramatizes a historical reference, although
the language of the play avoids such traditionally "historical"
details of date, place, or other localizing context. Rebecca relates, with delicate vagueness, her unsettling visit to this factory, which "wasn't the usual kind of factory" (*AA*, 23). Rows of
workers in caps removed their caps in apparent deference to
their commander, Rebecca's lover. She notes the factory was
cold and "exceedingly damp" but had no toilets: "I wanted to go
to the bathroom. But I simply couldn't find it" (27).

Rebecca's anodyne language conflicts with an eyewitness
view of conditions at Dora. According to Jean Michel, a French
slave laborer, the Nazis provided "No heat, no ventilation, not
the smallest pail to wash in. . . . [T]he latrines . . . were barrels
cut in half with planks laid across" (1980, 62–63). In *Albert
Speer*, Sereny allows Speer to give his version, querying him in
1978 about the 1943 visit to Dora. She describes his powerful
shame on the subject: "[I]mmediately and impossible to fake, his
face went pale; again he covered his eyes for a moment with his
hand" (1995, 404). Speer told her that at the time, "I was out-
raged. I demanded to see the sanitary provisions"; he ordered
that rations be increased, facilities built, and workers not be
threatened with execution as a motivating tool (405). In his
memoirs *Inside the Third Reich*, Speer portrays himself as the
recipient of such a salute as Rebecca describes: "Expression-
lessly, they [the prisoners] looked right through me, mechani-
cally removing their prisoners' caps of blue twill until our group
had passed them" (1970, 370). Not even Speer himself describes
this moment in the terms of respect and warmth evoked by the
image of these prisoners "doffing" their caps to him. The slave-
laborers' actions conflict in tone with Rebecca's account, pro-
viding an ironic contrast between differently narrated versions
of the same event, and illustrating that Rebecca herself adopts
Speer's ability to construct history in a way that is partial and
self-absolving.

Although there are so many facts—so many truths—available
in the historical record of the Holocaust, paradoxically, there is
no one truth that is generally agreed upon—if indeed the "truth"
concerning anything about the Holocaust can be understood by

those who did not live through it. In *Ashes to Ashes*, Pinter dramatizes facts of the Shoah as if they were one person's bizarre, vague, unverifiable stories—he "elides the historical referent" of Holocaust reality, in Geoffrey Hartmann's fine phrase (2000, 16). How one views the facts of the genocide is a problem of perspective, which Pinter confronts directly. If Pinter aims to compel attention to crimes of political murder, in *Ashes* and in his plays of the eighties and nineties, his audience might object that such nightmares of Nazi genocide have nothing to do with us—we aren't slave drivers like Speer; we aren't war criminals; we don't even know anyone who is. Through Devlin's attack on Rebecca's lack of authority to refer to the Holocaust, Pinter voices a likely response by an audience asked to ponder material that would assault its moral complacency. Thus, Pinter incorporates an attitude of resistance to the material the play explores, rendering problematic the process of opening oneself to knowledge of historical oppression. In delineating the factors that inhibit a wider knowledge of historical truth, Pinter investigates the conditions working to prevent and suppress a compassionate awareness of political victims. Specifically, Devlin believes Rebecca unreliable in how she uses language to formulate experience:

> DEVLIN. Now let me ask you this. What authority do you yourself possess which would give you the right to discuss such an atrocity?
> REBECCA. I have no such authority. Nothing has ever happened to me. Nothing has ever happened to any of my friends. I have never suffered. Nor have my friends.
> DEVLIN. Good. (*AA*, 41)

Rebecca's remarks reflect society's (or human beings') efforts to deny historical atrocities, even in the case of individuals who do try to "admit" them into consciousness. Lawrence Langer argues that human memory almost inevitably rejects extreme victimization. "[H]umiliated memory," he writes in *Holocaust Testimonies*, "negates the impulse to historical inquiry. Posterity not only can do without it; it prefers to ignore it" (1991, 79). Given how frequently the Holocaust has been documented and memorialized in recent years (through movies, television, museums, history books), however, everyone has access to images of the genocide; the issue is how deeply or seriously we permit them to inhabit our psyches, our moral imaginations.[4] Langer writes that the concern must be with how much we allow ourselves to absorb these images and their resonances. Devlin personifies a willed ignorance (a paradox, admittedly, but one Devlin is committed to). His behavior reveals the collusion between an autonomous, bourgeois self and a cultural preference for denying history. Devlin's behavior as a "repressive force" to Rebecca (Owens 2002, 90) is thus politically determined. Pinter himself experienced this kind of denial of actuality in the audiences at his political plays, as previously noted. According to the playwright, these audiences pretended they already knew and "did not need to be told" about the facts he was dramatizing (1986b, 18). (The author's decision to dramatize echoes of the Holocaust might be understood as a desire to confront the audience with horrors whose existence cannot be denied.) We flatter and lie to ourselves, Pinter suggests, if we believe our consciences extend further than Devlin's. Through him, Pinter illustrates how the atomized, insulated selves we seek out of self-protection or social conformity bar engagement with the depths of history. This is the blinkered, empirical, male mind-set that ratifies the misperception that historical atrocities "never happened," as Pinter expresses it in *Various Voices* (1998, 198). A society that values the truth and privacy of personal experience will only with difficulty be able to learn from the past.[5]

Contrary to Devlin's manner of rejecting experience he defines as outside his personal sphere of knowledge, Rebecca embraces a kind of historical determinism in which everyone's life is connected with everyone else's.[6] She tries to will historical fate into her personal life, attempting to know the past through emotion, imagination, and memory. Yet, though Rebecca wishes to connect with history, and specifically with the Holocaust, the play shows how this attempt is fraught with difficulty.

In his 1996 discussion of the play, Pinter asserted the moral heroism of Rebecca's actions but in a way that nearly characterizes her as obsessed. "We dare not think about these things," he said in reference to historical crimes, "but Rebecca can't *not* think about them." Pinter seems to suggest that personally to acknowledge such guilt as manifested in the Holocaust is to risk being overwhelmed. Such an attempt threatens our very selves, leading to an emotional state that Clendinnen identifies as "the Gorgon effect," a paralysis caused by Holocaust contemplation (1999, 18). Rebecca provides such an image of paralysis when describing a fellow cinemagoer:

But there was a man sitting in front of me, to my right. He was absolutely still throughout the whole film. He never moved, he was rigid, like a body with rigor mortis, he never laughed once, he just sat like a corpse. I . . . moved as far away from him as I possibly could. (AA, 65)

Though Rebecca apparently distances herself from this ostracized "corpse,"[7] it may, nevertheless, double for Rebecca herself, who also denies a capacity for humor and who is generally immobile and self-isolating.[8] We may conclude that she represents an impossible sort of freedom that requires remaining apart—a type of martyrdom, as it were. Rebecca's sense of obligation to others coincides with her estrangement from them; hence, it cannot be acted on and is difficult to emulate. Pinter attempts to estrange us from Rebecca's historical sympathy by associating it here with death and, in the passage on "mental elephantiasis" (51), with a disabling awareness of guilt.[9] To have guilt, or to experience responsibility for another, comes to connote paralysis and self-death. Pinter also qualifies Rebecca's compassion for others by placing this word in the context of the subjugation she imagines as part of her relationship with her lover. "No, no. He felt compassion for me," she says of her lover-oppressor, denying that the violence perpetrated against her can be seen as criminal aggression (45). This heterodox portrait of compassion is not Pinter creating a morally masochistic character, but rather a means of investigating skeptically the efficacy of empathy in life and in art. Pinter does not allow his audience to take consolation from a triumph of empathetic responsibility. He suggests that in a post-Holocaust world, redemption is illusory.

In previous criticism of *Ashes to Ashes*, empathy has been privileged as an effective route from suffering towards transcendence. In "Harold Pinter's *Ashes to Ashes*: Rebecca and Devlin as Albert Speer" (1998), Katherine H. Burkman argues that Rebecca's storytelling may lead to an existentially fuller life, perhaps to the ownership of suffering and to healing, loving capabilities. Burkman parallels the play to Gitta Sereny's biography; in so doing, she equates Speer's ability to love late in his life with Rebecca's growth at the end of the play: "Perhaps, like Speer, she will now be able to love" (1998, 94). Just as Speer is able to overcome the emotional paralysis that blinded him to his odious actions for the Third Reich, Rebecca makes a similar rediscovery of feeling and personal growth, leading to her expressions of empathy for the victims of history.[10]

The impulse to see empathy as transcendent parallels deep assumptions about art's moral efficacy. Theater, especially, is thought to offer moral benefits based upon its ability to bridge the gap between the experiences of differing selves. Additionally, when dealing with material as dark and depressing as the Holocaust, one experiences an impulse to escape from such darkness to a more hopeful, positive endpoint, thus leading Langer to prefer an artistic "discourse of ruin" to one of "consolation" fostering only our self-protection (1995, 6). Francis Gillen also seems driven to a more positive reading than the play warrants, claiming Rebecca strengthens herself (and us as viewers too) through identification and empathy. By means of empathy, he writes, she "discovers her own power . . . to reshape herself as non-victim" (1997, 91). Well, perhaps. This is a matter that, to speak strictly from the evidence of the play, is left unresolved. Both Gillen and Burkman note that Pinter provides Rebecca with one important triumph: she declines to kiss Devlin's fist when he emulates this tactic of her "lover." Devlin's action is more a stately mime of violence than the thing itself, emphasizing his impotency, especially compared to the violent images Rebecca evokes. However, this moment of resistance to Devlin need not be privileged as the definitive moment of his and Rebecca's relationship, nor should its meaning be overrated. Rather, it should be set against two other events: how Devlin (as representative of society) denies Rebecca a psychologically secure space in which she can utter testimony, and (as I shall examine later in this chapter) how Rebecca moves toward silence and withdrawal at the end of the play.

If critics of *Ashes to Ashes* valorize empathy and its empowering effects, the very possibility of real empathy has been questioned in important ways. Elaine Scarry argues throughout *The Body in Pain* (1985) that accounts of suffering always provoke doubt in their hearers: attending to reports of how others suffer is nearly impossible. Pointing to the difficulty of acknowledging another's pain, William James remarked that the trouble with human beings is that they cannot feel each other's toothaches. In *Regarding the Pain of Others*, Susan Sontag argues that even when we see precise, seemingly actual images of death and destruction, we ignore, brush aside, or misread this evidence of human pain (2003, 10–11). Geoffrey Hartmann acutely notes that empathy is a limited resource (2000, 17). The Holocaust's extreme subjugation brings the problem of identification with suffering to its highest pitch. Its victims were utterly stripped of will and were told that their narrations would never be believed. The Shoah's extremity as a vast criminal enterprise, arising not

from the margins of society but from the heart of a supposedly
civilized country, also uniquely endangers our view of ourselves
as moral individuals whose use of words like "compassion" and
"empathy" has been irrevocably altered by the fact of genocide.

Surely it is a mark of Rebecca's success in imagining the Holocaust if she can see herself as a victim, albeit a disabling "success." In considering the question of what Rebecca ultimately
becomes, I believe it is necessary to note two things about her
stories. First, they end in a way that impresses on us the fact and
finality of that ending; second, they narrate the abdication or
"denial" of moral responsibility. When Devlin confronts Rebecca about her lack of "authority," she seems to renounce her
own project of sympathetic historical knowledge. Possibly her
overall aim in the play is to complete this renunciation: she
speaks in order to be able to not speak. Although the final moments of the play, with Rebecca's narrative of abandoning her
baby and her denial that she has done so, may in Burkman's view
only "seem negative," it is instead a negativity that is both lasting and pervasive, engulfing any "possibility of redemption"
(1998, 94). Such redemption might represent the kind of inappro-
priate—yet understandable—consolation that Adorno, Langer,
and Cynthia Ozick have warned us against: "We want to escape
from the idea of having to quit in the bottomless muck of annihilation, with nothing else on the horizon" (Ozick 1988, 278).
But the nature of the Holocaust makes such escape false, wish-
ful. Pinter's consciousness of hate and violence—both its inten-
sity and persistence—means to disallow such escape. Moreover,
the critical desire to read Rebecca's engagement with suffering
as triumphant misrepresents its burden as a convenient step-
ping-stone to spiritual growth.

Pinter underlines Rebecca's closure and isolation through her
status as passive spectator in the stories she tells. From her window, Rebecca watches refugees being led into the sea. Likewise,
she hands over her baby without protest.[11] Her final renunciation of responsibility for the "baby" parallels her earlier retreat
under Devlin's attack. This movement is emphasized, as Merritt
notes, in the verbal shift from "your baby" to "what baby" and
then to "I don't know of any baby" (2000, 82)—it is significant
that the latter phrase is uttered twice. Rebecca's action of abandoning her own storytelling mirrors the abandonment she narrates. Even in her imagination, she cannot picture herself as
morally effective. Her inward turn, finally, comes up empty.
Both the plot of her narration and her cessation of that narrative

illustrate how Rebecca doubly internalizes the failure of moral outreach, the indifference that many historians have located at the heart of the genocide. The role she constructs is the mythically innocent, fatally ineffective bystander, whose complicitous acts of both commission and omission allowed genocide to proceed. Through her abandonment of narrative and narrative of abandonment Rebecca stands in both for the victims of atrocity and for its perpetrators, as Jessica Prinz observes (2002, 102).[12] Rebecca's final story inverts the consolatory narratives of rescue now so familiar to us from movies such as *Schindler's List* and *Life Is Beautiful*. Rainer C. Baum argues that the moral indifference that permitted the Final Solution is rooted in social circumstances deeply ordinary and absolutely contemporary: "modern life simply generates no demand for conscience" (1988, 82, 56). "[L]et us use memory," he posits, "to realize just how deeply we have woven the opportunities for amoral conduct into the social fabric of modern life, how easy we have made it for ourselves to adopt the role of passive bystander" (84). Our role as spectators to the play may even cruelly evoke this role of passive onlooker.

Rebecca's experience in the play confirms the notion of Zygmunt Bauman in *Modernity and the Holocaust* that the practice of morality is socially and temporally circumscribed: "Morality tends to stay at home and in the present" (1989, 200). Bauman argues that key aspects of social modernity represent a necessary condition of the Holocaust, maintaining that genocide could have occurred in any bureaucratically advanced Western nation. Bauman defines three methods by which society manages and restricts morality:

> social production of distance, which either annuls or weakens the pressure of moral responsibility; substitution of technical for moral responsibility, which effectively conceals the moral significance of the action; and the technology of segregation and separation, which promotes indifference to the plight of the Other. . . . (1989, 199)

These aspects of social practice are visible in *Ashes to Ashes* and in other Pinter plays. *Ashes* dramatizes the social distance and separation between "home" and "world," between oneself and others, a separation internalized by Rebecca, whose position in her stories is distanced and spectatorial. The "technology of segregation and separation" defines the settings of *Mountain Language* and *Party Time*—settings hidden from public view, serving in the first case as prison for the out-group and in the second as fortress for the in-group. Also, Albert Speer exemplifies what Bauman calls "the substitution of technical for moral responsibility." In Speer's words: "the habit of thinking within the limits of my own field provided me, both as architect and as Armaments Minister, with many opportunities for evasion" (1970, 113). Devlin, too, substitutes duty for conscience and thereby defends both indifference and aggression to others: "Fuck the best man, that's always been my motto. It's the man who ducks his head and moves on through no matter what . . . who gets there in the end . . . A man who doesn't give a shit. A man with a rigid sense of duty" (AA, 47). Devlin embodies mental habits that culminate in a plausible deniability of moral responsibility to others.

Bauman ties the Holocaust to the present day in ways that strengthen the link to prominent Pinter themes. In the present,

> the ancient Sophoclean conflict between moral law and the law of society shows no sign of abating. If anything . . . the odds are shifted in favour of the morality-suppressing societal pressures. . . . [M]oral behavior . . . means resistance to societal authority. (1989, 199)

His notions of morality and power describe Pinter's overall political stance that values outsiders against a morally deadening society forcing all to conform. An irony arises: antisocial behavior is moral, while actions conjoined by society may be immoral. Pinter expressed the necessity of such defiance, famously and economically, in Petey's plea to the defeated Stanley at the end of *The Birthday Party*: "Stan, don't let them tell you what to do" (*BP*, 86). This definition of morality as defiance roots Pinter's politics in Holocaust contemplation.

Ashes to Ashes illustrates the link between genocide and life in the now—a connection that is, paradoxically, both inescapable and tenuous. The fact of genocide has a lingering yet uncertain presence in contemporary consciousness. Late in the play, Pinter has Devlin (like Deeley in *Old Times*) join his mate in singing a romantic tune:

REBECCA. . . . (*singing softly*) "Ashes to ashes"—
DEVLIN. "And dust to dust"—
REBECCA. "If the women don't get you"—
DEVLIN. "The liquor must." *Pause.* I always knew you loved me.
REBECCA. Why?
DEVLIN. Because we like the same tunes. (*AA*, 69)

Despite Devlin's assertion of community, this moment illustrates fracture and misunderstanding. While Rebecca does not correct Devlin's musical memory, as she did earlier in the play (17), we still see that Rebecca's understanding of "ashes to ashes" has nothing to do with Devlin's. To Rebecca, obsessed by genocidal imagery, these ashes are the ashes of Jews (or Bosnians or Tutsis or Kurds). To Devlin, they are simply the cue for a popular (also misogynist) song, worthy of no more thought than one gives to any cliché.

The words that title Pinter's play evoke the Holocaust for Rebecca, measuring her psychological and epistemological distance from Devlin, to whom they evoke simply a sentimental song or a wistful allusion to love. Words that many of us think of as unexceptional are granted powerful meaning by Rebecca because these words are somehow, at least potentially, connected to the crimes of Nazism. In the same vein, Norma Rosen writes in "The Second Life of Holocaust Imagery" that particular words—"trains," "camps," and so forth—whenever they are uttered, in whatever context, may evoke memory of the Holocaust: "For a mind engraved with the Holocaust, gas is always that gas. Shower means their shower. Ovens are those ovens" (1987, 58). Possibly, such references—including that to the song lyric "ashes to ashes"—if woven into the texture of daily life by those who never stop contemplating the Holocaust, can be slight but effective memorials to its victims. Rosen's conception that everyday life affords opportunities for moral contemplation of the Holocaust enlarges the ways in which postgenocide generations may confront its legacy. And yet, the ever-present and omnipresent shadow of the Holocaust in our lives suggests that the residue of evil is all around us—there is no one who then can claim to be outside it, raising the problem of complicity, central to Pinter's political dramas, in a new and heightened form.

A specific political legacy of the Holocaust that is explored in *Modernity and the Holocaust* provides a key to Pinter's politics. According to Bauman, a necessary cause of the genocide was the modern, bureaucratic conception of human beings as subservient to political desires and calculations. Bauman quotes sociologist Joseph Weizenbaum on the importance of instrumental reason—the bureaucratic conception of human beings as objects to serve impersonal ends—in the Final Solution and its continued use by other, ostensibly less odious governments. Instrumental reason, indifference to the humanity of other humans, enables the crime of officialized murder: "The same logic, the same cold and ruthless application of calculating reason, slaughtered at least as many people during the next twenty years as had fallen victim to the technicians of the thousand-year Reich. We have learned nothing" (qtd. in Bauman 1989, 115). This idea parallels a prominent theme in Pinter's politics. For Pinter, instrumental reason is the fundamental attitude of criminality. Indifference to the particularity and moral worth of individual human beings defines the oppressive regimes of Pinter's political plays. His first directly political play, the sketch *Precisely*, features two bureaucrats who plan the death of millions of their own citizens according to a Cold War scenario pitting "us" against "them." Human beings in such a scenario become mere counters important only to the political goals of their alleged leaders, who are in fact their oppressors. While torture is the core of Pinter's political plays (*The Hothouse, One for the Road, The New World Order*), his political villains are bureaucrats as much as torturers. The application of instrumental reason, the vision of human beings as mere ciphers with no inherent moral rights, leads to acts that deserve to be termed criminal even though these acts may have public, governmental approval. The manipulation of instrumental reason and indifference defines numerous characters Pinter has dramatized, including the figure of Eichmann echoed by Adolf Dorff in Robert Shaw's *The Man in the Glass Booth* and extending to Devlin, with his parallel to Albert Speer and his evocation of a world composed of "winners" (who matter) and "losers" (who do not).

Pinter's work has always been seen as an exploration of how humans exercise power. One of the crucial insights Pinter provides in his political plays is that evildoers perceive themselves not as such but as agents of an ideology that is transparently unobjectionable, obviously moral. Here Pinter's overall political analysis of power aligns with Holocaust themes. We are used to the idea that some perpetrators of the genocide believed they were acting according to dictates of morality, in pursuit of clearly defensible goals and values, even when the actions taken to achieve such goals were so evidently sadistic and criminal. One commentator argues that the arbitrary inventiveness of Nazi cruelty afforded pleasure for its perpetrators—not merely the pleasure of sadism afforded through unrestrained capacity to perform violent criminal acts but also, perhaps more importantly, the pleasure that comes from the experience of righteousness. Fascism affords "the experience, for the powerful, of being on the right side" (Crouch 1990, 30). This "right side" is not just the morally correct one but takes shape as an affiliation with the inevitably all-powerful father of one's childhood conceived in oedipal terms (27). Self-perceived vulnerability thus drives obedience to oppression. Sociologist Jack Katz describes the moralistic appeal of being on the right side of (and through) violence: he argues that in many cases of murder the criminal experiences a feeling of righteousness based on the belief he or she is defending communally acknowledged values (1988, 12–42). This feeling enables the doer of a vicious deed to believe that he is doing something moral and just. Lionel and Des in *The New World Order* insist they are safeguarding "democracy" just as Nicolas defends his own godly state in *One for the Road*, just as Roote in *The Hothouse* cloaks himself in self-approval because he is carrying on the legacy of a sacred past.

Not everyone who is self-righteous is a tyrant, of course, but Pinter is surely accurate in pointing out that not only in the Holocaust but also in contemporary life, many who abuse power see themselves as just, legitimate, and benevolent. Devlin, though not necessarily a criminal or murderer, betrays a similar desire to present himself as righteous. He needs to find a rational, moral justification for his actions and attitudes. He notes carefully in defense of his antagonism to Rebecca: "I have the right to be very angry indeed. Do you realize that? I have the right to be very angry indeed. Do you understand that?" (*AA*, 69–71). An audience hearing these words will clearly understand this dialogue is itself an act of aggression. Despite this anger, or perhaps because of the guilt its presence might spark in Devlin, he argues absurdly that Rebecca "could have treated [him] like a priest" (45) by confessing to him. The claim to moralism is laughable to everyone but Devlin.

Pinter himself uses the fact of genocide to denounce the false moralism of contemporary Western governments, drawing a link between personal behavior in the play and the historical behavior of power in both the past and the present. In an interview with Mireia Aragay, he correlates Nazi oppression with the death-dealing actions of present nations: "It's not simply the Nazis that I'm talking about in *Ashes to Ashes* . . . it's also that what we call our democracies have subscribed to . . . repressive, cynical and indifferent acts of murder" (*VV*, 65). Pinter's eagerness to move from the Nazi genocide to contemporary political crimes suggests a move toward certitude and toward a particular abstract conclusion to Holocaust contemplation. This conclusion is at some temporal-historical distance from specifically

Nazi crimes, crimes that in Pinter's interpretation here figure as analogues to other acts of oppressive power. In contrast to Pinter's public pronouncements, the play itself resists such interpretive certainty (in other words, the play is at odds with its author—critics here must pay attention to the tale, not the teller). *"Keep watch over absent meaning,"* Blanchot warns those who would write about the Shoah (1986, 42)—do not rush to close the gap between event and meaning. In fact, *Ashes to Ashes* opens a space in which the Holocaust must, impossibly, be "thought" as an event that challenges and denies the assumptions that we can comprehend and interpret experience through language or in any other way.

This empty space is privileged in our experience of the play by its status as conclusion. Rebecca's attempts to merge self and history end in a final silence, memorably dramatized. Rebecca's final moment of renunciation lasts through the "[l]ong silence" specified in the penultimate stage direction (*AA*, 85). Rebecca has previously reminded us that an ending can be not a point in time, but a lasting process (67). Her final silence, in similar fashion, ends at great length, as the echo we have come to expect fails to arrive. The pause between her two denials, "I don't know of any baby," marks one utterance as being inside her story and the other outside it—that is, from Rebecca as "herself," emphasizing that she exits from storytelling as moral engagement and that the place she enters after this exit is one of silence. Silence is the ground from which language may or may not emerge; in Rebecca's final silence (mirroring the play's opening) Pinter makes us attend to the absence, the disappearance, of language. This empty space, characterized as void of language, is a site in which genocide (and its legacy) challenge our trust in meaning and articulation.[13]

Holocaust literature, writes Lang, is "always to be judged as having displaced the value of silence" (1990, 161). However, perhaps anything other than silence, any discourse at all, may have only negative value in this context; to return to Langer's terms, there may be no such thing as a "discourse" of ruin, in that any use of language implies reconstruction and consolation. Language always fails to communicate the truth of traumatic events, leaving silence (to return to Adorno's original insight) as the only mode of representing atrocity. Not only the Shoah itself but life after it can be expressed only by a form of inarticulation, by "drawing a blank" (Lacoue-Labarthe 1999, 18, 19). The untranslatability of trauma into words derives from the inarticulable essence of trauma: contemplation of extreme suffering escapes both recollection and words, leading to psychological numbness. That Pinter's Holocaust play ends in pronounced silence is aesthetically and morally appropriate as an index of a catastrophe about which one of its victims predicted, "The truth was always more atrocious, more tragic than what will be said about it" (Blanchot 1986, 83).

Acts of recollection and witness are themselves conditioned by the fact of silence. As Primo Levi writes in *The Drowned and the Saved* (a book for which Pinter has expressed admiration), the true witnesses of what happened in the concentration camps paradoxically cannot and could never utter testimony—both before and after their deaths a particular kind of Nazi victim was condemned to silence. In contemplating such a true witness, Levi evokes the *Muselmänner* of the concentration camps—those who endured a living death, a death in life, seemingly resigned to or unaware of their fate. These are the "drowned" of Levi's book title:

> I must repeat: we, the survivors, are not the true witnesses. This is an uncomfortable notion of which I have become conscious little by little. . . . We survivors are not only an exiguous but also an anomalous minority: we are those who by their prevarications or abilities or good luck did not touch bottom. Those who did so, those who saw the Gorgon, have not returned to tell about it or have returned mute, but they are the "Muslim," [*Muselmänner*], the submerged, the complete witnesses, the ones whose deposition would have a general significance. (1988, 83–84)

The *Muselmänner* (the origins of the term are obscure) were those prisoners on the verge of biological death who did not attend to their own lives. They were, as Levi recounts, without the ability to express their condition; indeed, the inability to express defined their condition: "Even if they had paper and pen, the drowned would not have testified because their death had begun before that of their body. Weeks and months before being snuffed out, they had already lost the ability to observe, to remember, to compare and express themselves." (84). The *Muselmänner* are generally described as walking corpses, or living dead, or mummy-men (Agamben 1999, 54). Levi notes with his usual honesty that other camp inmates did not want to acknowledge these people.

Given Rebecca's fixity throughout the play, her trancelike

stillness, the way in which she fearfully recognizes the "corpse" at the movie she has allegedly seen, and her ultimate descent into silence, it is possible to see her final condition as evoking the *Muselmänner*. The image resonates in several ways in *Ashes to Ashes*. First, the *Muselmänner* testify, even in their muteness, to the full extent of antihuman power:

> The *Muselmann* embodies the anthropological meaning of absolute power in an especially radical form. . . . The death of the other puts an end to the social relationship. But by starving the other, it gains time. It erects a third realm, a limbo between life and death. Like the pile of corpses, the *Muselmänner* document the total triumph of power over the human being. Although still nominally alive, they are nameless hulks. In the configuration of their infirmity, as in organized mass murder, the regime realizes its quintessential self. (Sofsky 1997, 294)

The fearsome capacity of entrenched power is the core problem of Pinter's political dramas. As evidenced by the *Muselmänner*, in the camps the Nazis did more than kill; they created new avenues for power to express itself, at the cost not only of human lives but also through the destruction of the very categories "death" and "life." The camps and especially the *Muselmänner* reveal how power can create the nonhuman out of the human: "There is thus a point at which human beings, while apparently remaining human beings, cease to be human"; "it is possible to lose dignity and decency beyond imagination, that there is still life in the most extreme degradation" (Agamben 1999, 55, 69). As we see Rebecca abandon both narration and articulation and slip into nonresponsiveness, the specter of the *Muselmänner* arises to haunt whatever existence she has left and to suggest that an image of the Holocaust and its revelations of power's dominance over the human has eerily reasserted itself in contemporary life.

The second relevance of the *Muselmänner* to the play relates to the paradoxical nature of testimony. In *Remnants of Auschwitz*, Giorgio Agamben plumbs Levi's statement that the true witnesses of the Shoah were the mute *Muselmänner*, in order to analyze the contradictory condition of these "Muslims" and the paradoxical implications of their presence for the act of witness. If authentic testimony may derive only from these speechless persons, as Levi argues, then there is a silence where we might expect witness of deepest horrors of the genocide. In this sense, as Laub writes, the Holocaust is an event without witnesses (1995, 65). (When Pinter speaks of our political responsibility, he invokes the necessity of witness and the fact of death, ascribing muted life and sight to the victims of oppression: "the dead are still looking at us, steadily, waiting for us to acknowledge our part in their murder" [*VV*, 199]. Rebecca's identification with Holocaust victims and her unfocused gaze at the end of the play evoke both death and the need to witness the dead.) In another sense, the existence of the *Muselmänner* reveals that all surviving testimony contains a blank or lacuna. Inmates of the lager did not want to see, encounter, or acknowledge the *Muselmänner*, who appear as "the *larva* that our memory cannot succeed in burying, the unforgettable with whom we must reckon" (Agamben 1999, 81). When Levi speaks of articulating by proxy the testimony of the drowned, other paradoxes are implicit. If Levi is to voice the *Muselmänner*, the true witnesses of the camps, who stand for the inhuman, the persistence of life outside the social frames of humanity, then "the one who truly bears witness in the human is the inhuman; . . . [therefore,] the human is nothing other than the agent of the inhuman. . . . Or, rather, . . . there is no one who claims the title of 'witness' by right" (Agamben 1999, 120). The act of witness that Rebecca embarks upon is subject to these paradoxes and difficulties. Witnessing means speaking while preserving a silence and being human while absorbing the inhuman. Furthermore, no one, properly speaking, has a preestablished right to utter such testimony, so it becomes vulnerable to an ontological or epistemological questioning of which Devlin's "What . . . would give you the right to discuss such an atrocity?" is simply a crude example.

The endpoint of such a project of witness might well be hazardous and difficult. It is here that the resemblance of Rebecca to previous Pinter characters—such as Beth in *Landscape* and Len in *The Dwarfs*—is relevant. By committing herself to witness in the form of imagination, and by separating herself from those around her, Rebecca risks the dangers of withdrawal, isolation, and perhaps loss of self or sanity—all risks encountered by Beth and Len. Relying on imagination frees Rebecca's moral self from the empirical limitations of the bourgeois ego, but it may also culminate in an "indeterminacy in which both 'reality' and the self are lost," as Gillen describes of Beth (2002, 62). Succumbing to this confusion between interior and exterior reality, Len skirts lasting mental imbalance, a fate that cannot be ruled out for Rebecca (although it must be remembered that this condition is the result of her empathetic project as attempted in her social context, not the cause of this project).

Rebecca's final state can be conceived as a silence that is externally imposed upon as well as internally sought by her. Maurice Blanchot suggests in *The Writing of the Disaster* that a unique type of silence is the condition of contemplating our survival after the Holocaust, a condition in which we cannot be ourselves. "The thought of the disaster," Blanchot writes, glossing the post-Holocaust moral philosophy of Emmanuel Levinas, removes us from conventional life (1986, 12).[14] "It replaces ordinary silence—where speech lacks—with a separate silence, set apart, where . . . the other, keeping still, announces himself" (12–13). The task of engaging with this moral other is fraught with intense difficulty. Moral responsibility for unspeakable atrocity destroys the foundation of our selves: "The Other calls me into question to the point of stripping me of myself" (22). In his 1996 public discussion, while describing the moral pressure Rebecca puts on herself in, Pinter noted that she strips herself naked, echoing the idea that Rebecca's project is about divesting herself of herself: "Passivity is . . . being worn down past the nub," a state composed of "anonymity, loss of self, loss of sovereignty but also of all subordination; utter uprootedness; exile" (1996c, 17–18). Rebecca carries this exile within her. She intensifies this condition for herself, even mourning over a police siren that moves away from her toward others, leaving her bereft, lonely, and, as she puts it, "insecure" (*AA*, 31). According to Blanchot, extreme suffering owns the individual who attempts to own it. Such is the end, the limit, and also the personal cost of empathizing with victims of the Holocaust. Acknowledging responsibility "interrupt[s] our speech, our reason, [and] our experience" (Blanchot 1986, 18). The impossibility of contemplating the Holocaust is that it separates us from our selves.

The theme of Pinter's political plays in the 1980s and early 1990s is the suppression of dissident voices by overwhelming structures of established power. Rebecca's can be seen as such a dissident voice, also ultimately stilled. As her attempts at imaginative empathy conclude, we witness what could be termed the end of witness as we enter a frozen world with little or no room for remembering atrocity. Contrary to earlier plays such as *Old Times* and *No Man's Land*, Pinter is no longer dramatizing the persistence of the past in the present; memory now can no longer sustain the presence, the presentness, of the past. Time's capacity to blunt horrifying historical pain is itself a tragic loss;

Ashes to Ashes evokes the terror of the past by showing it to be out of reach. "Never forget" is one famous purported lesson of the Holocaust. Pinter's play is a testament to the impossibility as well as the necessity of commemorating the dead. Rebecca's isolation indexes profound loss and gestures to the irremediable absence that both provokes, and concludes, engagement with atrocity's legacy. Faulkner wrote, "The past is never dead. It's not even past" (1966, 92), yet *Ashes to Ashes* refutes Faulkner's view. *Ashes to Ashes* summons us to make the past meaningful in our present as it simultaneously demonstrates how attempting to obey such a calling has complex, threatening, and self-destructive consequences.

The nature of the silence in which the play ends can also be approached from within Pinter's own conceptualization of dramatic silence, so frequently noted as his signature dramatic innovation. In his essay "Writing for the Theatre," Pinter elaborated upon silence and its relationship to human communication. His analysis can be regarded as an extension of the modern theater's discovery of what is called "subtext," following Stanislavsky and the myriad others inspired by his method. In making the point that communication, or revelation of self, is not dependent upon ordinary language, he implies that language continues (presumably in the forms of residue, memory, or habit) even in ostensible silence. It is as if this kind of silence is a mathematical limit that can be approached asymptotically but never reached:

> There are two silences. One when no word is spoken. The other when perhaps a torrent of language is being employed. This speech is speaking of a language locked beneath it. That is its continual reference. The speech we hear is an indication of that which we don't hear. It is a necessary avoidance, a violent, sly, anguished or mocking smoke screen which keeps the other in its place. *When true silence falls we are still left with echo but are nearer nakedness.* (Pinter 1964, 579; emphasis mine)

But what happens, we might ask, when echo ends? If "true silence" is everlastingly marked by "echo," then there would seem to be a purer and more absolute—more real—silence located beyond the cessation of echo. It is just this kind of absolute and irremediable post-echo silence that concludes *Ashes to Ashes*.

This permanent, irredeemable silence betokens the enduring

lack of connection and communication between individuals and across societies. As *Ashes to Ashes* concludes by issuing into a barren silence, obligation to social others fails to extend past the domestic sphere—the home, the now. Domestic spaces and the present define the aesthetic territory of realist dramaturgy as well as the actual limits to moral empathy as defined by Bauman. Rainer C. Baum pursues an analogous view as to the Holocaust's implications for the limits of our moral capacities. Citing the work of moral philosopher Lawrence Kohlberg, as well as the familiar if notorious psychological research conducted by Stanley Milgram and Philip Zimbardo, Baum argues that "most of us are and remain, throughout our lives, morally comparative simpletons," fixed at an early, conformist stage of moral development "originally thought appropriate for adolescents" (1988, 82). We "are able to conform to rules, as institutionalized in a given social setting, but we are unable to transcend them. Thus we can act with conscientiousness in a given role but remain unable to obey the imperatives of a postconventional conscience" (82). The conflict between individual conscience and social duty never arises, because conscience never even enters the playing field.

According to Pinter, this necessary but fatal conflict between morality and power continues. Time and again in Pinter, those exercising a "postconventional conscience" that conflicts with perceived social orthodoxy—Stanley, Petey, Rose, Sam, Victor, Jimmy, the unnamed victim in *The New World Order*, Rebecca—are in various ways (and to various extents) defeated by those who "act with conscientiousness" in roles sanctified by society. Viewed in this manner, *Ashes to Ashes* becomes an extremely dark political statement. The play reveals the centrality of Pinter's belief in the necessary martyrdom of dissent—in the paired yet contradictory ideas that dissent in practice becomes martyrdom but that it nevertheless must be attempted. "I can't go on, I must go on," as Beckett says. This paradox, implicit in all Pinter's politics, has never been stronger and located so close to home than it is in *Ashes to Ashes*.

In his 1961 essay "Writing for Myself," Harold Pinter remarked of his theater: "I'm convinced that what happens in my plays could happen anywhere, at any time, in any place, although the events may seem unfamiliar at first glance" (173). This statement links his political theater to his earlier works. Pinter's political theater challenges us to see the familiarity of oppression and abuse of power. It provokes us with the moral force of the assertion that repression can and does happen, and has happened, in the West as surely as it can, does, and has occurred anywhere else in the world. Political violence is a historical constant, which can take place now, then, or any time. This stark insight motivates the social and temporal range of Pinter's political art: from pre–World War II, to its aftermath, to unnamed, perhaps foreign countries, to what is recognizably contemporary Britain. Given the inevitability of the immoral use of power, Pinter asks his audience at least to begin accounting for its involvement in political abuses. Pinter is aware of the morally and theatrically problematic nature of seeing and understanding oneself through the representation of others. In an early, thoroughly skeptical view of theater's capacity to alter political morality, Jean-Jacques Rousseau wrote, "In the quarrels at which we are purely spectators, we immediately take the side of justice. . . . But when our interest is involved, our sentiments are soon corrupted . . . then we prefer the evil which is useful to us to the good" (1974, 295). The nature of Pinter's preferred theatrical images may, however, be at odds with his aim of political effectiveness. While the political actions and conditions Pinter dramatizes "may seem unfamiliar at first glance," the author knows that in the theater, one glance is all we get. This problematic relationship between the momentary glance and the lasting insight may obstruct the political self-awareness Pinter means to prompt. However, the author has persevered in his political theater, against both public and scholarly criticism, as Pinter has continued to expand the scope and depth of his political art. What surprised many readers of Pinter in the early 1980s is now a phase of Pinter's career that he is fully committed to, aesthetically and personally, and one that has embraced forms such as poetry, screenplays, directing, revue sketches, one-acts, and the full-length proscenium play. Pinter's political works are diverse in form and content—examining different issues, times, and locations through varying dramatic styles—yet they provide a coherent and compelling vision of the cruelty of political power.

The final silence of Rebecca in *Ashes to Ashes* is the paradoxical, ultimate statement of Pinter's political theater. Although Pinter recognizes the existence in theory of the individual voice in opposition, this voice is always silenced in the political plots he devises. His political theater ends in silence and, as do so many of his early plays, in the threatened destruction of potential counterforces to the status quo. In Pinter's later plays, the oppositional individual is marginalized on public and social rather than psychological or arbitrary grounds; the menace brought to bear on individuals is a matter of social generality. In *Party Time*, to emphasize the theme of silence, Pinter even allows his dissident character to speak about what it is like not to have a language. While silence may be a step toward distance from all that exists, or a token of resistance, it is ultimately a form of withdrawal from struggle, including social struggles. Not to speak is not to be fully human. Rebecca's ultimate silence, a silence beyond echo, is tinged with the specters of withdrawal and defeat. Its conscious, willed nature underscores the note of withdrawal. This final silence encourages us to read the silences which conclude *The Dumb Waiter, The Hothouse, Precisely, One for the Road, Mountain Language, The New World Order, Party Time,* and *Celebration* as the overwhelming triumph of power over dissidence. This triumph is the quintessential, unavoidable image of Pinter's political dramas. His political theater might be summarized as a warning to respect human rights, paired with a lament that such a warning may never be heeded. To emphasize the brute fact of power's triumph, Pinter barely adumbrates the principles that motivate dissidence. Dusty in *Party Time* flippantly links her brother Jimmy to an extinct brand of courtesy; the ironically named Victor in *One for the Road* stands only for the notion of intellectualism; Rebecca's principles amount only to a tentative, unconfident assertion of compassion. The unnamed and incapacitated victim in *The New World Order* stands only for opposition per se. The sketchy nature of oppositional values in Pinter's writing reveals his distance from other committed playwrights and emphasizes his vast political pessimism.

It is a familiar idea that political theater need only ask the right questions; it does not have to answer or solve them. Pinter's unique, even paradoxical style of political drama separates as far as possible the act of questioning from the existence of solutions. Pinter ends his political theater in silence because he has no answers to afford us.

Notes

Chapter 1. Harold Pinter and the Tradition of Political Theater

1. This thought received popular expression in the 1960's. For instance, in "My Back Pages" Bob Dylan fears that "I'd become my enemy in the instant that I preach."

2. Is the politicized Pinter, now partaking in public discourse over political issues, in danger of becoming such an ideologue, presenting statements that may be seen as reductive and unsubtle? Many of his recent statements, especially about America, are so strong that it seems Pinter may have abandoned worrying about potential dangers of presenting "ideological statements of any kind." I examine this question in chapter 6.

3. Quigley paraphrases this critique of political discourse as inevitably reductive: "Politicians consequently tend to display a readiness to settle for what is currently possible rather than to register a sustained determination to deal with all the imponderables of the actual or to confront the intractability of the necessary" (2001, 9). One might question the definition of politics here. Is politics not the art of the possible; do we properly ask politicians to spend time exhaustively analyzing the imponderable? On the question of hypocrisy, Pinter noted in a 1984 interview the hypocrisy of the U.S.S.R., America, and the United Kingdom in regard to Central America: "[T]here's nothing to choose between one side or the other" (Knowles 1989, 27). He assents to the interviewer's question "You're not lined up politically to East or West, Left or Right?" This position seems rather far removed from Pinter's more current political attitudes, which are strongly anti-American.

4. An interesting case here is Pinter's view of his vote for the Conservatives in 1979. He labels this one of the most stupid things he has ever done. Knowles is much more forgiving of Pinter than he is of himself, noting that many artists voted against Labour in this election because of the ongoing strike of theater technician unions (1990, 80).

5. In *The Life and Work of Harold Pinter*, Michael Billington argues this position strenuously. Critic Austin Quigley observes that Pinter's attempts to unify his works under the umbrella of politics are somewhat exaggerated and "belated" (2001, 8). Similarly, playwright David Hare discounts "current protestations that Harold was always a political playwright" (Eyre 2000, 20). Mark Batty notes that Pinter's own reinterpretation of his early plays in light of his later and explicit political investments is self-contradictory (2001, 90).

6. Nuclear weapons are, however, the subject of the first sketch of Pinter's political period, entitled *Precisely*.

7. "[T]he American writer in the middle of the twentieth century has his hands full in trying to understand, describe, and then make *credible* much of

American reality. . . . The actuality is continually outdoing our talents" (1961, 224).

8. The German writer referred to is Lutz Niehammer, and the essay quoted is "Posthistoire," in *Zones of Engagement*, edited by Perry Anderson (London: Verso, 1992).

9. Cf. O. K. Werckmeister: "The educational level and the intelligence of its [industrial democracy's] technical, social, and political elites are too highly developed to find their self-understanding in straightforward assertions of the values by which they live. These elites demand a culture which appears to do justice to the contemporary historical situation, or which even represents it as problematical as it is, but without making a problem of what its permanent crises have to do with their privileged conditions of existence" (1991, 14–15). Christopher Butler writes that audience of political theater is impervious to criticism, being composed of "anti-bourgeois bourgeois, who accept society more or less as it is, while at the same time entertaining a set of intellectual and artistic notions which are contradicted by [their] actual behavior" (1980, 122).

10. Critic Marc Silverstein even wonders whether Pinter's plays are in fact collusive with the ideologies and power structures they seek to oppose. In Pinter's plays, the power of "the cultural order" is "unshakeably homogenous and monolithic" to the extent that "the totalizing nature of [their] analysis of cultural power tends to reify that power" (1993, 142, 152). Here the assumption, a common one, is that political theater must provide tools for change or at least establish hope for change. Silverstein seems beholden to this assumption, even as his often brilliant analyses are grounded in postmodern social theory. Pinter writes a political theater which is heterodox, even heretical, on the basic assumption that such theatre encourages the hope for or possibility of social change. If political theater urges to revolt against what exists, Pinter's version obliges by rebelling against the prevailing definition and procedures of that political theater.

11. Pinter deals quickly with the notion of obviousness: "My plays are not political discussions. They are living things. They are certainly not debates" (*VV*, 60). He spends several sentences describing, in familiar fashion, the necessity of violence to any serious writer reflecting on contemporary life. Numerous political playwrights write "living" plays that include levels of explicit reference and debate Pinter does not.

12. "The past brings out our patriotism," novelist Don DeLillo reminds us; we give it an "undivided allegiance" (1997, 73).

CHAPTER 2. EARLY PLAYS AND RETROACTIVE READINGS: *THE BIRTHDAY PARTY, THE DUMB WAITER,* AND *THE HOTHOUSE*

1. Esslin notes the "racialist flavor" of Goldberg and McCann's attack upon Stanley (1993, 30). Knowles sees the play evoking the plight of deported Jews; we as audience are passive and complicit in Stanley's fate (1995a, 38).

2. Pinter discusses these vans with Mireia Aragay in *Various Voices* (65).

3. "Play up, play up, play the game" is a quote from Sir Henry Newbolt's patriotic poem "Vitai Lampada," a poem which urged courage on the battle-

fields of the Great War (World War I) by comparing war to school sports (www.firstworldwar.com/poets_and_prose/newbolt.htm).

4. Pinter's political interpretation of the 1994 production differs from that suggested by his 1958 poem "A View of the Party." This poem stresses the immateriality of Goldberg and McCann: "The thought that Goldberg was / Sat in the centre of the room," while the opposition between Stanley and his tormentors dissolves into a unity in the poem: "For Stanley had no home / Only where Goldberg was, / And his bloodhound McCann, / Did Stanley remember his name" (1991, 32–33). These lines suggest that the dissident Stanley needs his persecutors, that they are essential to his identity and being. Goldberg and McCann may even, on this reading, be psychological self-extensions of Stanley, as K.'s tormentors in *The Trial* are sometimes seen as manifestations of his own consciousness. (To take this point further, it is just possible that the ultimate irony of *The Trial* is that K. really is guilty; if so, the politics of *The Birthday Party* become even murkier.) These suggestions move toward a psychological thematic, thus, as Peacock notes, "seeming to deny the political content that [Pinter] was to claim for the play during the 1980s" (1997, 28).

5. The name Wilson can be taken as a political reference either to Woodrow Wilson, who promised to fight World War I to make the world safe for democracy, or to the Labour Party's Harold Wilson—two politicians Pinter might have had reason to view with contempt.

6. Hinchliffe (1967, 57) argues that the stress Ben displays in the play arises due to this call to murder Gus. Perhaps, but there is nothing in the play to prove this. As what anthropologist F. G. Bailey terms a "good follower," Ben must anticipate what to do in every situation to please his superiors, a condition that itself gives rise to perpetual stress—in other words, his displeased manner could be how he acts all the time; there need be nothing special about the day of the play's occurrences to cause his attitude (see Bailey 1988, 13, 27).

7. The high number of stage directions and Ben's recourse to violence as opposed to language suggest something crucial is at stake.

8. Gus's silence reverses the outcome of the famous battle about lighting the kettle versus the lighting gas (*DW*, 97–98). Gus's victory here is a red herring that distracts us from his more lasting defeat. Despite the dramatic satisfactions of Gus's linguistic triumph over Ben and his power, the true conditions of the world of the play emphasize a lasting and ritualized subjugation, one that appears natural, even invisible. The dramatic reversal of Gus's temporary victory should not mislead us. "Drama often obscures the real issues," as Jenny Holzer has it (installation at Boston MFA, December 28, 2002).

9. The play premiered in 1980.

10. It is not the case that Pinter himself has such a positive view of the family. As *Moonlight* demonstrates, the family is a way to perpetuate emotional inadequacy from one generation to the next. *The Homecoming* dramatizes the family as means to learn cruelty and exercise power—a place to acquire patriarchal roles. There are at least two implications for Pinter's political analysis here. First, the family is a major means of inculcating the patriarchal expectations of behavior and judgment, as a number of critics have noted recently. Second, the family is where one first experiences power—as a child looking up to figures of authority necessary for sustenance and life. This view of our relationship to power is supported by Freud. Experiences of power in childhood may provide a sort of blueprint for later experiences of power, especially explaining deference and the need to obey (Bailey 1988, 95).

CHAPTER 3. PINTER AGAINST THE (NEW) RIGHT: *PRECISELY*, *ONE FOR THE ROAD*, AND *MOUNTAIN LANGUAGE*

1. During the early 1980s various experts argued that the "first use" of a nuclear weapon was moral and proper. *Hiroshima in America: A Half Century of Denial* (by Robert Jay Lifton and Greg Mitchell) may be read in conjunction with *Precisely*, as it reminds us of the real-world references behind Pinter's satire. For instance, according to nuclear scientist Herman Kahn, "'if a president asks his advisers, 'How can I go to war—almost all American cities will be destroyed?' the answer should be, 'That's not entirely fatal; we've got some spares'" (Lifton and Mitchell 1995, 311). In another statement of the pronuclear stance, Joseph Nye in *Nuclear Ethics* argued that merely because nuclear war might lead to apocalypse was not, logically, a sufficient cause to reject it (see Lifton and Mitchell, 312). In a 1985 interview Pinter noted American physicist Peter Hagelstein's reference to nuclear weapons as "an interesting physics problem" (Knowles 1989, 28).

2. The medieval reference of Roger and Stephen above is continued in other of Pinter's political plays. In *Party Time*, one character asks about the streets, where the army may be putting down a popular insurrection, "What on earth's going on out there? It's like the Black Death" (*PT*, 6). This odd comparison evokes the Middle Ages, which in turn provides a model of corporate or group identity, a model popular in the social worlds Pinter portrays in these plays. To be a member of a group, especially a powerful one, is safety; to have an identity as an individual is dangerous to oneself and subversive of the social order.

3. See Esslin (1970, 25).

4. It is surprising how often this hope asserts itself in progressive discourse. For instance, in a 2002 conversation between novelist/commentator Arundhati Roy and historian Howard Zinn, Roy predicts that "hopefully" the fascists in India will "mess up" their attempts at domination. "Zinn: I think we can count on them to mess it up. Roy: I hope so. Zinn: We need that. We'll try our best. We'll accomplish a lot, but we do really need them to mess it up" (http://www.lannan.org/__authors/roy). Leftist discourse should, according to the paradoxical, self-questioning politics of Pinter, learn how to be more hardheaded and should not underestimate the strength of its enemy or merely stand by in hope of its defeat. Hope is not a strategy.

5. Nicolas in *One for the Road*, the next play in the author's sequence of protest works, puts this issue to his victim: "Who would you prefer to be? You or me? . . . I'd go for me if I were you. The trouble about you, although I grant your merits, is that you're on a losing wicket, while I can't put a foot wrong" (*One*, 50). Membership among the winning group is an antidote to the potential insecurities of power. Being part of the winning side is one way to subsume individual feelings of the anxiety of command—revenge is possible against a lone person but impossible against a large and strong enough group.

6. This point surely has extended application: we must take moral responsibility for public actions from which we fail to dissociate ourselves. The point surely applies, or applied, to the war on Saddam Hussein's Iraq in 2003 and 2004. We provide ourselves only a comforting, but certainly false, illusion, if we seek to separate ourselves from what is done in our name. If these wars are done in our name, what moral distance do we actually achieve from it by

muttering disgustedly about stupid Republicans as we read our newspapers (my reaction), or even by protesting publicly about it (that of people braver and more certain than myself)?

7. The Gestapo arrested not only the suspected individuals but also their entire families, a system called "kith and kin arrests," especially when persecuting the anti-Hitler conspirators (the subject of Pinter's *Reunion* screenplay). This system resembled ancient Germanic law that held a family or tribe responsible for the misdeeds of any of its members. "Not only the perpetrator of the deed, whether accomplished or attempted, was therefore to be persecuted and punished, but also the spirit of the deed. . . . Not merely individuals, therefore, but their 'kith and kin,' their families in which the spirit of freedom and resistance to injustice and arbitrary action had grown and been nurtured, were to be exterminated," Peter Hoffmann writes of the arrests carried out after the unsuccessful plot against Hitler's life on July 20, 1944 (1977, 519–20).

The regime of *One for the Road* seems to subscribe to similar methods. If Pinter's politics seem particularly apt at the current moment, it may be because he intuits that the behavior of those wielding reactionary power is driven not by principled opposition to certain opinions or deeds. It is not just that these reactionaries disagree with certain beliefs or notions, but they hate their very existence and everything about the existence of people who utter or perform these noxious thoughts or actions. "They" really do hate "us," if "us" means anyone who opposes society. The fact that Britons during the Falklands crisis and Americans during the Iraq war perceived those who opposed militarist policy as treasonous documents this phenomenon by which the powerful hate and demonize their opponents. This phenomenon explains why Pinter's political plays never specify the exact nature of the dissidence reigning power tries to crush. His villains do not have to ascribe particular beliefs or actions to these dissidents to hate them. Of course, this fact might well liberate opponents of the social order: if they are going to hate you merely because you are you, because you embody the taint of evil, you might as well speak up and cause a fuss and truly earn their hatred. It is a provocative subject of speculation to wonder if liberals or progressives do not hate their opponents this way. Perhaps their belief in human correctibility or in the efficacy of reason or in the notions of fair play and inclusion prevents this. Or perhaps (venturing further down the road of unprovable speculation) progressives should learn to play just as ruthlessly as their opponents.

8. The (apparently initial) holograph draft does not contain these lines. This draft makes Nicolas's devotion to "God" more emphatic—the regime is more openly theocratic than Pinter eventually decided upon. "We are as one, we all pray to the same God," says Nicolas in the holograph, later noting of his interview chamber, "God is here" (PA, Box 43).

9. This moment bears out Joseph Brodsky: "In the case of a tyrant, time to think of the soul is always used for scheming to preserve the status quo" (1986, 113).

10. Ronald Knowles argues that one reservation about Silverstein's sophisticated and insightful analysis is that perhaps he has "reconstituted the plays as a Lacanian mirror image of his own intellectuality, indicating as much the critic's as the dramatist's procedure" (1995b, 738). Colette Stoeber makes a similar observation in her own highly positive review (1995, 219).

11. Pinter arrived at this version of the scene after writing two separate drafts in which the mother does speak. In one she addresses her son in conven-

tional dialogue; in another there is a moment near the end of the scene where it appears she speaks through voice-over (PA, Box 36).

12. As Jeanette Colleran notes, this line echoes what a privileged audience is likely to say about welfare recipients; thus Pinter brings the play home in a brief but powerful way (1993, 60).

13. It is, of course, possible to give too much emphasis to Pinter's comments on his own plays. Artistic creation is not defined by rational intentions, and Pinter has spoken of the unconscious element in his playwriting, the duty to allow his characters to speak as they wish. Yet, Pinter has also proclaimed that he has put his art at the service of his public positions—he has something to tell us. The idea that Pinter's creative impulse eschews reflection is something of an overstatement: "Looking at the texture of the plays more closely, one detects a planning and a building method which proves that the dramatic texts are not as random and unpreconceived" as sometimes assumed (Sakellaridou 1989, 45). Gillen makes a similar point about Pinter's attention to craft and conscious shaping, selection, and revision (2002, 55). The plays often bear clear resemblances to their sources or inspiration. Compare his account of a 1985 meeting with Turkish writers who had been tortured with the final image of *Mountain Language*: "Those who had been tortured in prison were still trembling. . . . One of the writer's wives was mute. She had fainted and lost her power of speech when she had seen her husband in prison" (http://www.haroldpinter.org). This is not to say that Pinter's proffered meanings for his plays are to be regarded as authoritative, of course, but only that they are worthy of consideration as one possible reading among others.

14. In fact, Pinter has at times suggested the play is not about the Kurds in Turkey, but rather it is truly about the abuse of power to restrict civil liberties and freedoms in Britain (Knowles 1989, 29). Not surprisingly, given such a statement, his next play, *Party Time*, depicts an England under martial law.

15. Frank Gillen argues so far as to argue that seeing the play in terms of definitive reference to a particular situation is itself fascist (1988, 4), but this is a rather restrictive view of language, as it denies even a possible distinction between language as ideology and language as information.

16. Watt sees *The Homecoming* as modernist in its concern with depth psychology, as opposed to the more postmodern *No Man's Land* (1998, 95). The pairing of *One for the Road* and *Mountain Language* can be seen analogously in terms of this shift from late modernism to incipient postmodernism.

17. If in some formal matters the play appears Brechtian, in other ways it is not. Above I discussed the universalism of the play, the sense that oppressions disparate in place and time are being addressed without distinction or in light of their (assumed) commonalities. This method is the very opposite of Brecht's notion of historicism, that is, seeing each historical situation as unique, as Sakellaridou suggests: "Rationality and historicity . . . are alien" to *One for The Road* and *Mountain Language* (1989, 44).

18. Quoted in Martin P. Golding's "On the Idea of Moral Pathology," from *Echoes from the Holocaust: Philosophical Reflections on a Dark Time*, edited by Alan Rosenberg and Gerald E. Myers (1988, 144).

19. Why do we fall for this just-world concept? Crelinsten and Schmid, historians of torture, offer a theory: we imbibe "Manichean" myths of good triumphing over bad when we are young (1994, 8). A sense that the world is properly ordered provides psychological security. Recall the childishness of Ben and Gus, who need to believe the system they live in (and for) is benefi-

cent. Are we unable to be politically mature because our relationship to power is fundamentally childlike or influenced by the relation we had with power as children? The issue here is the grounds why people accept the world as it is, living within its given conditions of power. Do they do so because of something called "ideology"? Ideology is always conceived of as a structured set of ideas, feelings, and predispositions inculcated into rational. Our fear of randomness and our unwillingness to see power as inimical or to confront it if it is so become parts of our psyches during childhood, occurring before we even have a chance to be "ideologized" by pro–status quo arguments and assumptions. According to Judith Butler, these early experiences structure and abet future subjectification: "this situation of primary dependency [of the child] conditions the political formulation and regulation of subjects and becomes the means of their subjection" (1997, 7).

20. This book was published as *Der Begriff des Politischen* in 1928. For more on Schmitt's ideas and their relation to Nazism, see Paul Edward Gottfried's *Carl Schmitt: Politics and Theory* (Greenwood Press, 1990) and Joseph W. Bendersky's *Carl Schmitt: Theorist for the Reich* (Princeton University Press, 1983).

21. If the idea of a state justifying all uses of power, including lethal power, to defend itself against diffuse enemies suggests post-9/11 America almost as much as it does Nazi Germany, Pinter could hardly be displeased. In fact, a *New York Times* Sunday Magazine column from June 2003 notes (with disapproval) that many on the left are offering Weimar Germany as an analogy to America during the administration of George W. Bush (Traub 2003a). Is there a danger in such analyses of blurring the moral distinctions between things one does not like? The implications of this question for Pinter's public politics are taken up in chapter 6.

Chapter 4. Pinter and the Permanence of Power: *Party Time, Celebration, Press Conference,* and *The New World Order*

1. Discussion at 92nd Street Y, New York City, October 1996. Of course, Pinter might mean "Conservatives" with a capital *C*, meaning Thatcher's Conservative Party. These neoconservative cultural warriors of the 80s and early 90s are to be distinguished, in some ways and certainly nominally, from the contemporary (circa 2002 and 2003) group of politicians who espoused "regime change" in Iraq as part of a hoped-for democratization of the Middle East.

2. This quote appears in *The French Lieutenant's Woman* by John Fowles (1981, 193.) It does not appear in Robert C. Tucker's edition of *The German Ideology* in *The Marx-Engels Reader* (1978).

3. Terry's voice in his central monologues, his use of repetition, his use of verbal violence and profanity, his self-assurance, and his sexual scatology are echoed in Pinter's poem "American Football" (quoted from Pinter's *Collected Poems*). This piece was written in 1991 to protest the Gulf War:

> Hallelujah!
> It works.
> We blew the shit out of them.

We blew the shit right back up their own ass
And out their fucking ears.
. . . . . .
We blew their balls into shards of dust,
Into shards of fucking dust.

(1991, 55)

Pinter assumes that a political animus is focused on the body of the hated other: political violence equals sexual control.

4. Watt notes that a concept of heroic maleness is vital to the legitimation of these repressive regimes (1998, 108, 118). However, the males in *Party Time* are flat, banal, far from imposing. Either heroism has been debased, or male heroism is not necessary for the perpetuation of this society.

5. Pinter's first title for this play was *Normal Service*. The Gavin character says in a draft version, "We want the world to run in a normal manner, on normal lines, on paths of what we understand to be normality, paths which would be recognized as legitimate paths by the man on the Clapham Omnibus" (PA, Box 44).

6. Charlotte sees a punning complexity in her husband's death being described as "slow and quick" (quick as in alive) that Fred does not, for an example of one joke the disempowered use to poke at the privileged.

7. Watt mentions allied figures in the New Right, such as Dinesh DeSouza and Robert Kimball who attacked diversity, feminism, and postmodern relativism (1998, 121).

8. Watt sees these two methods of legitimation as logical opposites (1998, 106–7); Lifton sees them as complementary.

9. This supposed weakness in the operations of power can be utilized to portray the powerful as victims; in later plays, especially *Celebration*, elites complain about how they are abused by others. The moral odiousness of this portrayal is obvious. Beckett captures the outrageousness of masters-as-victims in *Waiting for Godot*. When Pozzo first enters with Lucky, Estragon and Vladimir are angry at Pozzo's inhuman and cruel treatment of his servant. After Pozzo describes how Lucky no longer provides quality service, Vladimir forgets his outrage at Pozzo and turns on Lucky—rebuking him for daring to "[c]rucify" his master (Beckett 1954, 23a). Beckett satirizes how Vladimir's instinct for empathy (or his desire to display such an instinct) leads him to a false position.

10. See Didion's "Fixed Opinions, or the Hinge of History," *New York Review of Books*, January 16, 2003. She goes on to write that the abandonment of inquiry made it "seem as if we had been plunged at one fell stroke into a premodern world. The possibilities of the Enlightenment had vanished" (2003, 55). Such a world is one autocrats inherently prefer.

11. If Pinter's plays delineate the justifications by which the powerful rationalize themselves, as Quigley argues (2001, 10), *Celebration* shows how the empowered have their own brand of *ressentiment*.

12. Here the play seems to mock the many critics who have noted that Pinter's rooms are places of refuge and protection akin to the womb as ultimate sanctuary, by blatantly and banally expressing these ideas on the surface of the play. The characters allude to other themes often held to compose the "Pinteresque." Suki refers to the persistence and intermixing of the past into the present: "I sometimes feel the past is never past" (C, 56). "You mean that yes-

terday is today?" asks Julie, and Suki assents. Julie mocks her husband for no longer being able to exercise cruelty indirectly through sophisticated language. Lambert discusses the tragedy of life according to the absurdist model by which all individuals are monads unable to know, communicate with, and care for others. To make a different point, the word "boot" recurs in the Waiter's fears—the same one "itching to squash" that Pinter mentions in his letter to Wood about *The Birthday Party*. Richard Sennett writes of the origin of the phrase "giving someone the boot" to describe oppression. In the nineteenth century, it became unpopular to discipline servants corporally (as with a whip) such that the master drew blood—piercing the skin of servants and inferiors came to be regarded as déclassé, unwise and immoral. With whipping no longer a respectable option, "the violence adults inflicted on other adults came through the boot or the use of the hands" (Sennett 1980, 93–94). Of course, the contemporary decrease in direct physical discipline should not be understood as a lessening of coercion.

13. The phrase "mystery of life" might be connected with this book's initial distinction between Pinter as an absurdist versus a political writer. If one wanted a quick tag line for all that absurdist theater gives us and political theater supposedly slights, it might be "the mystery of life"—the sense of what is uncertain, unquantifiable, difficult to categorize and verbalize. Nightingale uses the word "mystery" to label what Pinter's political works lack in comparison with the depth of the previous plays (1990, 149).

14. Pinter's revision methods bear comparison to Beckett's. As suggested, in various manners, by S. E. Gontarski, Ruby Cohn, and Deirdre Bair, Beckett's writing process embodies what Gontarksi terms an "intent of undoing." Earlier drafts of a work are often more thematically clear, more "realistic, traditional, and even sentimental," than the final products; during revision, the work becomes more abstract and unspecific, organized more complexly, thus subverting "what we have traditionally called meaning or content" (1985, 228). Bert O. States analyzes how in *Waiting for Godot* Beckett introduces the mythical theme of Cain and Abel and then attempts to "take back" or retract the reference, and its implications, by submerging it within the play's ostensible subject of waiting (1978, 9). Beckett castigates thematic obviousness through *Catastrophe*'s Director: "This craze for explicitation! Every i dotted to death!" (1984, 269). The Director (portrayed by Pinter in a 1999 video version of the play directed by David Mamet) is generally labeled a fascist, but the aesthetic point he makes here captures Beckett's movement away from specificity. In considering Pinter's revisions whereby Jimmy in *Party Time* was originally located in prison, it is interesting to note that during rehearsal for a production of *Waiting for Godot*, Beckett pondered having the shadows of prison bars on the stage floor (Graver 1989, 27).

15. Nazim Hikmet is a Turkish poet whose anti-American poem "A Sad State of Freedom" appears in *99 Poems in Translation*, edited by Pinter, Anthony Astbury, and Geoffrey Godbert (1994, 42–43). By Jorge Ellecuria, Pinter apparently is referring to Ignacio Ellecuria, a Jesuit priest in El Salvador, an outspoken opponent of the Salvadorian right and a theologian and philosopher active in liberation theology.

16. The locution "peasant theology" evokes "liberation theology." Pinter has referred to the American sponsorship of the overthrow of Chilean President Salvador Allende as one spark to his politicization.

17. It is tempting to conclude that these qualities of torture also characterize the manner in which Pinter's plays have been said to operate.

18. *Victoria Station* (1981) is something of a transitional piece in this regard. The silences of the Driver (a character perhaps evoking a latter-day Jack the Ripper) are both canny and confused. The Driver destabilizes his boss the Controller, provoking the latter's recognition that his life is limited and barren. But the Driver seems also to provoke physical punishment from his boss—and to be waiting for it at the end of the play.

Chapter 5. Pinter at the Movies: *The Comfort of Strangers* and *Victory*

1. Pinter does not appear in the film's final credits.

2. The precise nature of this satire is difficult for Pinter as screenwriter to portray in the film script—as he and others have pointed out, it is the narrative voice of a novel that most resists being captured on screen. The location of this satire might be in the performances of Natasha Richardson and Rupert Everett as Mary and Colin. Richardson's acting projects a kind of girlish preciousness, while Everett seems to be suggesting that he realizes, as should we, that he is more intelligent than the character he is playing.

3. As Daniel Mendelsohn notes, Robert's appearance should set off alarm bells: he looks exactly like Christopher Walken in a white suit (2001, 28).

4. Penelope Prentice cites an e-mail exchange between her and Pinter: what positive political action can we take at the current time, she asked him. Pinter answers, "Before we can defeat an enemy, we have to know them" (2002, 194).

5. For an excellent analysis of this theme see Raymond F. Armstrong's *Kafka and Pinter: Shadow-Boxing: The Struggle Between Father and Son* (1999).

6. As striking and direct as Pinter's language is here, there is one question his theories do not answer. Are there tremendous incentives provided by society not to care about the wider world—or is it our fundamental desire as individuals not to care about the world? That is, is political indifference determined by nurture or nature? If the latter, constructing a politics of caring and morality must defeat human nature itself. However, compassion or solidarity does not have to arise from contemplation of the oppressed. Bentham once said of John Stuart Mill that he rather hated the ruling few than loved the suffering many, a characterization that I sometimes think might also apply to Pinter. Pinter's own political dramas disdain the high society that ignores the suffering many around it—recall the callous indifference of *Party Time*'s characters and the violent scheming of *The Hothouse*'s staff (the latter play does not depict any social victims).

7. This scene is not included in the 1990 Faber and Faber edition, but it does appear in the screenplay in *Collected Screenplays 3*, published in 2000.

8. Billington: "McEwan is perfectly happy with Pinter's political interpolation. 'It's not there . . . in the novel, but it fits perfectly well with the general nature of the tension between Robert and Colin . . . '" (1996, 319). Well, maybe. But, what else is McEwan going to tell Billington? And, if the particular reference is so apt, why didn't McEwan choose to make such a one in the first place? According to Gale and Hudgins (1996, 109, 110), Pinter's drafts of this scene contained also a conversation about gays and lesbians raising children.

9. Politically speaking, there is always the possibility that Robert will be read strictly in terms of his psychological aberrance. This focus on aberrance might well detract from the "political" force of the film, just as it did in Pinter's *One for the Road*. Here the psychological focus might allow a "common sense" view of patriarchy—as ordinary, normal—to be recuperated from the extreme, obsessive version Robert professes. Is the ideology of patriarchal sexism monstrous in itself—or can it, in either good or bad faith, be seen in exculpatory fashion merely as possibly yielding to monstrous interpretations?

10. *Victory* has, in fact, been a popular Conrad novel on the screen. Three English-language versions exist (a 1919 silent and versions done in 1930 and 1940); a live American TV version was done in 1960, a 1986 German adaptation starred Sam Waterston as Jones, and a 1995 French-German production featured Willem Dafoe as Heyst (Moore 1997, 224–29).

11. Both works are metapolitical in that they deal with this transition rather than the specific ideologies that might follow the process of "becoming political." In his screenplay adaptation of *Accident*, Pinter writes the character Stephen, an Oxford don, in more negative tones than does Nicholas Mosley in the novel exactly on this issue of avoiding reality. "Pinter's [Stephen] is an Oxford nearly-man who retreats behind the ambiguities of philosophy and who is forced—by accident, as it were—to engage with the real world" (Billington 1996, 186).

12. Conrad portrays Heyst's reaction internally: "Doubt entered him— . . . It seemed to spread itself all over him, and lodge in his entrails. He stopped suddenly, with a thought that he who experienced such a feeling had no business to live" (1924, 391–92). This doubt is not a new thing in Heyst's evaluation of Lena. Hudgins points out that his initial impulse to rescue Lena is termed "pity," a quality that to Heyst's father, and to thinkers such as Blake and Nietzsche, is merely a form of contempt (1991, 25).

13. The moral status of such privacy and isolation is not without its complications, of course. Pinter does equate this self-isolation away from social and political conflicts as an immaturity or insufficiency that must be transcended, somehow. The plots of *The Comfort of Strangers*, *The Dumb Waiter*, and *The Dreaming Child* dramatize a coming forth of the individual from a self-willed separation from sociality into engagement with or awareness of wider social and political forces. Yet, the humanitarian thrust of Pinter's politics, noted by Knowles and Batty, assert that the State or other power should not impose upon the life and dignity of the individual (Knowles 1995a, 189; Batty 2001, 120). This position implies that privacy is a goal of political action—not just a bar to it.

14. This is not to deny that there is a kind of anti-intellectualism in Pinter—as there is in the genre of modern drama as a whole. Andy's speech about the futility of thinking from *Moonlight* and Ruth's disquisition on the movements of her lips as more important than her words are generally cited in Pinter criticism in this regard. Of course, the kind of anti-intellectualism Pinter (and Beckett) display is likely to be of a paradoxical, intellectual sort.

15. Also, Billington and Antonia Fraser, Pinter's wife, credit his happy marriage with allowing him to expand his career in different ways (Billington 1996, 235, 255), suggesting that the security of a relationship of love and mutuality (rejected by Heyst, accepted by Pinter) aids in the task of engaging with the world.

Chapter 6. Pinter and the Politics of Fascism: *Reunion, Taking Sides,* and *The Trojan War Will Not Take Place*

1. No such comparable political facts are included in Uhlman's novella, underscoring Pinter's commitment to historical specificity. Pinter has Hans turn the radio off (*R*, 82), just as he later snaps the TV off when it shows the Nazi judge Roland Freisler (*R*, 59), creating through visual rhyme a correspondence between Henry and his younger self.

2. This scene was developed through several draft versions. In handwritten, early draft material, Pinter sketches out a scene in which the announcer, as in the final screenplay, explicitly invites his audience to see Freisler as an actor covering up his real self (see Gale and Hudgins 1996, 129). The first screenplay draft contains a scene in which Henry watches TV and hears "A political discussion (naturally in German). Henry clearly understands the argument" (PA, Box 49). Other notes sketching out this scene specify the program's audience as young people (Box 50). Pinter has an interesting view of this scene. He sees Henry as recognizing Freisler's voice "through a sort of osmosis" (Pinter 1989c, 26). Later Pinter curiously maintains that Henry, at this point, has a subconscious or intuitive awareness of the fact that his friend took part in the Resistance: "De toute evidence Henry ne sait pas ce qui est arrive a son ami, qu'il faisait partie du complot contre Hitler, qu'il y eut un proces que dirigeait Freisler, et pourtant dans son subconscient" (26). ["By all the evidence Henry does not know upon his arrival that his friend was part of the plot against Hitler, but the image of Freisler begins a process of awareness in his unconscious"; my translation.]

3. This sadistic fact is fairly well known. Uhlman inserts it in an early draft of his novella ("Konrad's Letter"). This version takes the form of a long letter Konradin writes, just before his execution, to Hans. "Now I know that I shall die in a few hours, slowly. . . what horrifies me is the manner in which I shall die: by strangulation, slowly, hanging from a butcher's hook, squirming till death ensues" (PA, Box 49).

4. There is no evidence that concludes that Hitler conceived the Final Solution as an anticipatory response to Russian military savagery, as Nolte argues, and even if Hitler did think this way, such an idea would not pertain to the Nazi destruction of Jews in Poland, Germany, Hungary, and so forth. See Maier 1988, 28–31 and 66–84 for analysis of Nolte's arguments and Habermas's responses.

5. Robert C. Reimer and Carol J. Reimer note that, when one looks at films about the Nazis, "one would assume that every German family had a Jewish friend whom it sought to protect" (1992, 9).

6. It may be that even to use the term "German Resistance" represents something of an overstatement. Günter Grass notes, "By the end of the war, doubts arose, but no resistance to speak of. It was—is—all too tempting to count yourself among the liberated, hiding the painful knowledge that a majority of the German people did their utmost to prevent liberation." In 1988, politician Philipp Jeininger described the passivity of the German nation in response to Nazi anti-Semitism: "[T]here was no rejection, no resistance worthy of mentioning. . .. [O]nly a few were sympathetic, gave practical solidarity, assistance or help. All saw what happened, but the majority of them looked

away and said nothing" (Reimer and Reimer 1992, 85). In less measured tones, Daniel Cohn-Bendit compares 1970s German environmentalism to the lack of anti-Nazi resistance in the Third Reich: "It is easier to find 200,000 people fighting against the destruction of 6 million trees than 200,000 people fighting against the destruction of six million Jews." (The Grass and Bendit-Cohn quotes are from Marcel Ophul's documentary *Hotel Terminus: The Life and Times of Klaus Barbie.*)

7. The immediate aftermath of Stauffenberg's failed assassination attempt illustrates the historical ambiguity surrounding the actions and motivations of the 20 July group. Hitler's ministry of propaganda termed the conspirators a "small group of blue-blooded swine" (Reimer and Reimer 1992, 99). The view of the Allies was not so different—Churchill had in fact denied previous requests for help from German dissenters, while the U.S. Office of War Information also called Stauffenberg's circle "a small group of blue-blooded reactionaries" (Rothfels 1962, 123).

8. Several conspirators wrote statements about their conduct and beliefs as part of the investigation against them. Hamerow concludes that these statements are more or less reliable—since the conspirators knew they were going to be executed, there was little reason for them to be untruthful (1997, 376). In connection with the issue of the plotters' motivations, Uhlman revises interestingly. In "Konrad's Letter," Konrad addresses this matter directly: "It was a terrible decision [to oppose Hitler]. In a thousand years no Hohenfels [Konrad's family name] had ever betrayed in time of war. But here . . . the point was to save millions of lives. As soon as we were sure that we could not win the war, we decided to act. One last point, but the most important: I must repeat it to you once more. I had never heard of the gas chambers. I knew that there were concentration camps but I knew nothing of the gas chambers. It was only a few months before the attempt against Hitler's life that I learned of those horrible things. It only reinforced my determination to kill the monster" (PA, Box 49). In the published *Reunion*, Uhlman strikes any such specific language. Konrad's explanations in this early version may have appeared to Uhlman to smack too much of special pleading and to underscore the Resistance's central motive of minimizing the consequences of Germany's military losses: "As soon as we were sure we could not win the war, we decided to act." This bald statement that for the conspirators, to win the war was more important to counter evil, surely qualifies in a large way a positive assessment of the Resistance.

9. Fest ultimately sees the July 20 plot as a work of "conscience" that cannot be fairly "measured by the futility of its efforts or by its unfulfilled hopes" (1997, 341–42). Shirer puts the matter quite succinctly: "better late than never" (1960, 1047). The central dilemma of perceiving the Resistance involves this theme of belatedness. Like Heyst in *Victory*, the conspirators finally took action only when it was overdue.

10. Recently Pinter joined an atheist protest. He and other intellectuals, including playwright Arnold Wesker, asked the BBC to supplement its "Thought of the Day" program, which deals with religious issues, with a program that looked at the world from an atheist perspective. (See BBC New World Edition, August 14, 2002, by Torin Douglas, accessible on http://news.bbc.co.uk/2/hi/entertainment/2192086.stm.)

11. Bailey's definitions again resemble Jean-Paul Sartre's classic analysis of anti-Semitism in *Anti-Semite and Jew*. The rational man, Sartre writes, knows

that drawing conclusions about the world is an uncertain and tenuous process; the anti-Semite by contrast desires to possess (and does possess) certain truth. Such a person will "tell you that he wants a strong authority to take from him the crushing responsibility of thinking for himself" (1995, 31). The novella and screenplay compound this irony, as Konradin tells Henry in a farewell letter that Henry "taught me how to think. You have. Truly" (R, 90).

12. Pinter remembers how people forget oppression that is done to others.

13. This scene is apparently one of the first that Pinter worked on as he began the screenplay. In initial drafts, it occurs before the boyhood flashback begins. Pinter also plays with phrasing, first writing "It's no good" in reference to Henry's parents' past (PA, Box 49), later replacing that with the more articulate "They died of despair." The first version of the scene, as Gale and Hudgins note, does not have Henry responding to the driver's failure to understand (1996, 128). As Pinter revised, he shifted all scenes in which Henry can be seen as German to the latter section of the screenplay, after the childhood flashback.

14. *Ashes to Ashes* similarly conjoins the personal and the historical, as will be analyzed in chapter 7.

15. Another Holocaust play Pinter directed, Robert Shaw's *The Man in the Glass Booth*, considers social factors affecting remembrance of the genocide. Pinter directed *The Man in the Glass Booth* by Robert Shaw in London (1967) and New York (1968); he also helped rewrite the script during rehearsals. In a grotesque inversion, Arthur Goldman, a Jewish businessman, assumes the identity of Colonel Dorff, a sadistic Nazi. Unlike Adolf Eichmann, Dorff at his trial revels in his viciousness. He calls the Jews sheep, mocks them as the chosen people, and refers to the cooperation of the *Judenraete* with the Final Solution—one thinks of Hannah Arendt's controversial discussion of Jewish complicity in *Eichmann in Jerusalem*. Part of his motivation for this imposture is the unemotional, euphemized, sanitized way Germans spoke about their genocidal conduct during postwar trials such as Nuremberg and the Eichmann trial. The Judge at the trial points to the insufficiency of such legal events: "I understand his need to put a German in the dock—a German who would say what no German has said in the dock" (R. Shaw 1968, 71). Goldman/Dorff, angered also by the world's forgetting of what happened in the Holocaust, wants the world to witness and be appropriately shocked by a German who admits to the pleasure of sadism. However, there is a touch of sadism in Goldman. He claims that if Hitler had chosen the Jews to lead, they would have followed. This assertion of moral equivalence leads an Old Woman to unmask Goldman as not Dorff, but a Jewish survivor. Even when unmasked as innocent, Goldman continues his charade—reviewer Walter Kerr noted Pinter's direction emphasized a wish for martyrdom, perhaps inspired by survivor's guilt, as a reason for Goldman's impersonation. This compelling play is often revived. However, literary critic Robert Skloot claims that the play evades honest engagement with the moral issues of the Holocaust (1982, 83–87). Edward Isser observes that Goldman's anti-Semitic accusations of Jewish complicity and moral equivalence between Jews and Nazis are never rebutted in the play and argues that these themes typify British Holocaust drama (1997, 51). Seeing oppression as universal leads Pinter to present Nazism as example rather than as singularity. If the Holocaust is not essentially unique, it is not necessarily unforgivable. Michael Billington recounts how Pinter and Shaw, in a TV interview, used *The Man in the Glass Booth* to assert that it was time for

the Germans to "be absolved for the killing of the Jews" (1996, 194). But justice can never be simply equated with the passage of time. Furthermore, as Pinter in fact suggests through the latter third of his *Reunion* screenplay, memory and time operate differently for perpetrators and victims. For perpetrators, their deeds fit squarely into the past that ever recedes from the present; victims, on the other hand, experience what was done to them as part of a perpetual present that never disappears into the past. The memory of suffering reemerges into consciousness involuntarily.

16. Harwood omitted this part of his plot when he adapted his play into a 2003 movie (directed by Istvan Szabo with Harvey Keitel as Arnold and Stellan Skarsgård as Furtwängler). In the movie's last moments, Arnold notes in voice-over: "I didn't nail him [Furtwängler]. But I sure winged him." Harwood means to suggest the value of the kind of skepticism Arnold has about the attempted self-absolution of Furtwängler—or of anyone who benefits from or participates in oppression of others.

17. Pinter has criticized this trial as bogus, because Milosevic was sent to The Hague after the U.S. gave ex-Yugoslavian authorities a large amount of direct foreign aid. In the November 17, 2003, the *New Yorker*, Peter J. Boyer minimizes the causal link between NATO's bombing campaign and the fall of Milosevic (70–88).

18. Quoted in Thomas L. Friedman's column in the *New York Times*, November 20, 2003, A33. The letter appeared in the *Guardian* of November 18. It's the kind of statement that your friends will ask you about if they know you're writing a book about Pinter's politics. It is an exceedingly harsh characterization, obviously, bound to be provocative. Pinter's comments, from the sixties and even later, about distrusting general statements and ideological language come to mind: is Pinter now embracing generality and ideology? Maybe not, for his statement, while vivid, has a direct and specific content: that Bush violated international laws in beginning the 2003 war against Iraq. Many people would agree with this statement.

19. In 1998 Pinter is quoted, in a news story reporting on a protest of renewed hostilities against Saddam Hussein: "I am not a pacifist. I am rational" (http://haroldpinter.org; see the section "Nato and the Gulf.") With this statement, Pinter attempts to prevent a possible indictment of his position as moral perfectionism.

20. Every once in a while in debates about American foreign policy one hears a remark so stunning that the extreme statements of someone like Pinter do not seem like hyperbole at all. For an example: it is generally accepted that in air warfare, ninety percent of casualties are civilians not combatants. (The latest location in which I have seen this statistic is "What Sport!" by Paul Laity [2003] in the *London Review of Books*). For another: as of summer 2004, there is no official count of Iraqi military or civilian casualties resulting from the U.S.-led war against Hussein's regime—nor, again as far as I am aware, has the American government promised that one is forthcoming.

21. My thanks to Steven Price for a conversation in which he noted this aspect of Pinter's anti-interventionist stance.

22. The debate over military action against Saddam Hussein's regime in Iraq evoked many of the same dilemmas for the left as did the issue of responding to Milosevic's atrocities. Again, Pinter's stance, echoed by many Americans and Europeans, was roundly against the war. Others on the left felt greater ambivalence or even took prowar stances. Pinter's friend and political cohort Sal-

man Rushdie argued the desirability of freeing Iraq from Hussein's leadership: "There is a strong, even unanswerable case for regime change in Iraq that ought to unite Western public opinion and all those who care about the brutal oppression of an entire Muslim nation" (2002, 35).

CHAPTER 7. *ASHES TO ASHES:* MORALITY AND POLITICS AFTER THE HOLOCAUST

1. Adorno also writes in "Commitment": "the abundance of real suffering tolerates no forgetting. . . . It is now virtually in art alone that suffering can still find its own voice, consolation, without immediately being betrayed by it" (1977, 188).

2. October 21, 1996, at the New York 92nd Street Y.

3. Laudatory reviews include those by Dennis L. Noble (*Library Journal,* October 15, 1995, 74) and Boyd Tonkin (*New Statesman and Society,* December 8, 1995, 32).

4. There is a general sense that now the Holocaust is adequately, even repetitively represented in our culture. It is interesting to note that Pinter did not write a "Holocaust play" until remembrance attained its current level of ubiquity. Clendinnen writes that one danger of selecting events of the genocide as artistic material is that we may merely "flick to the identikit image of 'The Holocaust' we carry in our heads—and are relieved . . . of the terrible burden of specific, systematic imaginings" (1999, 165). Rebecca allows her imaginings of the Holocaust to go beyond such standard images.

5. There is, as other critics have noted, an irony here: Even as Devlin privileges "privacy," he nevertheless pursues verification of Rebecca's stories as if they had meaning. While Devlin's sense of self makes him unwilling to credit Rebecca's experience, he queries her stories constantly, perhaps precisely because of their supposed status as forbidden or (a word he uses in the play) "illegitimate" (*AA,* 11). While Devlin lightly mocks his own limited life as a scholar, even denying he has a past worth talking about (45), he nevertheless seems to need access to Rebecca's past. See Marc Silverstein's "'Talking About Some Kind of Atrocity': *Ashes to Ashes* in Barcelona" (1998, 74–85) for an astute analysis of this aspect of Devlin and of other issues in the play.

6. There are other ways to read the split between Devlin and Rebecca. According to Quigley, Pinter in his personal life has moved from perhaps being too ignorant of politics to being overly concerned with them (2001, 11), suggesting an analogy to the apolitical Devlin versus the obsessed Rebecca. Pinter is too cunning and cautious merely to recommend Rebecca's state of concern and compassion; he teases out its inner conflicts and difficulties. If Devlin parallels Albert Speer, as other critics have noted and as I do, we can see another distinction in the couple, between the collective, generalized guilt Speer admitted to versus the extremely personal and specific guilt Rebecca feels. Such impersonal "guilt" serves as bad faith. Arendt was first among commentators to notice that after the war many Germans accepted a collective guilt while remaining antagonistic to the concept of personal guilt and knowledge (Agamben 1999, 95).

7. Later, I will argue that this "corpse" figure (a figure Rebecca herself resembles, especially as the play progresses) evokes the *Muselmänner* of the con-

centration camps—those who endured a living death, a death in life, seemingly resigned to or unaware of their fate. There is another Holocaust reference in the term "corpse." The Germans often used the word *Befehlnotstand* to describe the state of compulsion one goes through when obeying an order. Adolf Eichmann glossed this condition of obedience by noting that he and others obeyed commands "*kadavergehorsam*, like a corpse" (Agamben 1999, 78).

8. This impression was reinforced for me by this moment as performed by Anastasia Hille in the production of the play at Lincoln Center's 2001 Pinter Festival (directed by Katie Mitchell). Hill gave a short, cautious smile here, as if Rebecca found a moment of subtle humor in the implied relationship between herself and the moviegoer. Both throughout and especially in the final moments of the play, also, Hill's physical pose evoked paralysis and rigidity. Her version of Rebecca was always quiet, never overtly dramatic, and yet extremely intense; one was aware of the audience leaning toward her to catch her words. It seemed as if she never acknowledged Devlin's existence in the same space as her; it was not worth it for her to reach him, to communicate with him, even through aggression. When the echo talked to her, its voice was a sly, quiet whisper—a taunting call to conscience that Rebecca clearly experienced as painful.

9. "This mental elephantiasis means that when you spill an ounce of gravy, for example, it immediately expands and becomes a vast sea of gravy. It becomes a sea of gravy which surrounds you on all sides and you suffocate in a voluminous sea of gravy. It's terrible. But it's all your own fault. You brought it upon yourself. You are not the *victim* of it, you are the *cause* of it," Rebecca says (*AA*, 51). Pinter may have gathered the basis for this image from a Sereny anecdote. When Nazi official Hans Fritzsche was forced to watch movies of the death camps at the Nuremberg trials, he responded to his personal guilt with a description of his own horror, saying with a mixture of remorse and self-pity, "I have . . . the feeling . . . I am drowning in filth . . . I'm choking in it. . . . I cannot go on. . . . It is a daily execution" (1995, 341).

10. If Burkman reads Sereny partially and overoptimistically, it may also be that Sereny herself tells the story of Speer too reassuringly. Sereny does quote one observer who, contrary to Sereny's own view, credited neither Speer's "good faith" self-examination nor his disavowal of complicitous knowledge (1995, 699). It is ironic that Sereny deludes herself as to Speer's taking responsibility for his guilt, in that it is she who disproved Speer's claim that, at the time they were being carried out, he did not know about genocidal policies. Her argument that Speer was present at Himmler's Posen speech, explicitly announcing the Final Solution, is regarded as definitive.

11. Susan Hollis Merritt made the fascinating discovery that Rebecca's final story is adapted, and rather faithfully so, from the words of a Holocaust survivor (2000, 81). The survivor in question (dubbed Bessie K.) preserved her story as part of the Fortunoff Video Archives for Holocaust Testimony at Yale University. Geoffrey Hartmann points to two books by Lawrence Langer which reproduce Bessie's words, *Admitting the Holocaust* and *Holocaust Testimonies: The Ruins of Memory*, books which I portray as interpretive frames for Pinter's play. Hartmann assumes Pinter read one or both of these books; it is *Admitting the Holocaust* that has the fullest excerpt of Bessie K.'s words. However, *Admitting the Holocaust* does not reproduce all of the story that Merritt quotes in her article. In *Holocaust Testimonies*, Langer writes how Bessie's experiences have caused a lasting rupture in both her memory and her

confidence in life—she did not even share her story with her husband, also a survivor, until years after their marriage. This is how she sums up the effects of her experiences: "To me, I was dead. I died, and I didn't want to hear nothing and I didn't want to know nothing" (Langer 1991, 49; 1995, 143). Bessie K.'s full words show how far her condition was from the kind of existential growth some critics see in the arc of Rebecca's character.

12. It might also be that the terms "perpetrator" and "bystander" are insufficiently nuanced in terms of the category of "evil." Both are assumed to have a clear will: the perpetrator wills and then accomplishes evil, knowing it is evil, while the bystander quashes his will to intervene and so does nothing. As Hannah Arendt argues, modern evil is such that it may well be done in routinized ways, difficult to interpret in terms of will. Figures such as Eichmann abetted genocide without exhibiting outward indications of being a moral monster. People may commit harmful actions without believing themselves to have evil intent.

13. Craig Owens argues insightfully that in Pinter's plays surface meaning is always undercut by another force that disrupts completion and coherence (2002, 83). I am locating this logically disruptive force that threatens "nothingness . . . pointlessness, loss, or absence" precisely in the silence that has been postulated as the origin and end of authentic contemplation of genocide. Owens goes on to argue that Rebecca's consciousness embodies abjection as defined by Julia Kristeva. Her abject consciousness, composed of "rupture, anguish, fear, and disgust" and expressing itself through verbal mechanisms of "lapses, lacunae, aphasia, jokes, ruptures, songs, and disarticulations" allows her an escape from the logical, limitedly empirical symbolic order represented by Devlin (2002, 84). My feeling is that Owens slights the negative aspects of existing outside the symbolic order. There may be a kind of freedom there— but whom would you talk to? How would you communicate? Pinter's play asserts not just that Rebecca needs to escape from Devlin's mental habits, but that this place of refuge is itself difficult and problematic. Put the other way round, the play delimits an inevitable choice between unrestrained speech versus conventionally accessible language.

14. Levinas places the philosophical prioritization of ontology (the definition of identity) over ethics at the causative root of the Holocaust. By concerning ourselves with individual identity, we restrict our moral imaginations to us and people like ourselves. This process, the play shows, accompanies basic ones of socialization and language ability. Rebecca's nephew is learning to speak, saying "things like 'My name is Ben.' Things like that. And 'Mummy's name is Mummy.' Things like that" (AA, 57). As we grow up we learn to recognize as humans, as moral entities, only those closest to us, inhibiting the kind of moral-historical awareness Rebecca attempts.

Works Cited

Adler, Thomas P. 1991. "The Embrace of Silence: Pinter, Miller, and the Response to Power." *Pinter Review: Annual Essays*: 4–9.

Adorno, Theodor. 1977. "Commitment." Trans. Frances McDonagh. In *Aesthetics and Politics*, ed. Ernst Bloch et. al., 177–95. London: New Left Books.

Adorno, Theodor, et al. 1950. *The Authoritarian Personality*. New York: Harper & Row.

Agamben, Giorgio. 1999. *Remnants of Auschwitz: The Witness and the Archive*. Trans. Daniel Heller-Roazen. New York: Zone Books.

Alleg, Henri. 1958. *The Question*. Trans. John Calder. New York: G. Braziller.

Almansi, Guido, and Simon Henderson. 1983. *Harold Pinter*. London: Methuen.

Altemeyer, Bob. 1996. *The Authoritarian Specter*. Cambridge, MA: Harvard University Press.

Amend, Victor. 1967. "Harold Pinter—Some Credits and Debits." *Modern Drama* 10:165–74.

Arendt, Hannah. 1966. *The Origins of Totalitarianism*. New edition. New York: Harcourt, Brace & World.

———. 1977. *Eichmann in Jerusalem: A Report on the Banality of Evil*. Rev. ed. New York: Penguin.

———. 2000. *The Portable Hannah Arendt*. Ed. Peter Baehr. New York: Penguin.

Armstrong, Raymond. 1999. *Kafka and Pinter Shadow-Boxing: The Struggle between Father and Son*. New York: St. Martin's Press.

Ash, Timothy Garton. 1999. "Vivid, Dark, Powerful and Magnificent—But Wrong." *Independent* (London), May 4, Comment section, 4.

Bailey, F. G. 1988. *Humbuggery and Manipulation: The Art of Leadership*. Ithaca: Cornell University Press.

Baker, William, and Stephen Ely Tabachnick. 1973. *Harold Pinter*. Modern Writer Series. New York: Barnes & Noble.

Barker, Howard. 1982. *The Hang of the Gaol* and *Heaven*. London: John Calder.

Barthes, Roland. 1972. *Mythologies*. Trans. Annette Lavers. New York: Hill and Wang. (Orig. pub. 1957.)

Batty, Mark. 2001. *Harold Pinter*. Horndon, U.K.: Northcote House.

Baudrillard, Jean. 1983. *Simulations*. New York: Semiotext(e).

———. 1992. "Transpolitics, Transsexuality, Transaesthetics." Trans. Michel

Valentin. In *Jean Baudrillard: the Disappearance of Art and Politics,* ed. William Chaloupka and William Stearns, 9–26. New York: St. Martin's.

———. 1994. *The Illusion of the End.* Trans. Chris Turner. Stanford: Stanford University Press.

Baum, Rainer C. 1988. "Holocaust: Moral Indifference as the Form of Modern Evil." In *Echoes from the Holocaust: Philosophical Reflections on a Dark Time,* ed. Alan Rosenberg and Gerald E. Myers, 53–90. Philadelphia: Temple University Press.

Bauman, Zygmunt. 1989. *Modernity and the Holocaust.* Ithaca: Cornell University Press.

Bearak, Barry. 2003. "Unreconstructed." *New York Times Magazine,* June 1, 40.

Beckett, Samuel. 1954. *Waiting for Godot.* New York: Grove Press.

———. 1958. *Endgame.* New York: Grove Press.

———. 1984. *Collected Shorter Plays.* New York: Grove Press.

Bigsby, C. W. E. 1981. "The Politics of Anxiety: Contemporary Socialist Theatre in England." *Modern Drama* 24: 393–403.

———. 1984. "The Language of Crisis in British Theatre: The Drama of Cultural Pathology." In *Modern British Dramatists: New Perspectives,* ed. and introd. John Russell Brown, 161–76. Englewood Cliffs, N.J.: Prentice-Hall.

Billington, Michael. 1996. *The Life and Work of Harold Pinter.* London: Faber and Faber.

Blanchot, Maurice. 1986. *The Writing of the Disaster.* Trans. Ann Smock. Lincoln: University of Nebraska Press.

Boyer, Peter J. 2003. "General Clark's Battles." *New Yorker,* November 17, 70–88.

Brecht, Bertolt. 1964. *Brecht on Theatre: The Development of an Aesthetic.* Ed. and trans. John Willett. New York: Hill and Wang.

Brodsky, Joseph. 1986. *Less Than One: Selected Essays.* New York: Penguin.

Budick, Emily Miller. 1998. "Acknowledging the Holocaust in Contemporary American Criticism." In *Breaking Crystal: Writing and Memory After Auschwitz,* ed. Efraim Sicher, 329–43. Urbana: University of Illinois Press.

Burke, Kenneth. 1957. *The Philosophy of Literary Form: Studies in Symbolic Action.* Rev. ed., abridged by the author. New York: Vintage Books.

Burkman, Katherine H. 1993. "Harold Pinter's *Death in Venice:* The Comfort of Strangers." *Pinter Review: Annual Essays 1992–93:* 38–45.

———. 1998. "Harold Pinter's *Ashes to Ashes:* Rebecca and Devlin as Albert Speer." *Pinter Review: Collected Essays 1997 and 1998:* 86–96.

Butler, Christopher. 1980. *After the Wake: An Essay on the Contemporary Avant-Garde.* New York: Oxford University Press.

Butler, Judith. *The Psychic Life of Power: Theories in Subjection.* Stanford: Stanford University Press, 1997.

Camus, Albert. 1991. *The Rebel: An Essay on Man in Revolt.* Trans. Albert Bower. New York: Vintage International.

Canetti, Elias. 1962. *Crowds and Power.* Trans. Carol Stewart. New York: Viking.

Carpenter, Charles. 1979. "*The Dumb Waiter.*" In *Analyses of Modern British and American Drama,* ed. Hermann J. Weiand, 112–18. Frankfurt am Main: Hirschgraben-Verlag.

Caruth, Cathy. 1995. *Trauma: Explorations in Memory.* Baltimore: Johns Hopkins University Press.

Chancer, Lynn S. 1992. *Sadomasochism in Everyday Life: The Dynamics of Power and Powerlessness.* New Brunswick, NJ: Rutgers University Press.

Clendinnen, Inga. 1999. *Reading the Holocaust.* Cambridge: Cambridge University Press.

Cohen, Nick. 2002. "Why It is Right to be Anti-American." *New Statesman,* January 14, 10–12.

Colleran, Jeanne. 1993. "Disjuncture as Theatrical and Postmodern Practice in Griselda Gambaro's *The Camp* and Harold Pinter's *Mountain Language.*" In *Pinter at Sixty,* ed. Katherine H. Burkman and John L. Kundert-Gibbs, 49–65. Bloomington: Indiana University Press.

Conrad, Joseph. 1924. *Victory.* New York: Doubleday.

Crelinster, Ronald D., and Alex P. Schmid. 1994. Introduction to *The Politics of Pain: Torturers and their Masters,* eds. Crelinsten and Schmid, 1–11. Boulder, CO: Westview Press.

Crouch, Mira. 1990. "The Oppressors and the Oppressed in Interaction: A Shared Dimension of Everyday Life." In *The Attractions of Fascism: Social Psychology and the Aesthetics of the "Triumph of the Right,"* ed. John Millful, 21–31. Providence, RI: Berg Publishers.

Davidson, Eugene. 1997. *The Trial of the Germans: An Account of the Twenty-Two Defendants before the International Military Tribunal at Nuremberg.* Columbia: University of Missouri Press. (Orig. pub. 1966.)

DeBord, Guy. 1983. *Society of the Spectacle.* Detroit: Black & Red.

DeLillo, Don. 1997. *Underworld.* New York: Scribner.

Didion, Joan. 2003. "Fixed Opinions, or The Hinge of History." *New York Review of Books,* January 16, 54–59.

Dinesen, Isak. 1942. *Winter's Tales.* New York: Random House.

Dylan, Bob. 1964. "My Back Pages." In *Another Side of Bob Dylon.* Columbia Records, PC 8993. Published 1964 by Columbia Records.

Edgar, David. 1988. *The Second Time as Farce: Reflections on the Drama of Mean Times.* London: Lawrence and Wishart.

———. 1989. *Shorts [Ball Boys, The National Theatre, Blood Sports, The Midas Connection, Baby Love].* London: Nick Hern Books.

Ellul, Jacques. 1965. *Propaganda: The Formation of Men's Attitudes.* Trans. Konrad Kellen and Jean Lerner. New York: Knopf.

Engelmann, Bert. 1986. *In Hitler's Germany: Daily Life in the Third Reich.* Trans. from the German by Krishna Winston. New York: Pantheon Books.

Esslin, Martin. 1961a. "Pinter and the Absurd." *Twentieth Century* 169 (February): 176–85.

———. 1961b. *The Theatre of the Absurd.* New York: Anchor Books.

———. 1970. *The Peopled Wound: The Work of Harold Pinter.* New York: Doubleday.

———. 1990. "Creative Process and Meaning—Some Remarks on Pinter's 'Letter to Peter Wood.'" In *Pinter at 70: A Casebook,* ed. Lois Gordon, 3–12. New York: Routledge.

————. 1993. "Harold Pinter's Theatre of Cruelty." In *Pinter at Sixty*, ed. Katherine H. Burkman and John L. Kundert-Gibbs, 27–36. Bloomington: Indiana University Press.

Eyre, Richard, ed. 2000. *Harold Pinter: A Celebration*. London: Faber and Faber.

Faulkner, William. 1966. *Requiem for a Nun*. New York: Random House.

Fest, Joachim. 1997. *Plotting Hitler's Death: The Story of the German Resistance*. Trans. Bruce Little. New York: Henry Holt.

Fineman, Howard. 1984. "The Virtuecrats." *Newsweek*, June 13, 30–36.

Fischer, Klaus P. 1995. *Nazi Germany: A New History*. New York: Continuum.

Fish, Stanley. 2002. "Postmodern Warfare." *Harper's*, July, 33–40.

Foucault, Michel. 1979. *Discipline and Punish: The Birth of the Prison*. Trans. Alan Sheridan. New York: Vintage.

————. 1984. *The Foucault Reader*. Ed. Paul Rabinow. New York: Pantheon.

————. 1991. "Governmentality." In *The Foucault Effect: Studies in Governmentality*, ed. Graham Burchell, Colin Gordon, and Peter Miller, 87–104. Chicago: University of Chicago Press.

Fowles, John. 1981. *The French Lieutenant's Woman*. New York: Signet. (Orig. pub. 1970.)

Friedlander, Saul. 1979. *When Memory Comes*. Trans. from the French by Helen R. Lane. Original title *Quand vient le souvenir . . .* New York: Farrar, Straus, Giroux.

Friedman, Thomas. 2003. "You Gotta Have Friends." *New York Times*, November 20, A33.

Gale, Steven H., and Christopher C. Hudgins. 1996. "The Harold Pinter Archives II: A Description of the Filmscript Materials in the Archive in the British Library." *Pinter Review: Annual Essays 1995 and 1996*: 101–42.

Ganz, Arthur. 1995. Review of *Pinter at Sixty*, ed. Katherine H. Burkman and John L. Kundert-Gibbs. *Modern Drama* 38:429–31.

Gellately, Robert. 2002. *Backing Hitler: Consent and Coercion in Nazi Germany*. Oxford: Oxford University Press.

Gillen, Francis. 1988. "From Chapter Ten of *The Dwarfs* to *Mountain Language*: The Continuity of Harold Pinter." *Pinter Review* 2:1–4.

————. 1989. Review of *Mountain Language/The Birthday Party*. *Pinter Review: Annual Essays*: 93–97.

————. 1997. "History as a Single Act: Pinter's *Ashes to Ashes*." *Cycnos* 14:91–97.

————. 2002. "'The Shape of Things': *Landscape* in Draft, Text, and Performance." *Pinter Review: Collected Essays 2001 and 2002*: 55–65.

Giraudoux, Jean. 1955. *La guerre de Troie n'aura pas lieu*. Trans. Christopher Fry [as *Tiger at the Gates*]. Oxford: Oxford University Press.

Goldhagen, Daniel Jonah. 1996. *Hitler's Willing Executioners: Ordinary Germans and the Holocaust*. New York: Knopf.

Golding, Martin P. 1988. "On The Idea of Moral Pathology." In *Echoes from the Holocaust: Philosophical Reflections on a Dark Time*, ed. Alan Rosenberg and Gerald E. Myers, 128–48. Philadelphia: Temple University Press.

Gontarski, S. E. 1985. "The Intent of Undoing." In *Modern Critical Views: Samuel Beckett*, ed. Harold Bloom, 227–45. Philadelphia: Chelsea House.

Gordon, Robert. 2000. "*Celebration* in Performance: The Drama of Environment." *Pinter Review: Collected Essays 1999 and 2000*: 66–72.

Graver, Lawrence. 1989. *Samuel Beckett: "Waiting for Godot."* Cambridge: Cambridge University Press.

Gray, Simon. 1985. *An Unnatural Pursuit and Other Pieces*. London: Faber and Faber.

Gussow, Mel. 1988. "Pinter's Plays Following Him Out of Enigma and into Politics." *New York Times*, December 6, Section III, 17, 22.

———. 1994. *Conversations with Pinter*. New York: Limelight.

Haffner, Sebastian. 2000. *Defying Hitler: A Memoir*. Trans. Oliver Pretzel. New York: Farrar, Straus and Giroux.

Hall, Ann C. 1998. "Looking for Mr. Goldberg: Spectacle and Speculation in Harold Pinter's *The Birthday Party*." *Pinter Review: Collected Essays 1997 and 1998*: 48–56.

———. 2001. "Daddy Dearest: Harold Pinter's *The Comfort of Strangers*." In *The Films of Harold Pinter*, ed. Steven H. Gale, 87–98. Albany: State University of New York Press.

Hamerow, Theodore S. 1997. *On the Road to the Wolf's Lair: German Resistance to Hitler*. Cambridge: Belknap Press of Harvard University Press.

Hampson, Robert. 1992. *Joseph Conrad: Betrayal and Identity*. New York: St. Martin's.

Hare, David. 1978. Afterword [A Lecture Given at King's College, Cambridge, March 5, 1978] to *Licking Hitler*, by Hare, 57–71. London: Faber.

Harwood, Ronald. 1995. *Taking Sides*. London: Faber and Faber.

Hatley, James. 2000. *Suffering Witness: The Quandary of Responsibility after the Irreparable*. Albany: State University of New York Press.

Hartmann, Geoffrey. 2000. "Memory.com: Tele-Suffering and Testimony." *Raritan* 19 (Winter): 1–20.

Haugaard, Mark. 1997. *The Constitution of Power*. Manchester: Manchester University Press.

Hilberg, Raul. 1961. *The Destruction of the European Jews*. New York: Quadrangle Books.

Hinchliffe, Arnold P. 1967. *Harold Pinter*. New York: Twayne Publishers.

Hindess, Barry. 1996. *Discourses of Power: From Hobbes to Foucault*. Cambridge, MA: Blackwell Publishers.

Hoffman, Eva. 2000. "The Uses of Hell." *New York Review of Books*, March 9, 19–23.

Hoffmann, Peter. 1977. *The History of the German Resistance 1933–1945*. Trans. Richard Barry. Cambridge: The MIT Press.

Holderness, Graham. 1992. Introduction to *The Politics of Theatre and Drama*, ed. Graham Holderness, 1–17. New York: St. Martin's.

Hollis, James R. 1970. *Harold Pinter: The Poetics of Silence*. Carbondale: Southern Illinois University Press.

Horowitz, Sara R. 1998. "Auto/Biography and Fiction after Auschwitz: Probing the Boundaries of Second-Generation Aesthetics." In *Breaking Crystal:*

Writing and Memory After Auschwitz, ed. Efraim Sicher, 276–94. Urbana: University of Illinois Press.

Hotel Terminus: The Life and Times of Klaus Barbie. 1989. Produced and directed by Marcel Ophuls. 267 min. Los Angeles: Virgin Vision, Samuel Goldwyn Home Entertainment.

Howard, Tony. 1996. "'No One Outside These Arms': Edward Bond's *The War Plays.*" In *Acts of War: The Representation of Military Conflict on the British Stage and Television Since 1945*, ed. Tony Howard and John Stokes, 127–40. Aldershot, Hants, UK: Scolar.

Hudgins, Christopher C. 1984. "Dance to a Cut-Throat Temper: Harold Pinter's Poetry as an Index to Intended Audience Response." In *Drama in the Twentieth Century: Comparative and Critical Essays*, ed. Clifford Davidson, C. J. Gianakaris, and John H. Stoupe, 275–93. New York: AMS Press.

———. 1991. "*Victory*: A Pinter Screenplay Based on the Conrad Novel." *Pinter Review: Annual Essays*: 23–32.

Hughes, Catharine. 1973. *Plays, Politics, and Polemics.* New York: Drama Book Specialists.

Innes, Christopher. 1992. *Modern British Drama 1890–1990.* Cambridge: Cambridge University Press.

Ionesco, Eugene. 1964. *Notes and Counter-Notes: Writings on the Theatre.* Trans. Donald M. Allen. New York: Grove Press.

Isaacson, Walter. 2003. "Fighting Words." *New Yorker*, July 14 & 21, 94–98.

Isser, Edward R. 1997. *Stages of Annihilation: Theatrical Representations of the Holocaust.* Madison, NJ: Fairleigh Dickinson University Press.

Jameson, Fredric. 1981. *The Political Unconscious.* New York: Cornell University Press.

Katz, Jack. 1988. *Seductions of Crime: Moral and Sensual Attractions in Doing Evil.* New York: Basic Books.

Kershaw, Baz. 1997. "Fighting in the Streets: Dramaturgies of Popular Protest, 1968–1989." *New Theatre Quarterly* 13: 255–72.

King, Kimball. 2001. "Harold Pinter's Achievement and Modern Drama." In *Pinter at 70: A Casebook*, ed. Lois Gordon, 243–56. New York: Routledge.

Knowles, Ronald. 1989. "Harold Pinter, Citizen." *Pinter Review* 1:24–33.

———. 1990. "Harold Pinter 1990." *Pinter Review: Annual Essays 1990*: 79–87.

———. 1991. "Harold Pinter 1991." *Pinter Review: Annual Essays 1991*: 64–73.

———. 1992. "Harold Pinter 1992." *Pinter Review Annual Essays 1992–93*: 85–95.

———. 1995a. *Understanding Harold Pinter.* Columbia: University of South Carolina Press.

———. 1995b. Review of *Harold Pinter and the Language of Cultural Power*, by Marc Silverstein. *Modern Language Review* 90 (3): 737–39.

———. 2000. "Harold Pinter 1998–2000." *Pinter Review: Collected Essays 1999 and 2000*: 169–90.

Koestler, Arthur. 1977. Introduction to *Reunion*, by Fred Uhlman, 7–9. New York: Farrar, Straus and Giroux.

Kohler, Klaus. 1984. "The Establishment and the Absurd." *Zeitschrift für Anglistik und Amerikanistik* 32 (4): 315–29.

Kren, George. 1988. "The Holocaust as History." In *Echoes from the Holocaust: Philosophical Reflections on a Dark Time*, ed. Alan Rosenberg and Gerald E. Myers, 3–50. Philadelphia: Temple University Press.

Kristeva, Julia. 1982. *Powers of Horror: An Essay on Abjection*. New York: Columbia University Press.

Lacoue-Labarthe, Philippe. 1999. *Poetry as Experience*. Trans. Andread Tarnowski. Stanford: Stanford University Press.

Laity, Paul. 2003. "What Sport!" *London Review of Books*, June 5, 13–14.

Lamont, Rosette C. 1993. "Harold Pinter's *The Hothouse*: A Parable of the Holocaust." In *Pinter at Sixty*, ed. Katherine H. Burkman and John L. Kundert-Gibbs, 37–48. Bloomington: Indiana University Press.

Lang, Berel. 1990. *Act and Idea in the Nazi Genocide*. Chicago: University of Chicago Press.

Langer, Lawrence L. 1991. *Holocaust Testimonies: The Ruins of Memory*. New Haven: Yale University Press.

———. 1995. *Admitting the Holocaust: Collected Essays*. New York: Oxford University Press.

Laub, Dori. 1995. "Truth and Testimony: The Process and the Struggle." In *Trauma: Explorations in Memory*, ed. Cathy Caruth, 61–75. Baltimore: Johns Hopkins University Press.

Levi, Primo. 1985. *Survival in Auschwitz and The Reawakening: Two Memoirs*. Trans. Stuart Woolf. New York: Summit Books.

———. 1988. *The Drowned and the Saved*. New York: Vintage.

Levinas, Emmanuel. 1993. *Collected Philosophical Papers*. Trans. Alphonso Lingis. Dordrecht, The Netherlands: Kluwer Academic Publishers.

Lewis, Anthony. 2003. "On the West Wing." *New York Review of Books*, February 13, 4–7.

Lifton, Robert Jay. 1986. *The Nazi Doctors: Medical Killing and the Psychology of Genocide*. New York: HarperCollins.

———. 1993. *The Protean Self: Human Resilience in an Age of Fragmentation*. New York: HarperCollins.

———. 1995. "An Interview with Robert Lifton [conducted by Cathy Caruth]." In *Trauma: Explorations in Memory*, ed. Caruth, 128–47. Baltimore: Johns Hopkins University Press.

Lifton, Robert Jay. and Greg Mitchell. 1995. *Hiroshima in America: A Half Century of Denial*. New York: Avon Books.

London Theatre Record. 1983. Reviews of *The Trojan War Will Not Take Place* also known as *Tiger at the Gates*. May 7–20, 362–66.

McEwan, Ian. 1981. *The Comfort of Strangers*. New York: Vintage.

———. 1983. *Or Shall We Die? Words for an oratorio set to music by Michael Berkeley*. With an introduction by McEwan. London: J. Cape.

Magurshak, Dan. 1988. "The 'Incomprehensibility' of the Holocaust: Tightening Up Some Loose Usage." In *Echoes of the Holocaust: Philosophical Reflections on a Dark Time*, ed. Alan Rosenberg and Gerald E. Myers, 421–31. Philadelphia: Temple University Press.

Maier, Charles S. 1988. *The Unmasterable Past: History, Holocaust, and German National Identity*. Cambridge: Harvard University Press.

Mailer, Norman. 2003. "Only in America." *New York Review of Books*, March 27, 49–53.

Malkin, Jeanette R. 1992. *Verbal Violence in Contemporary Drama: From Handke to Shepard*. Cambridge: Cambridge University Press.

Marcuse, Herbert. 1964. *One-Dimensional Man: Studies in the Ideology of Advanced Industrial Society*. Boston: Beacon Press.

Marx, Karl and Friedrich Engels. 1975. *Collected Works*. Volume 5. New York: Norton.

Mendelsohn, Daniel. 2001. "Harold Pinter's Celebration." *New York Review of Books*, October 4, 28–31.

Merritt, Susan Hollis. 1986. "Pinter's 'Semantic Uncertainty' and Critically 'Inescapable' Certainties." *Journal of Dramatic Theory and Criticism* (Fall): 49–76.

———. 1994. "The Pinter Archive: Description of the Archive in the British Library." *Pinter Review: Annual Essays 1994*: 14–53.

———. 1995. *Pinter in Play: Critical Strategies and the Plays of Harold Pinter*. Durham, NC: Duke University Press.

———. 2000. "Harold Pinter's *Ashes to Ashes*: Political/Personal Echoes of the Holocaust." *Pinter Review: Collected Essays 1999 and 2000*: 73–84.

Michel, Jean. 1980. *Dora*. Written in association with Louis Nucera and trans. Jennifer Kidd. New York: Holt, Rinehart and Winston.

Miller, Arthur. 1978. *The Theater Essays of Arthur Miller*. New York: Viking Press.

Moore, Gene M., ed. 1997. *Conrad on Film*. Cambridge: Cambridge University Press.

Morrison, Kristin. 1983. *Canters and Chronicles: The Use of Narrative in the Plays of Samuel Beckett and Harold Pinter*. Chicago: University of Chicago Press.

Mulgan, Geoff. 1994. *Politics in an Antipolitical Age*. Cambridge, UK: Polity.

Naimark, Norman M. 2002. *Fires of Hatred: Ethnic Cleansing in Twentieth-Century Europe*. Cambridge, MA: Harvard University Press.

Nightingale, Benedict. "Harold Pinter/Politics." In *Around the Absurd: Essays on Modern and Postmodern Drama*, ed. Enoch Brater and Ruby Cohn, 129–54. Ann Arbor: University of Michigan Press, 1990.

Noakes, Jeremy. 1987. "Social Outcasts in the Third Reich." In *Life in the Third Reich*, ed. Richard Bessel, 83–96. Oxford: Oxford University Press.

Noble, Dennis L. 1995. Review of *Albert Speer: His Battle with Truth*, by Gitta Sereny. *Library Journal* 120: 74.

Norris, Christopher. 1990. *What's Wrong with Postmodernism: Critical Theory and the Ends of Philosophy*. Baltimore: Johns Hopkins University Press.

O'Toole, Fintan. 1999. "Our Own Jacobean." *New York Review of Books*, October 7, 28–32.

Owens, Craig N. 2002. "The *Unheimlich* Maneuver: *Ashes to Ashes* and the Structure of Repression." *Pinter Review: Collected Essays 2001 and 2002*: 78–96.

Ozick, Cynthia. 1988. "Roundtable Discussion." In *Writing and the Holocaust*, ed. Berel Lang, 277–84. New York: Holmes and Meier.

Page, Malcolm. 2000. "Pinter's Politics and Pinter's Plays: A Brief Survey." Paper reading. "Pinter at 70 Conference." Russell Hotel, London. June 16.

Pamuk, Orhan. 2001. "The Anger of the Damned." *New York Review of Books*, November 15, 12.

Parks, Tim. 2000. *Destiny.* London: Vintage.

Pawel, Ernst. 1977. "Nostalgia for the Old Germany." Review of *Reunion*, by Fred Uhlman. *New York Times* April 24, sec. 7, 15, 35.

Peacock, D. Keith. 1997. *Harold Pinter and the New British Theatre.* Westport, CT: Greenwood Press.

Perloff, Carey. 1988. "Keeping Up the Mask: Some Observations on Directing Pinter." *Pinter Review* 2:60–65.

Peters, Edward. 1985. *Torture.* New York: Basil Blackwood.

Phillips, Gene D. 1995. *Conrad and Cinema: The Art of Adaptation.* New York: Peter Lang.

Pinter, Harold. 1961a. *The Birthday Party and The Room.* New York: Grove Press.

———. 1961b. *The Caretaker and The Dumb Waiter.* New York: Grove Press.

———. 1961c. "Writing for Myself." *Twentieth Century* 169 (February): 172–75.

———. 1962. *Three Plays: A Slight Ache, The Collection, The Dwarfs.* New York: Grove Press.

———. 1964. "Writing for the Theatre." In *The New British Drama*, ed. Henry Popkin, 574–80. New York: Grove Press.

———. 1965. *The Homecoming.* New York: Grove Press.

———. 1967. Interview by Lawrence Bensky. In *Writers at Work: "The Paris Review" Interviews*, intro. Alfred Kazin, 347–68. Third Series. New York: Viking Press.

———. 1978. *Complete Works: Three.* New York: Grove Press.

———. 1980. *The Hothouse.* New York: Grove Press.

———. 1981. *Complete Works: Four.* New York: Grove Press.

———. 1985. *Precisely. Harper's*, May, 37.

———. 1986a. *One for the Road.* New York: Grove Press.

———. 1986b. "A Play and its Politics: A Conversation between Harold Pinter and Nicholas Hern." In *One for the Road*, by Pinter, 5–23. New York: Grove Press, 1986. [Year of interview 1985.]

———. 1987. "The US Elephant Must be Stopped." *Guardian*, December 5, 16.

———. 1988a. "Language and Lies." *Index on Censorship* 17 (6): 2.

———. 1988b. Letter. *Times Literary Supplement* October 7–13, 1109.

———. 1989a. *Mountain Language.* New York: Grove Press.

———. 1989b. "Visually Speaking: Harold Pinter Interviewed by Michel Ciment." *Film Comment* 25 (May/June): 20–22.

———. 1989c. "Entretien avec Harold Pinter." [Conversation with Harold Pinter and Michel Ciment.] *Positif* 339 (Mai): 23–27.

———. 1990. *The Comfort of Strangers and Other Screenplays*. New York: Grove Press.

———. 1991. *Collected Poems and Prose*. London: Faber and Faber.

———. 1993a. *Moonlight*. New York: Grove Press.

———. 1993b. *Party Time and The New World Order*. New York: Grove Press.

———. 1996a. *Ashes to Ashes*. London: Faber and Faber.

———. 1996b. *Collected Poems and Prose*. New York: Grove Press.

———. 1996c. Remarks in conversation with Austin Quigley. 92nd Street Y, New York. October 21.

———. 1998. *Various Voices: Prose, Poetry, Politics*. New York: Grove Press.

———. 1999. Letter. *Independent* (London), May 11, Comment section, 2.

———. 2000a. "Anniversary of Nato Bombing of Serbia." A speech given at the Committee for Peace in the Balkans Conference, The Conway Hall, June 10, 2000. [Distributed by Pinter at the 2001 Pinter in London Conference.]

———. 2000b. *Celebration and The Room*. London: Faber and Faber.

———. 2000c. *Collected Screenplays 3*. London: Faber and Faber.

———. 2001. "Unthinkable Thoughts." [Interview of Pinter by David Edwards]. October 24. http://www.squall.co.uk.pinter2.html.

———. 2002a. "Pinter on Pinter: The Lincoln Center Interview." Conducted by Mel Gussow. Transcribed (with the assistance of Sean Donnelly) and ed. by Susan Hollis Merritt. *Pinter Review: Collected Essays 2001 and 2002*: 14–37.

———. 2002b. *Press Conference*. London: Faber and Faber.

———. 2002c. "What We Think of America." *Granta* 77 (Spring): 66–69.

———. 2003. "While We Have Your Attention, Mr. President . . . " *Guardian*, November 18, Features Pages, 2.

———. n.d. The Pinter Archives. Modern Manuscripts Collection, British Library, London.

———. n.d. http://www.haroldpinter.org.

Pinter, Harold, Anthony Astbury, and Geoffrey Godbert, comps. 1994. *99 Poems in Translation*. New York: Grove Press.

Plantinga, Carl. 1999. "The Scene of Empathy and the Human Face on Film." In *Passionate Views: Film, Cognition, and Emotion*, ed. Carl Plantinga and Greg M. Smith, 239–55. Baltimore: Johns Hopkins University Press.

Prentice, Penelope. 1994. *The Pinter Ethic: The Erotic Aesthetic*. New York: Garland Publishing.

———. 2002. "*Mountain Language* and *Ashes to Ashes*: A Playwright/Director's Perspective." *Pinter Review: Collected Essays 2001 and 2002*: 192–96.

Probyn, Elspeth. 1992. "Technologizing the Self: A Future Anterior for Cultural Studies." In *Cultural Studies*, ed. Lawrence Grossberg, Cary Nelson and Paula Treichler, 501–11. New York: Routledge.

Prinz, Jessica. 2002. "'You Brought It Upon Yourself': Subjectivity and Culpability in *Ashes to Ashes*." *Pinter Review: Collected Essays 2001 and 2002*: 97–105.

Quigley, Austin E. 1978. "*The Dumb Waiter*: Undermining the Tacit Dimension." *Modern Drama* 21:1–11.

——. 2001. "Pinter, Politics, and Postmodernism (I)." In *The Cambridge Companion to Harold Pinter*, ed. Peter Raby, 7–27. Cambridge: Cambridge University Press.

Rabey, David Ian. 1986. *British and Irish Political Drama in the Twentieth Century: Implicating the Audience*. New York: St. Martin's.

——. 1990. "Images of Terrorism in Contemporary British Drama: Unlocking the World." In *Terrorism and Modern Drama*, ed. John Orr and Dragan Klaic, 151–59. Edinburgh: Edinburgh University Press.

Regal, Martin S. 1995. *Harold Pinter: A Question of Timing*. New York: St. Martin's.

Reimer, Robert C., and Carol J. Reimer. 1992. *Nazi-Retro Film: How German Narrative Cinema Remembers the Past*. New York: Twayne Publishers.

Riddell, Mary. 1999. "The *New Statesman* Interview: Harold Pinter." *New Statesman*, November 8.

Roof, Judith. 1988. "Staging the Ideology Behind the Power: Pinter's *One for the Road* and Beckett's *Catastrophe*." *Pinter Review* 2:8–18.

Rosen, Norma. 1987. "The Second Life of Holocaust Imagery." *Midstream* 33 (4): 56–59.

Rosenfeld, Alvin H. 1979. "The Problematics of Holocaust Literature." In *Confronting the Holocaust: The Impact of Elie Wiesel*, ed. Alvin H. Rosenfeld and Irving Greenberg, 1–30. Bloomington: Indiana University Press.

——. 1980. *A Double Dying: Reflections on Holocaust Literature*. Bloomington: Indiana University Press.

Ross, Lillian. 1999. "The Talk of the Town: The Boards: The Things that Haunt Harold Pinter." *New Yorker*, February 1, 22–23.

Roth, Philip. 1961. "Writing American Fiction." *Commentary* (March): 223–33.

Rothfels, Hans. 1962. *The German Opposition to Hitler*. Chicago: Regnery.

Rousseau, Jean-Jacques. 1974. "Politics and the Arts." In *Dramatic Theory and Criticism: Greeks to Grotowski*, ed. Bernard F. Dukore, 293–97. New York: Holt, Rinehart and Winston.

Roy, Arundhati. 2001. *Power Politics*. Cambridge, Mass.: South End Press.

——. 2003. "Come September." June 6, 2003. http://www.lannan.org/__authors/roy/. [Transcription of Arundhati Roy reading and Ms. Roy and Howard Zinn in Conversation, September 18, 2002.]

Rushdie, Salman. 2002. "A Liberal Argument for Regime Change." *Washington Post*, November 2, A35.

Ruthven, Malise. 1978. *Torture: The Grand Conspiracy*. London: Weidenfeld and Nicolson.

Sakellaridou, Elizabeth. 1989. "The Rhetoric of Evasion as Political Discourse: Some Preliminaries on Pinter's Political Language." *Pinter Review: Annual Essays 1989*: 43–47.

Sartre, Jean-Paul. 1958. Introduction to *The Question*. New York: G. Braziller.

——. 1995. *Anti-Semite and Jew: An Exploration of the Etiology of Hate*. New York: Schocken Books. (Orig. pub. 1948.)

Sarup, Madan. 1993. *An Introductory Guide to Post-Structuralism and Postmodernism*. Second edition. Athens: University of Georgia Press.

Scarry, Elaine. 1985. *The Body in Pain: The Making and Unmaking of the World*. New York: Oxford University Press.

Schell, Jonathan. 2003. "No More Unto the Breach [Part One]." *Harper's*, March, 33–46.

Sennett, Richard. 1980. *Authority*. New York: Norton.

Sereny, Gitta. 1995. *Albert Speer: His Battle with Truth*. New York: Knopf.

Shaw, George Bernard. 1913. *The Quintessence of Ibsenism, Now Completed to the Death of Ibsen*. New York: Hill and Wang.

———. 1958. *Shaw on Theatre*. Ed. E. J. West. New York: Hill and Wang.

———. n.d. *The Complete Plays of Bernard Shaw*. London: Oldhams Press.

Shaw, Robert. 1968. *The Man in the Glass Booth*. New York: Samuel French.

Shirer, William L. 1960. *The Rise and Fall of the Third Reich: A History of Nazi Germany*. New York: Simon and Schuster.

Sicher, Efraim. 1998a. "The Holocaust in the Postmodernist Era." In *Breaking Crystal: Writing and Memory After Auschwitz*, ed. Sicher, 297–328. Urbana: University of Illinois Press.

———. 1998b. Introduction to *Breaking Crystal: Writing and Memory After Auschwitz*, ed. Sicher, 1–16. Urbana: University of Illinois Press.

Silverstein, Marc. 1993. *Harold Pinter and the Language of Cultural Power*. Lewisburg, PA: Bucknell University Press.

———. 1998. "'Talking About Some Kind of Atrocity': *Ashes to Ashes* in Barcelona." *Pinter Review: 1997 and 1998*: 74–85.

Sierz, Aleks. 1994. "Polishing the Kitchen Sink." *New Statesman & Society*, March 11, 34–35.

Skloot, Robert. 1982. *The Theatre of the Holocaust*. Madison: University of Wisconsin Press.

Slay, Jack Jr. 1996. *Ian McEwan*. New York: Twayne Publishers.

Sloterdijk, Peter. 1987. *Critique of Cynical Reason*. Trans. Michael Eldred. Minneapolis: University of Minnesota Press.

Sofsky, Wolfgang. 1997. *The Order of Terror: The Concentration Camp*. Trans. William Templer. Princeton: Princeton University Press.

Sontag, Susan. 2003. *Regarding the Pain of Others*. New York: Farrar, Straus and Giroux.

Speer, Albert. 1970. *Inside the Third Reich*. Trans. Richard and Clara Winston. New York: Collier.

States, Bert O. 1978. *The Shape of Paradox: An Essay on "Waiting for Godot."* Berkeley and Los Angeles: University of California Press.

Steiner, George. 1967. *Language and Silence: Essays on Language, Literature, and the Inhuman*. New York: Atheneum.

———. 1977. "Unsentimental Education." Review of *Reunion*, by Fred Uhlman. *New Yorker*, August 15, 85–89.

Stoeber, Colette. 1995. Review of *Harold Pinter and the Language of Cultural Power*, by Marc Silverstein. *Essays in Theatre* 13: 218–20.

Stoppard, Tom. 1972. *Jumpers*. New York: Grove Press.

———. 1978. *Every Good Boy Deserves Favor and Professional Foul*. New York: Grove Press.

Strunk, Volker. 1989. *Harold Pinter: Towards a Poetics of His Plays*. New York: Peter Lang.

Styron, William. 1979. *Sophie's Choice*. New York: Random House.

Taking Sides. 2003. 108 min. Directed by Istvan Szabo.

Tonkin, Boyd. 1995. "Remembering the Reich." *New Statesman & Society*, December 8, 32.

Traub, James. 2003a. "Weimar Whiners." *New York Times Magazine*, June 1, 11–12.

———. 2003b. "Temperament War." *New York Times Magazine*, July 6, 9–10.

Tucker, Robert C., ed. 1978. *The Marx-Engels Reader*. New York: Norton.

Uhlman, Fred. 1971. *Reunion*. New York: Farrar, Straus and Giroux.

Urquhart, Brian. 2003. "The Rights Stuff." *New York Review of Books*, May 15, 39–41.

Van der Vat, Dan. 1997. *The Good Nazi: The Life and Lies of Albert Speer*. Boston: Houghton Mifflin.

Van Laan, Thomas F. 1987. "*The Dumb Waiter*: Pinter's Play with the Audience." In *Harold Pinter: Modern Critical Views*, ed. Harold Bloom, 117–26. New York: Chelsea House.

Variety. 1989. Review of *Reunion*, May 17, 32.

Watt, Stephen. 1998. *Postmodern/Drama: Reading the Contemporary Stage*. Ann Arbor: University of Michigan Press.

Weiss, Peter. 1971. *The Persecution and Assassination of Jean-Paul Marat as Performed by the Inmates of the Asylum of Charenton Under the Direction of the Marquis de Sade*. [*Marat/Sade*.] New York: Pocket Books. (Orig. pub. 1965.)

Werckmeister, O. K. 1991. *Citadel Culture*. Chicago: University of Chicago Press.

Weschler, Lawrence. 1990. *A Miracle, A Universe: Settling Accounts with Torturers*. New York: Pantheon Books.

Wiesel, Elie. 1978. *A Jew Today*. Trans. Marion Wiesel. New York: Random House.

Wittgenstein, Ludwig. 2003. *Tractatus Logico-Philosophicus*. Trans. C. K. Ogden. (Orig. pub. 1922.)

Zeller, Eberhard. 1969. *The Flame of Freedom: The German Struggle Against Hitler*. Coral Gables, Fla: University of Miami Press.

Index